PUBLIC ADMINISTRATION
AS A DEVELOPING DISCIPLINE

POLITICAL SCIENCE AND PUBLIC ADMINISTRATION
A Program of Textbooks and Monographs

Executive Editors

KENNETH FRIEDMAN
Department of Political Science
Purdue University
West Lafayette, Indiana

NICHOLAS L. HENRY
Center for Public Affairs
Arizona State University
Tempe, Arizona

Further volumes in preparation

PUBLIC ADMINISTRATION AS A DEVELOPING DISCIPLINE

(in two parts)

Part 1

PERSPECTIVES
ON PAST AND PRESENT

Robert T. Golembiewski
The University of Georgia
Athens, Georgia

MARCEL DEKKER, INC.   New York and Basel

Library of Congress Cataloging in Publication Data

Golembiewski, Robert T
    Public administration as a developing discipline.

    (Political science and public administration ;
v. 1)
    Includes index.
    CONTENTS: Pt. 1. Perspectives on past and
present.
    1. Public administration. I. Title. II. Se-
ries.
JK1351.G625   350   76-50383
ISBN 0-8247-6565-6

MARCEL DEKKER, INC.
270 Madison Avenue, New York, New York 10016

Current Printing (last digit):
10 9 8 7 6 5 4 3 2 1

PRINTED IN THE UNITED STATES OF AMERICA

To Geoff
> whose development brings pleasure,
> whose growth astounds,
> whose ambition vaults, and
> whose interests reflect a big man
> off the court as well as on,
> in his being as well as in his
> moves and motives

Preface

What has been in public administration and what may come to be—these are essential burdens of a pair of complementary volumes devoted to the theme *Public Administration as a Developing Discipline*. The two volumes are subtitled:

- *Perspectives on Past and Present*
- *Organization Development as One of a Future Family of Miniparadigms*

The first focus, clearly, is on how public administration got where it is. The second focus is on one approach toward further disciplinary development.

This pair of volumes is the result of a longish development which at once had many unexpected features, and yet seems to reflect a progression that is implicit even in my earliest published works. My two earliest books represent a tooling up in the behavioral sciences;* several intervening volumes reflect a fascination with theoretical orientations to a range of related phenomena, at least related as I see them;† and several recent book-length efforts have dwelt on aspects of using the methods and orientations of the behavioral sciences to approach what I and others consider empirically and normatively attractive conditions in the real world, especially in large organizations.‡

From my point of view, this two-volume effort is significant in that it is less generic and more rooted in a disciplinary tradition than most of my other

---

The Small Group (Chicago: University of Chicago Press, 1962); and *Behavior and Organization* (Chicago: Rand McNally, 1962).

†*Men, Management, and Morality* (New York: McGraw-Hill, 1965); *Organizing Men and Power* (Chicago: Rand McNally, 1967); and *A Methodological Primer for Political Scientists* (Chicago: Rand McNally, 1969).

‡(With Arthur Blumberg), *Sensitivity Training and the Laboratory Approach* (Itasca, Ill.: F. E. Peacock, 1970, 1973, 1977); *Renewing Organizations* (Itasca, Ill.: F. E. Peacock, 1972); and (with Arthur Blumberg), *Learning and Change in Groups* (London: Penguin, 1976).

work. Interpreters of cues may variously read these professional tea leaves. As usual, I am not overly concerned with my real motivation, whatever that is. I believed, and still believe, that this job requires doing, and about at this time. Indeed, I had several times started this project and put various sections of it into variously final form, only to retreat when inner urgings recommended pause. Sometimes, this caution was more or less clearly based on my need to know more and do more than I had done relevant to some facet of the book; and at other times, most public administrationists seemed to me too preoccupied with pressing practical needs to be very reflective about their field's developmental history. But most of the time my inner self urged respite, and I simply complied, without any real concern about the causes of that effect.

In any case, once the subtle and recurring logjam, or whatever it was, was somehow no longer a presence, the book was put into final shape in short order, given herculean efforts by Mrs. Sandra Daniel and her smoking electric typewriter.

I hope this pair of volumes on a common theme is better for this long and substantially inexplicable process of becoming. I only know that the product is more detailed and complex than it would have been had I finished it earlier. No one will ever know whether it will be more useful now than it would have been then. But the project's development seems somehow right to me; at least it seems time to say, in effect: "It is finished enough for now."

This pair of volumes is also different in that they, far more than most of my other books, rest on so many diverse contributions over such long periods. It would be onerous and perhaps maudlin to dwell on those whose intellectual and emotional support comes to mind and heart. Suffice it to say that those persons are numerous and that their aid was substantial; hopefully few will be surprised about how and when they helped. Specific intellectual indebtednesses are acknowledged in context. In addition, explicit thanks are due to Dr. Keith G. Baker, who granted permission to draw upon his work in the field of political economy, which enriches Chapter 5 in this volume. I hope I have been faithful about real-time acknowledgement of more personal indebtednesses.

Robert T. Golembiewski
Athens, Georgia

Introduction

For me, it has been an interesting and useful practice to write two introductions for each book-length project I undertake. One introduction is written early in the game, and the other after the book is essentially done.

Lengthy projects typically take on a kind of life of their own, and the two introductions often differ in surprising and sometimes even pleasing ways. It is as if in deleafing an artichoke, one comes to find that it sometimes transforms into a pomegranate, sometimes into a lemon.

For whatever it is worth, the present project has been in process in complex ways for a number of years, the end result of which is a substantial variability in detail within a basically constant framework. Thus the projected single book turned into a two-volume set, after I had spent much time and effort on trying to hide the seam between what were clearly two distinct parts of a single book. Although I believed the two parts should be unified not only in treatment but also in a single volume, reasonable practicalities finally got the better of my romanticism. However, I still believe the fit between the two volumes is both good and necessary.

More specifically, numerous signs of similarity and difference characterize the two volumes. For example, the tables of contents of the two volumes are very different from their earliest predecessors. However, the introduction I wrote when I started the project is essentially the one you as a reader see now. The reader can decide whether this reflects mere inflexibility, or a central idea that is vital enough to resist being substantially warped by the complex processes of researching, mulling, and writing that underlay this effort.

So this project ends about where it began, although its detailed route of travel is very different from the one I originally planned. The overriding goal here is to build upon the past development of public administration, to be critical without being a common scold, and to highlight developmental culs de sac, but only for the purpose of indicating how they might be bypassed or improved upon. More specifically, six goals further motivate this project.

First, this pair of volumes seeks to sketch the broad context of the conceptual development of public administration, as well as to detail one of the specific approaches that will permit further development. This volume tackles the first task of providing historical context for public administration's conceptual development. Specifically, this first volume emphasizes three major themes:

- Where Public Administration Came From: Perspectives on the Past
- Where Public Administration Is: Evaluations of the Present
- Where Public Administration May Go: Toward Miniparadigms in the Future

The second volume will elaborate one specific approach to facilitating the conceptual development of the discipline—the "laboratory approach to organization development," or OD. Its single theme is:

- Where Public Administration Can Go: Organization Development as a Miniparadigm

Second, the specific approach selected for emphasis in the second volume—organization development—bears a relation to the broad context of this first volume somewhat as a refillable cartridge is related to some modern pens. That is to say, many specific approaches might even today fit the broad developmental context sketched in this volume, even though the present focus is on only one such approach. Over time, without doubt, many other specific approaches will become appropriate, even vital, for the further development of public administration. But that is for the future. This book is written for now— no ifs, ands, or buts.

The basic orientation implies the intent and purpose of this volume and its companion. The volumes urge the relevance of a specific approach, *today,* to pressing needs in public administration. Hence this two-volume project may be characterized by these three themes:

- It accepts the sense of the common characterizations that public administration as a field is ". . . in 'drift,' as being in an 'intellectual crisis,' as in the need of a 'new' perspective, as 'coming apart,' and as 'in a period, of stress and change. . . .' "*
- It seeks to be sensitive to the fact that proposed solutions to the field's problems are often "so foreign to [public administration's] traditions or so rooted in other disciplines that their adoption would destroy the integrity of the field as a separate focus of inquiry."†

*Charles H. Levine, Robert W. Backoff, Allan R. Cahoon, and William J. Siffin, "Organizational Design: A Post Minnowbrook Perspective for the 'New' Public Administration," *Public Administration Review* 35 (July 1975): p. 425.
†Ibid., p. 425.

- It details how one approach—organization development—relates directly to public administration's needs and historical evolution, at the same time that organization development is still in its earlier years, is not rooted in any particular discipline, and serves several traditional fields.

Organization Development is *not* the exclusive vehicle for resolving public administration's developmental impasse—not even for today and most definitely not for the future. That is, this pair of volumes has no necessary quarrel with available and alternative specific approaches—"public choice" or "political economy" or whatever. The present purpose is only to establish that one specific approach does fit the developmental needs of public administration. Proponents of other specific approaches may be able to establish a similar or better fit for their own approach. Hopefully, they can and will. So be it. Terrific, in fact. Rather than excluding such other specific approaches, indeed, this pair of volumes basically desires to motivate their expression and testing against the developmental needs of public administration. In this sense—although I much prefer success—this volume may be helpful generally even if it fails specifically.

Third, the specific approach here is not chosen casually. Personally, the content of the two volumes reflects the better part of a decade of thought, developing and testing skills for intervention as well as for analysis, and using organizations as the site for applying thought, interventions, and analysis.

From an analytic perspective, the choice of a specific approach is strategically significant in coming to grips with some managerially relevant phenomena, while the focus is also tactically manageable *at this time* in the developmental history of public administration. Put in other words, the specific approach here is very far from the last word in the field's evolution. But it is a useful and even convenient way to get from where we are to wherever that "last word" will eventually take public administration.

The tactical virtue of the specific approach here, patently, is also its vice. Specifically, there are many other possible specific approaches that are strategically attractive, and some far more so than the present focus. Consider, for example, the mega-attractiveness of being able to meet the awesome challenge implicit in the contemporary dictum that in our day a theory of administration also requires a theory of politics. Unfortunately, *that* approach is not even remotely manageable today. Moreover, taking a tactical advantage does not mean strategic disadvantage or failure. In contrast, the chapters of this volume will argue that a fixation today on a global paradigm for public administration will only further delay the future development of our capability for dealing with target phenomena in effective ways.

In summary, there is no way to get from where we are now to that "theory of politics," whatever that is understood to mean. Moreover, at least in an analytical sense, fixation on the macro-challenges is likely to be counterproductive. It is likely to discourage the development of the traditions and processes of integrated empirical and normative inquiry that alone over time will permit the piecemeal development of a network of ideas and relationships that can lay distant-future development claim to being considered a "theory of politics" or a "theory of administration."

Fourth, this pair of volumes seeks to provide a model for testing the usefulness to the development of public administration not only of the specific approach here but also of several other possible specific approaches. The point applies in several senses. Hopefully, overall, the broad context of the developmental history of public administration will be shown to imply a set of guidelines or criteria for conceptual progress beyond the present condition. More specifically, this volume argues that any strategically and tactically significant specific approach must at least meet the following general standards:

- It must be shown to deal with some relevant values defining "good administration" and its relationship to a "just state."

- It must be based on some substantial if partial and variously consistent model of relationships in nature.

- It must have enough capacity for manipulating relationships in nature so as to permit some confidence about our ability to approach desired end states defining "good administration" or a "just state."

Many of the terms just used, of course, do not have concrete meanings. "Some relevant values," "substantial if partial," "enough capacity," and so on, clearly cannot be measured against analogs of that "standard foot" in the National Bureau of Standards. At the same time, however, these general standards clearly are not without substance. They rest on the complex and tedious testing of intersubjective consensus that is the basis of all accumulation of knowledge and progress in theoretical development. And like any good theory, the basic test is whether it works, whether it provides a useful map for reaching some desired outcomes.

Fifth, this pair of volumes sees more of a failure of will and skill in contemporary public administration than it does of the much ballyhooed and imprecisely designated "crisis of identity." And too often, the circular demand seems to be for a "new and more relevant identity" that is somehow to be generated by doing the same conceptual and analytical things.

In contrast, the view here is that concerns about identity and relevance are direct functions of what you do and how well, not vice versa. This first volume isolates the conceptual and analytical things that can be done to improve that crucial sense of identity and relevance; and the second volume concentrates on a specific approach that is at once rooted in the valuable developmental history of public administration but that also hopefully stretches most existing notions of what is a legitimate focus for inquiry.

Sixth, these two volumes propose a replacement for the pursuit of the "new paradigm" that is so central in the aspirations of so many public administrationists. This volume will attempt to show that public administration has had variously unsatisfactory experiences with three purportedly comprehensive paradigms, for one basic reason. Public administration as a field is now both too complex and undeveloped even to aspire to a "comprehensive paradigm." Hence, the constructs that have passed for "comprehensive paradigms" have basically been broad ideational networks whose basic common attribute has been longevity, and these constructs have been more mischievous than helpful, on balance.

It even seems that the intensity of today's expressed need for a new comprehensive paradigm—what Garson recently called expressions of "the intellectual modes and ideological needs of the time"—is in major respects a reaction to earlier efforts toward the "scientific" analysis of public administration. That emphasis on scientific analysis, in turn, was a reaction against still earlier intellectual modes and ideological needs, a reaction that trumpeted its "value-free" status as a kind of conceptual insulation against the preferences and values inherent in those modes and needs. And so the cycle is set, only to repeat itself. What Garson sees as the global tendency in political science applies generally to much of the developmental history of public administration, as well as to other social-behavioral areas of inquiry. He observes that the "discipline vacillates between these poles" of modes and needs and scientific inquiry, rather than seeking an integration of theory and practice, which necessarily requires "a base in normative theory." Garson concludes: "In the process the hopes for 'scientific' advance are surrendered to the gradual encroachment of ideas, each of which in turn is treated as if it were better than the last, and the fittest theories are equated with those which have survived."*

In capsule, this pair of volumes seeks to break that cycle by self-consciously stressing the strategic and tactical attractions of one approach to marrying theory and practice in public administration. It seeks to illustrate the complex relationshps between what is and what should be, leavened by an expanding sense of what could be and can be.

*G. David Garson, "On the Origins of Interest-Group Theory," *American Political Science Review* 68 (December 1974): 1506.

Contents

Contents of Part 2

WHERE PUBLIC ADMINISTRATION CAME FROM
Perspectives on the Past

Chapter 1

PUBLIC ADMINISTRATION AS A FIELD
Four Developmental Phases

If scholars live or die in terms of the images they create, students of public administration are clearly in trouble even if some hope still exists. This is the theme of this book.

The chapters of this volume deal with the full trouble-hope spectrum, but with definite emphasis on the former. Specifically, the first five chapters attempt some heavy critical work. They present and analyze the mix of attractions and problems that characterize major concepts used by public administrationists to define their field and themselves. These five chapters pose formidable challenges that a second volume seeks to meet, with the help of Chapter 6. That concluding chapter of this volume is transitional: it is designed to isolate some guidelines for future development implicit in Chapters 1 through 5, whereas the second volume single-mindedly illustrates one way of approaching those guidelines.

In a perhaps corny but real sense, this volume is one kind of conceptual bridge over troubled analytic waters. It proposes to stand on its own merit, of course. But far more profoundly, it seeks to encourage other bridges over these same waters, other specific ways of providing content for public administration as a field. "Content" in this case includes not only an orientation to analysis, but also the skills and technologies necessary for supporting cumulative traditions of research and application.

Phases as a Focus

The immediate emphasis is on four developmental phases that have shaped public administration's guiding concepts.[1] Awareness of these developmental phases is important, perhaps even critical, for two reasons: (1) valuable perspective on where the field is can be gained from tracing how it got there; and (2) getting where you want to go is easier if you are clear on where you have been and where you are.

The goals of this chapter can be stated more concretely. Especially in the last decade, public administration has come to emphasize a "public policy" concept of its scope and methods. How this came to be is a matter of substantial intellectual and practical interest in its own right. Although the "public policy" approach has been little analyzed, it has had a significant impact on which scholars do what work in which ways. This combination of scanty analysis and significant impact provides substantial motivation for this chapter. Finally, the "public policy" approach has certain unintended and largely unanticipated consequences that deserve explicit analysis, especially as regards the assertion that these consequences could mean the doom of public administration.

Three limitations must be acknowledged. First, this chapter does not pretend to provide a resolution of the contemporary concern about public administration as a field. Rather it sketches how the field developed, beginning with the early years and extending through the 1960s. Other chapters will extend the analysis through the present and also will attempt to develop useful leading ideas for the public administration of the future. Second, this chapter does not do justice to such developments as the "new" public administration, whose major thrusts need fuller treatment than is possible here. That treatment is reserved for Chapters 4 and 5. Third, this initial effort is unabashedly impressionistic in generalizing about the character and relative dominance of four developmental stages in defining a complex field. This chapter attempts to compensate for the inevitable loss of nuance and qualification by emphasis on an important set of intellectual dynamics underlying public administration.

Précis of a Predicament

Two opposed trends serve tolerably well to characterize the public administration of yesterday and today. They get brief attention here in separate sections.

Early Manifest Destiny

Public administration's early history is studded with symbols testifying to its rich destiny and performance. Not only were all problems ultimately administrative problems, for example, but the very existence of our civilizations depended upon the success with which we learned to cope with the administrative ultimates. Woodrow Wilson put the matter directly nearly a century ago: "It is getting harder to *run* a constitution," he noted, "than to frame one."[2] Wilson stressed the need to augment legal-institutional analysis with the panoply of science and art required to manage complex organizations of men and machines. His influential conclusion was echoed by many others.

Public administration seldom was seen as wholly able to guarantee the safety of our civilizations, but it was considered to play an important role in resolving major components of that challenge. "If those who are concerned scientifically with the phenomena of getting things done through cooperative human effort will proceed along these lines," read the Foreword to the monumental 1937 *Papers on the Science of Administration,* "we may expect in time to construct a valid and accepted theory of administration."[3] The measured confidence of these words had a firm basis. Public administration was then by common consensus at the top of the heap of analytical competence in dealing with matters administrative.

Today's Crisis of Identity

More recently, observers have tended toward greater pessimism. "For a variety of reasons," Frederick Mosher concluded, "public administration stands in danger of ... senescence."[4] Similarly, Martin Landau expressed a deep concern. As he put it, public administration, "that lusty young giant of a decade ago, may now 'evaporate' as a field."[5] The core difficulty is widely perceived to be the lack of an organizing focus. Without such a focus, research loses coherence and lacks cumulative relevance. The danger is particularly great today, given the manifold approaches to public administration that are both possible and necessary, as Mosher emphasized:

> More is now known about public administration than was the case twenty years ago. But there is a great deal more to know. There are more depths to probe than were then visualized, and more different perspectives from which to start the probing. This field need bow to no other in respect to its sophistication about its subject matter. But such sophistication can senesce into mere dilettantism unless it is grounded in premises and hypotheses that are in some degree ordered and tested and that are continuously refreshed with new data and experience.[6]

Dwight Waldo brought such considerations to a conclusion that has wide currency. He asserted that if a healthy discipline "has a solid center as well as an active circumference," the state of public administration is disturbing. "I have a nagging worry of late," Waldo confessed, "a fear that all is not as healthy as it should be at the center of the discipline."[7] Some years later, matters had only worsened appreciably from Waldo's perspective, to judge from his reference to a "crisis of identity for public administration."[8]

Assigning dates to historical events is always hazardous, but the relative disadvantage of public administration became apparent after World War II. There were many signs of this disadvantage, but the most obvious were the massive differences in the kind and quality of self-scrutiny in business schools and in public administration that followed World War II. The business-school effort was long run, well financed, and comprehensive, as well as searching and even searing. Two hefty volumes resulted that soon became required reading in business schools and motivated major changes in curriculum, staffing, and teaching methods.[9] That self-review took a decade, more or less. The comparable effort in public administration was Lilliputian. It generated a single, less-distinguished, and tamer volume of analysis[10] and very little change in teaching or research. And no wonder. That volume inspired only very faint praise, as in the comment that its "very triteness and superficiality . . . made it important."[11]

Overall, these two trends reflect the same tension as the Chinese picture-word for change. That picture-word is formed of two other symbols, one for "opportunity" and the other for "danger." So it is that today's public administration as a foundation for that of tomorrow has elements of both opportunity and danger.

The danger to public administration has been alluded to earlier, but the opportunity is no less obvious. Overall, that is to say, this seems an inopportune time for public administrationists to lose heart. The flurry of reorganizations, the new programs, the search for efficiency and economy because of the growing need to justify each dollar of expenditures, the rapid obsolescing and/or impending retirement of the bulk of our top-level civil servants, and the growing competition for tax resources: these are among the factors that have contributed to the swinging of the pendulum of attention back toward administration.

Many other signs of growing interest and need might be cited, but they support a common conclusion. Public administration is again beginning to churn with activity, for the first time since the Hoover Commissions. The research literature has vividly come alive. And progress in training and development of public officials has, if anything, been even more bullish.[12] Perhaps most usefully, substantial attention has recently been focused on the central assumptions and concepts underlying the field, a critical self-analysis that has been too long in coming.[13]

Consequently, there are those who argue that obituaries for public administration are premature, and some even imply that birth announcements are more appropriate. The late John Pfiffner and Robert Presthus are basically in the former camp. They observe that "much of this anguish" about a disciplinary "solid center" and an "active circumference" for public administration "seems misplaced." In support of their position, they note the results of a survey of the opinions of political scientists. When the question concerned who was doing the "most significant" work within political science, these professionals ranked public administration "squarely in the middle of the various subareas of the discipline." Although we should "not therefore be content to rest on our laurels," Pfiffner and Presthus conclude, "there seems no need for despair" about the future of public administration.[14] More ebullient observers see a new dawn for public administration just around a developmental corner.

How the Predicament Came to Be: Four
Developmental Phases in Defining Boundaries

Whether one is optimistic or pessimistic about the future, however, public administration today faces a basic predicament. This section outlines the dimensions of that predicament by describing four phases in the development of public administration. From one perspective, to preview the argument, the conceptual development of public administration leaves some of its adherents fainthearted when they should be bold, and concerned about their legitimacy when they should be striding confidently toward the demanding research and training objectives that recently have sprung into prominence. From an alternative perspective, that conceptual development leaves other specialists buoyantly expecting too much; consequently they are vulnerable to major disappointment, if not something worse.

This is one hell of a predicament, in sum, which this first volume will try to understand and with which the second volume will seek to cope, however incompletely.

A 2 X 2 Matrix

There are many ways of schematizing the development of public administration, and the choice here is convenient and revealing. Essentially, the conceptual development of public administration is viewed as being encompassed by the four cells of the 2 X 2 matrix in Figure 1.1. "Focus" refers to the analytical targets of public administration, the "what" with which specialists are concerned. "Locus" refers directly to the "where," to the contexts that are conceived to yield the phenomena of interest. Both focus and locus are crudely distinguished here as "relatively specified" and "relatively unspecified."

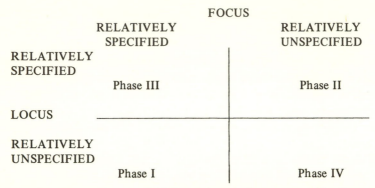

Fig. 1.1   The four cells of a 2 X 2 matrix relating two combinations of locus and focus.

This simple 2 X 2 matrix accounts for much of the historical variation in the conceptual development of public administration. Roughly speaking, the contemporary condition of the field is the result of its having passed through four major stages of phases of conceptual development that differ both in locus and focus, and sometimes radically so. These phases correspond to the four cells of the matrix shown in Figure 1.1.

Overview of Developmental Phases

It is possible, in brief outline, to provide detail for these four cells, drawing on the literature of the last half-century or so. The basic themes of each phase follow:

Phase I. The *analytic* distinction of politics from administration, interpreted as ideal categories or functions of governance, which functions are performed in different institutional loci in varying degrees

Phase II. The *concrete* distinction of politics from administration, with the former conceived as having a real locus in the interaction between legislatures and high-level members of the executive, and the latter as having a real locus in the bulk of the public bureaucracy

Phase III. A *science of management,* which emphasizes the isolation and analysis of administrative processes, dynamics, activities, or "principles" that are seen as universal or at least as having applicability in many organizations

Phase IV. The pervasive orientation toward *"public policy,"* in which politics and administration commingle and which has an unspecified locus that encompasses the total set of public and private institutions and processes that are policy relevant

The basic argument here is that public administration was significantly influenced by these four major concepts of the scope of the field. The focus is on a typology that is not dependent on time. That is, movement from one phase to another was not prompted by some sudden and collective decision among scholars at a specific time. Each concept did peak at a different time, but major proponents of each remained after the dominant emphasis had shifted toward the succeeding concept. Moreover, some students reflect aspects of several phases, either as stages in their own development or as eclectic combinations of approaches.

Properties and Problems of the Four Phases

To provide detail for the 2 X 2 table in Figure 1.1 is to sketch much of significance in the development of public administration. At the most general level, the dual choice of locus and focus helped determine the kind of work done in the field and who did it. At first, the field moved toward a sharper definition of a distinct "vital center," but by Phase IV, the concept of the field was broadened radically. Hence the contemporary concern that public administration does not have a distinctive vital center and active periphery at just the time when concerted research and applied effort are vital. Much detail about each of the conceptual phases is necessary to support this broad conclusion.

Phase I: Analytic Politics/Administration

Frank Goodnow's *Politics and Administration* provides the essential content for Phase I. The analytical focus of public administration is reasonably precise in that volume, as a first approximation, but the real locus of the appropriate phenomena is not specified.

Basically, Goodnow conceptually distinguishes "two distinct functions of government," which he designates politics and administation. "Politics has to do with policies or expressions of the state will," Goodnow explains. "Administration has to do with the execution of these policies." The heart of his distinction lies in the classic separation of powers, which prescribes the desirability of entrusting "in large measure" the expression or formulation of the "will of the sovereign" to "a different organ" than is charged with executing that will.[15]

Goodnow's basic distinction is not as crude as many imply. For example, his distinction is not monolithic, either in locus or focus. The two functions are *not* performed in different loci. "More or less differentiated organs" of government are established to perform the two functions, Goodnow notes, but no such organ is "confined exclusively to the discharge of one of these functions." Complexity does not permit such tidiness. For Goodnow, that is, students of public administration would seek their phenomena and cope with them in the executive or judicial branches, at state, local, or federal levels, and in matters both great and small. Not that all real loci are equally likely to produce phenomena of politics and administration. Goodnow's obscure terminology sometimes gets in the way of his argument on the matter of locus. But if we concede to him an inept usage or two, he consistently conceives of the three branches of federal government as having different loadings of politics and administration. For example, the legislative branch, as concrete locus, is mostly politics, whereas the lower bureaucratic levels are largely administration. Whatever the loading in a real locus, however, public administration is concerned with the administration component wherever it appears.

Relatedly, administration for Goodnow is neither homogeneous nor sealed off from politics. Thus, administration includes the "function of executing the law," as well as "semi-scientific, quasi-judicial, and quasi-business or commercial" functions. The latter functions are "a large part of administration" that is "unconnected with politics" and consequently should "be relieved very largely, if not altogether, from the control of political bodies." As for the "executive function," Goodnow notes oppositely, there can be no question about subjecting it to the "body entrusted ultimately with the expression of the state will."

Goodnow's conceptual concern with the analytical focus but not the locus of public administration may be brought to a summary conclusion. Wherever they occur, Goodnow argues, the target phenomena in public administration are defined as those activities of governance that possess "internal" criteria of correctness, which includes "semi-scientific, quasi-judicial, and quasi-business or commercial activity." Moreover, the target phenomena include activities that have "little if any influence on the [political] expression of the true state will" and consequently require little if any "external" control, as by legislatures. "External" or political control is appropriate only when no "internal" criteria of success exist, or when some measure of broadly political consensus about the degree of correctness must suffice or is desirable, as in the case of the "executive function" component of administration.

Goodnow's basic approach has a major attractive feature that is too little noted. Essentially, he contributed to the superficially easy differentiation of the provinces of public administration and political science and yet provided a stout umbilical. Landau notes that in terms of central tendencies, Goodnow's politics and administration each "referred to a different class of behavior and each presented a different set of problems." However, the total operations of government cannot be assigned completely to different agencies of government. Landau put the matter in these terms: ". . . the empirical processes of politics were far too complex to be discharged by any single governmental body and, similarly, administrative functions could not be deemed exclusive to any specific agency."[16] Differences in central tendencies, in short, coexisted with major conceptual overlap.

Goodnow's analytical distinction is a difficult one with which to live, despite its attractions, and the magnitude of these difficulties may be indicated economically. For example, Goodnow provides only general leads for isolating the central phenomena within the analytical province of administration. This unspecificity is compounded by the fact that Goodnow urged upon public administration a cosmopolitan view of its real locus. Oppositely, most fields in political science have a single locus, despite some strong contemporary intentions to become "truly comparative." Goodnow's concept of public administration, consequently, would require that students confront legislative specialists, for example, with a claim on the latter's real locus. An analytical distinction is no match for a distinction based on concrete locus, however. This was particularly the case in Goodnow's time. No substantial body of knowledge about "administration" then existed for whose broad applicability in various loci one could make a strong case.

Such perceived difficulties, by hypothesis, motivated search for another guiding concept. As will be seen in the following description of three such conceptual stages, that movement did not stop until the field was defined so as to encompass virtually the whole of political science. Of course, this did not happen in one fell swoop. But it happened quickly. The eyes of students of public administration were bigger than their stomachs, in short, and analytical appetites were awesome. This characterization helps us understand important components of the history of public administration that we shall summarize in thumbnail fashion: why ambitions were so expansive; why the pace of pushing forward the scope of the discipline was so rapid; and why a kind of dyspepsia resulted from, and persists after, this attemp of scholars to force their concepts of public administration to swallow too much too quickly.

Phase II: Concrete Politics/Administration

Phase II in the search for public administration's boundaries had a long-lived impact on the field and can be described briefly. Phase II proposed a sharp and concrete separation between "politics" and "administration." Basically, it is definite about the locus of relevant phenomena and vague about its focus.[17] As such, Phase II disingenuously caricatures Goodnow's basic distinction. The locus of public administration is restricted to the governmental bureaucracy, but within the locus the discipline knows no analytical limits. Everything is its meat. Administrative case law and administrative behavior, for example, are put cheek by jowl at a common trough in Phase II. In contrast, Phase I has a sharper analytical focus, but its locus is relatively unspecified.

The difficulties with Phase II are significant, both practically and conceptually. Primarily, a real locus is given to the analytical distinction between politics and administration. This left proponents of Phase II with no defense against the correct charge—and it was leveled time after time—that "things are not that way" within the executive and its bureaucracy. The way things "really are" became a datum to be interminably discovered and rediscovered over two decades or so: That the formulation of public policy typically involves complex combinations of bureaucrats and politically responsible officials, with the former not always clearly "on tap rather than on top"; and that "policy" is typically a product of "administration" as well as its tether.

Relatedly, Phase II encouraged neglect of relevant phenomena in other loci, especially in business. The lessening, but still very real, isolation of business administration from public administration stands as perhaps the most unfortunate by-product of Phase II's defining the discipline in terms of a specific locus. This left many scholars out of intimate touch with the revolutionary developments that have taken place very recently in many schools of business.[18] Finally, in its very emphasis upon locus rather than focus, Phase II assumes that where phenomena occur is more significant than what the phenomena are. This seems a procrustean basis for differentiation, although some building of common identifications among public administrationists did result from this parochialism.

In any case, Phase II significantly shaped the development of public administration. "For a half-century or so while political science was developing as a distinct discipline," Appleby concluded in 1949 about the academic staying power of Phase II, "much of its literature tended to accept as substantially real a separation of powers which excluded from administration any—or at least important—policy-making functions."[19]

The impact of Phase II was both profound and pervasive. For example, Phase II encouraged two major emphases: (1) the "neutral specialist" as the answer to the world's administrative problems,[20] and (2) the bureau movement that assumed that hyperfactualism was the simple road to the good administrative state.[21]

Like all ideas that gain currency, these two had a valid central theme. Given the relevations of the muckrakers, for example, pleas for more data and more trained personnel in public management were reasonable. Also like most ideas that gain wide currency, however, that valid central theme was over-extended by the conceptually careless and naïve. Only slight exaggeration or conceptual carelessness about reliance on experts and on facts was required, that is, to pair the separation of politics and administration with an equally sharp separation between value and fact. Many observers provided that exaggeration and carelessness. Needless to say, the distinction between fact and value was perhaps *the* dominant issue in public administration for two decades.

Phase III. A Science of Management

Expansionist tendencies in definitions of the boundaries of public administration also were manifest in Phase III's emphasis on a "science of management" in two opposite ways. From one perspective, Phase III agrued for a deepening of the analytical focus of the field. But another kind of expansionism was still the order of the discipline, for Phase III was rejected generally and early.

The reaction to Phase III may be phrased in bold terms without sacrificing essential accuracy. The concept had a short reign as king of the mountain, even though its fling was glorious while it lasted. Moreover, Phase III did not capture public administration as did naïve politics/administration, although it had many powerful proponents then and still retains some of them. Essentially, Phase III today gets its strongest support in business schools and in various academic units organized around a focus on generic management.

Both the briefness and the brilliance of the ascendancy of Phase III in public administration have similar roots. Roughly, Phase III may be characterized as a concern with managerial phenomena, that is, with the administration component of Phase I. Phase III was variously restricted, but in an imperialistic sort of way. To sample facets of the paradox: Phase III often was expressed in terms of a concrete working locus at lower levels of organization, and it proposed to deal with specific but diverse phenomena within that locus. Yet, Phase III asserted that its results applied to all or many organizations and not only to public ones.

Diverse Forms and Impacts

Providing details about Phase III is complicated by the variety of forms in which it appeared, as well as by the fact that some of its forms are still evolving. Broadly, the Phase III spirit is reflected early in the "principles" literature. Later, that spirit was forcefully expressed in the decision-making schema of Herbert Simon, which sought to encompass a central and generic managerial process from mathematical and statistical and also behavioral perspectives.[22] And the Phase III spirit also is clear in contemporary work on organization change and renewal,[23] which stresses behavioral learning designs that lead to changes in interaction as well as in policies, procedures, and structures.

Such complicating factors notwithstanding, Phase III's status as the guiding concept for public administration was determined by reactions to three major technologies or orientations as they existed in the 1930s and 1940s. They are:

- Scientific Management, as typified by time-and-motion studies
- Early work in Human Relations, largely in sociological studies that emphasized the limitations of Weber's bureaucratic model and stressed "informal organization
- the focus on Generic Management

Consider several significant commonalities of these major early expressions of Phase III. Paramountly, all three varieties are based on faith that a science of administration is both desirable and possible. Moreover, all three share the view that "administration is administration," wherever it is found. Proponents of Phase III did not place exclusive or even great stress on public *or* business contexts.

These three major expressions of Phase III also reflect an incredible diversity, both among the three types and among several proponents of the same orientation. Scientific Management, for example, shared a low-level bias—both conceptually and in level of the hierarchy stressed—with early work in Human Relations. Both of these Phase III varieties also treated values similarly, and unsatisfactorily. Garden-variety approaches to Scientific Management obscured the role of values by carelessly arguing that there is a "one best way" to organize work that inheres in specific situations. Similarly, early Human Relations work—often called "cow sociology"—typically reflected the implicit goal of molding humans to more or less hostile but inviolate technological requirements. In crude but useful summary, technological values simply overshadowed the values of man, and men adapted to the technology, whether willingly or kicking and screaming. At the same time, work in the early Human Relations tradition was largely a reaction against the mechanistic bias of Scientific Management. So great was this reaction that work in the Human Relations tradition has only recently given major attention to the technological contexts within which behavior at work occurs.[24]

Generic Management contrasted strongly with the other two varieties of Phase III work. It focused on processes and activities—leadership or planning or whatever—that were considered common to many or even all realms of the management of men and that might appear at many or all levels of any organization. Moreover, Generic Management also was seen as integrating the behavioral, the mechanical-procedural, and the substantive as they interact at work. This is clearly the thrust of Marshall Dimock. He explains:

> Administration is both social engineering and applied psychology. It is apparatus and mechanics, incentives and human nature. Let no one think it is merely the former. Nowhere is the need for psychology greater than the organization, direction, and inspiration of men working in large groups. Outstanding administrative results are products of psychological mainsprings and invigorating incentives. . . . Modern governmental administration is a new synthesis. It is necessarily concerned with all fields of knowledge and all matters which enter into the carrying out of official policies and programs.[25]

In simplified but meaningful contrast, Generic Management is to Scientific Management more or less as Fayolism is to Taylorism.[26] Taylor's Scientific

Management emphasizes mechanical or technical features at low levels of industrial organizations and generally excludes all but a narrow range of values centering on "economy." In contrast, Fayol was concerned with processes such as leadership that encompass mechanical and technical but also behavioral aspects, that exist at all levels of every human organization, and that patently must treat issues of value as well as empirical questions. At the same time, both Fayolism and Taylorism were motivated by the common goal of a science of management.

No doubt the key difference between Generic Management and Scientific Management or Human Relations lies in the treatment of values. Much longstanding work in the tradition of Generic Management made clear provisions for disciplining the use of empirical knowledge by suitable values. Basically, analysis and application were seen as posing different issues concerning values. Thus only a very narrow range of values was relevant for *analysis,* that is, for work leading to the development of an *empirical theory* of what conceptual entities covary in organizations. Consistently, Urwick announced in the major *Papers on the Science of Administration* that:

> there are principles which can be arrived at inductively from the study of human experience of organization which should govern arrangements for human association of any kind. These principles can be studied as a technical question, irrespective of the purpose of the enterprise, the personnel comprising it, or any constitutional, political or social theory underlying its creation.[27]

The key words are *can be studied.* At the same time, values were seen as crucial in the *application* of any results of study. That is, values are crucial in developing *goal-based, empirical theories* of how organization men must go about getting what it is they they value, based on empirical knowledge of what covaries with what. The key words at this second level are *can be applied.*

Given that there is no simple description of Generic Management, then, it is characterized by a marked deepening of analysis following the model of Phase I. Generic Management does emphasize the "internal" aspects of administration, "the carrying out of official policies and programs." However, that emphasis is no monomania, being a pragmatic judgment about where continued effort is most likely to generate early results of broad applicability. The judgment often was confirmed, as in the case of "group dynamics" and its development of major theoretical networks and applied technologies for organizational and personal change. Moreover, Generic Management packed great conceptual content into this narrowed focus, and also sought near universal generality. That is to say, Phase III proponents see themselves as handling matters that are practically and theoretically formidable. With varying justice, a charge of trifling could be made against Scientific Management and early work in Human Relations, two other varieties of Phase III work.

The impact of Phase III, in whatever form, can be evaluated only in terms of polarities. When the seminal *Papers on the Science of Administration* appeared, public administration was by general consensus at the top of the heap in terms of competence in comprehending large-scale organizations.[28] A rash of published and unpublished work spanning the period between the Great Depression and World War II established this superiority definitely over what was going on in business administration.

But early Phase III was more faith than good works. It was stronger on preaching about general "management principles" than in discovering specific ones. Moreover, the early work on Human Relations and the fantastic interest in Scientific Management had two features—a low-level bias as well as a markedly manipulative and unilateral character—that implied a wide range of difficulties for students of public administration whose professional socialization emphasized a normative ethos built around representative democracy.

A Common Fate for Diverse Forms

Polarities are not necessary in evaluating the fate of Phase III as the dominant concept for public administration, however. The early successes under Phase III proved no match for the allures of a broader definition of the scope of public administration. Less moderately, both proponents and opponents tended to view the three varieties of Phase III work as both more or less undifferentiated and inadequate.

Martin described the doomed character of Phase III, which he said "approached full fruition" with the 1927 publication of W. F. Willoughby's *Principles of Public Administration* and "achieved its pinnacle" with Gulick and Urwick's *Papers on the Science of Administration* (1937). Martin at once accurately illustrates the common lack of differentiation of Phase III efforts and also contributes to it by his use of the blanket term "scientific management" to encompass all Phase III work, including that specific variety commonly called Scientific Management. Martin notes:

> As applied to public administration, the credo of scientific management came in time to be characterized by attention to administration without much stress on the *public* part of the term, by faith in "principles," by emphasis on science in administration, and by divorce of administration and values. . . .
>   In the atmosphere provided by scientific management, a mechanistic concept of public administration came to prevail widely and in important circles. Administration was separated from the legislative. . . . "Politics" was anathema—not the politics practiced by administrators, but the politics of the "politicians". . . . Champions of the new order wrote and spoke . . . as though man were nothing more than "administrative man," eager to spring to his

place in the organization table and fall to on his appointed segment of POSDCORB.[29]

Later Phase III varieties in public administration—especially Simon's decision-making schema—had to swim against the substantial and general tide of opinion represented here by Martin. Simon's *Administrative Behavior* was published just as the mass of specialists in public administration were gathering momentum for their rush into Phase IV, which will be discussed in detail later. Simon left no doubt as to his hunches about what was happening around him. He opted for Phase III, as specifically defined in terms of his decision-making schema, and he recognized its ties to Phase I.

These summary statements may be supported economically. Simon predicted that the redefinition of the scope of public administration in terms of public policy implied the end of the golden days of Phase III, whose fuller flowering he correctly perceived as being just around the analytical corner. Unfortunately, for Simon at least, he was a little too far ahead of the research that would substantiate his hopes. That fuller flowering did not occur until the late 1950s, of course, basically in schools of business or industrial administration. Being a decade or so ahead of the field, Simon's argument was an easy target. And so much more the pity, for his instincts often were right-on. For example, even then he warned that the public-policy orientation would set scholars in flight after multiple analytical will-o'-the-wisps, thereby destroying that "center" so vital to a healthy discipline. Simon held out little promise for the success of the effort, but he thought he knew what success in public-policy terms required: ". . . nor can it stop when it has swallowed the whole of political science; it must attempt to absorb economics and sociology, as well."[30] That is, in Simon's eyes, the maw of the public-policy approach was cavernous.

Simon did more than point with alarm. He provided an alternative definition of the scope of public administration in terms of focus. As Landau observed, Simon's contribution was "all the more significant in the face of the general disorganization which had occurred. Simon was trying to redefine a public administration so as to give it a 'solid center,' a standard of relevance, a set of operating concepts—to make it, in short, a 'field' of inquiry. This was the function of the decision-making schema."[31]

Simon's decision-making schema may be described briefly, toward dual ends: (1) The description will sketch the Phase III variant of the scope of public administration he proposed as an alternative to the public-policy orientation; and (2) it will outline the senses in which Simon interpreted Goodnow's analytical distinction between politics and administration. Simon saw "deciding" rather than "doing" as the heart of administration and focused generally on the "premise of decision" rather than on "decision." The distinction was deliberate and consequential, for it reveals Simon's generic and synthetic emphases, as opposed to an empirical one rooted in specific decisions and as contrasted with an interest in a public or business locus. For Simon, decision making involves both factual and ethical elements. "Facts" and "values" differ fundamentally. The former may be validated by empirical tests, whereas the latter are imperatives beyond empirical proof or disproof. In Simon's terms, "different criteria of 'correctness' . . . must be applied to the ethical and factual elements in a decision."[32]

The basic distinction between factual and ethical elements is analytic or synthetic, as Simon recognizes. Reality does not always divide so neatly. Given that behavior in organizations is intentionally purposive at multiple levels, an "end" in some immediate means-end linkage may be a "means" in a more distant means-end linkage. Simon's decision rule for applying his analytical distinction is this: As far as decisions lead to the selection of "final goals," they are considered to be "value judgments" beyond empirical validation. When decisions implement any final goals, they are "factual judgments."[33]

Simon explicitly noted that this schema paralleled Goodnow's analytical distinction between politics and administration. Remember that Goodnow had proposed that politics and administration be distinguished in terms of different criteria of correctness. Administrative issues are beyond politics in that they "do not require external control because they possess an internal criterion of correctness," embracing as administrative issues do the "fields of semi-scientific, quasi-judicial, quasi-business or commercial activity" which all have "little if any influence on the expression of the state will." Political issues, in contrast, are value-loaded and beyond scientific standards. Simon sees a transparent parallel here with his decision-making schema. "The epistemological position of [Administrative Behavior] leads us to identify [Goodnow's] internal criterion of factual correctness and the group of decisions possessing this criterion with those that are factual in nature."[34] "If it is desired to retain the terms 'politics' and 'administration,' " Simon concluded, "they can best be applied to a division of the decisional functions that follows these suggested lines. While not identical with the separation of 'value' from 'fact,' such a division would clearly be dependent upon the fundamental distinction."[35] Significantly, Simon is also careful to discourage the reader from interpreting his analytical distinction as one of locus, as a latter-day concrete separation of politics and administration based on differences between value and fact. The point is patent in his discussion of democratic institutions, which he notes "find their principal justification as a procedure for the validation of value judgments." Simon continues:

> If the factual elements in decision could be strictly separated, in practice, from the ethical, the proper roles of representative and expert in a democratic decision-making process would be simple. For two reasons, this is not possible. First, as has already been noted, most value judgments are made in terms of intermediate values, which themselves involve factual questions. Second, if

factual decisions are entrusted to the experts, sanctions must be available to guarantee that the experts will conform, in good faith, to the value judgments that have been democratically formulated.[36]

Six Factors Reinforcing a Common Fate

Only conjectural explanations are possible about why a common grave was dug for the three early varieties of work in Phase III, as well as for later varieties such as Simon's decision-making schema. But communal gravedigging it was, and at least six reinforcing factors seem both probable and significant in its short reign.

First, the demise of Phase III seems in large part to be a result of intellectual leadership from political science, which all but unanimously took to the public-policy track of Phase IV. Keeping up with respected scholarly Joneses no doubt was a potent factor, given public administration's subordinate status within political science, and given the organizational ties common between the two areas.

Second, the demise of Phase III seems due to a common feeling among students that they had gone about as far as they could go with it.[37] The fascination with the mnemonic POSDCORD, to exaggerate the point somewhat, suggested to some that there was nothing really new in public administration. This was reasonable enough a reaction in the early flush of discovery, and in the absence of tools for intensive behavioral and mathematical/statistical analysis. The manifold senses in which a Phase III concept could support theoretically and practically significant work became manifest only in the late 1950s and early 1960s, and by then most students identified with public administration passed essentially into the hands of researchers in numerous schools of business and in departments of industrial administration, where major advances were made in mathematical and behavioral extensions of administration as viewed internally.

Public administration, which started it all, quickly became a bastard child at a family outing featuring a feast of managerial research. An increasing number of students trained in political science but having particular interests in administration did the reasonable but difficult thing, beginning especially in the 1950s. They sought, or were seduced into, employment in schools of business or generic administration.

Third, the eclipse of Phase III can be attributed to the general unavailability in public administration of the enhanced analytical skills required by the concept, but for which no real groundwork had been laid. Simon described the training required to exploit Generic Management as follows: "For the man who wishes to explore the pure science of administration, it will dictate at least a thorough grounding in social psychology."[38] But few students of public administration could boast such a background. More significantly, before World War II, little motivation and less opportunity to develop such competencies existed.

With few exceptions, the usefulness of social psychology in public administration was little explored in specifics.

This condition had two prime consequences. In the first place, Phase III was vulnerable to "put up or shut up" challenges. For example, Wallace S. Sayre in 1958 dismissed Phase III "prophets" as having offered "a new administrative science" that was not widely accepted because of the patent failure of the concept to produce new and useful results.[39] In addition, and far more critically, the providing of appropriate skills and training for Phase III was left essentially to the other social sciences, especially to business schools, whose adherents got an enormous head start in the behavioral and mathematical analysis of organizations. This head start led to increasingly active poaching on the disciplinary turf of public administration, which of late has encouraged a few public administration specialists to develop some of that "thorough grounding" that Simon correctly perceived as necessary some two decades ago.[40]

Fourth, Phase III had a short run because it was thought to narrow sharply the scope of public administration. Values were neglected in much work in Phase III, for example, particularly in Scientific Management and in early Human Relations. This neglect was unacceptable to many students of public administration, especially those steeped in the normative ethos of political science.[41] The reactions of many political scientists no doubt also were exacerbated by the likelihood that this neglect of values was seen as confirmation of the prevailing political science-public administration pecking order, in that such neglect seemed to be further proof of the superiority of political science. Dwight Waldo highlighted one major attitudinal consequence of the political scientist's "humanistic ethos and related conception of liberal education as concerned with 'higher things.' " The public administration specialist was commonly assigned a derivative "second-class citizenship status" within political science, because such a specialist generally was seen as dealing with the nuts and bolts of day-to-day public management rather than with "the great and persistent problems of government."[42]

Whatever the exacerbating conditions, Phase III's apparent neglect of value issues induced vigorous reactions and overreactions. The deep concern felt by many capable students did not encourage the drawing of fine distinctions, and, as typically happens, popularizers of the basic issues exaggerated the real points of difference. Consequently, the deep concern of value-conscious scholars tended to take the form of sharp denunciation, which was extended more or less uniformly to all three early varieties, including Simon's decision-making approach.

Fifth, Phase III in many respects seemed a bad bargain, as a brief catalog of particulars implies. Perhaps primarily, Phase III had some patent parallels with the naïve separation of politics and administration. These parallels include the common emphasis on internal administrative processes, as well as the common avoidance of value issues reflected in much of Stage II. The analytic guns being leveled against Phase II during the period around World War II thus often hit Phase III targets, even if they were sometimes innocent ones. Relatedly, Herbert Simon, a major Phase III proponent, tied his early work to Goodnow's *analytical* distinction between politics and administration.[43] Only a little overexuberance was required to conclude—as many did—that Simon was merely resurrecting the *concrete* distinction between politics and administration *à la* Phase II, which many political scientists were zestfully attacking even as Simon wrote.

The character of the resulting debate can be suggested by one case. One political philosopher chided another for raking Simon over the coals for being an inadequate political philosopher. That was manifestly unfair, the chider noted, as unfair as it would be to criticize a fire chief for being imprecise and inaccurate as a theorist of combustion. And so it went, with zesty thrusts and energetic parries reflecting that the issues were very serious and the combatants were most incensed.

Some observers also saw Phase III as more of a scholarly suicide pact than an analytical promised land. They argued, for example, that (1) Phase III required commitment to a science but did not furnish specific direction to attain it; (2) that the several varieties of Phase III work required new competencies that either were being handled well by other specialists or whose contribution to the study of public administration was unclear; (3) that all varieties of Phase III tended to cut off public administration from vast areas of traditional concern; and (4) that Phase III offered science as a colorless substitute for the rich prescriptive and normative concern that is so vital a part of the heritage of Americal political science and public administration.

Sixth, Phase III advocates hardly presented a unified front. For example, Herbert Simon, the major post-World War II advocate of a science of administration, delivered the most powerful indictment against the very "principles" that were long accepted by earlier preachers of the gospel of administrative science.[44] Such an indictment could be interpreted as reflecting either the logic by which science progresses, or the improbability or impossibility of an administrative science.

The latter interpretation was most prevalent, and neither proponent nor opponent was much given to generosity or forbearance. Furthermore, nuances had a way of becoming mammoth differences of principle. For example, Simon argued for his "pure science of administration" in terms that commonly were interpreted as severing public administration from the consideration of values, as well as from broad areas of political science.

However, Simon's major thrust was not always as sweeping as his interpreters claimed. At least part of the time, that is, Simon clearly labored only to establish that there are at least two major kinds of work to be done in public administration and that these two types of work must be distinguished. In addition, Simon did not see the two types of work as mutually exclusive. Indeed, they might be mutually stimulating. Thus Simon in 1947 saw two groups of students in public administration. One group sought after the "pure science of administration," which required "at least a thorough grounding in social psychology." The other, and far larger, group was deeply concerned with a broad range of values and was eager about "prescribing for public policy." In Simon's view, the latter ambition implied an enormous analytical range that cannot "stop when it has swallowed up the whole of political science; it must attempt to absorb economics and sociology as well." Simon saw real danger of a loss of identity for public administration in the latter approach, but he did not see the matter in win-or-lose terms. "If my analysis is correct," he explained, "there does not appear to be any reason why these two developments in the field of public administration should not go on side by side, for they in no way conflict or contradict. But the workers in this field must keep clearly in mind in which area, at any given time, they propose to work."[45] The din of analytic combat, however, was too great to allow the voice of reason to be heard.

A Massive Monolithic Interest?

These six reinforcing factors may explain the demise of Phase III to some observers, but others may still puzzle over the general lumping together of the conceptual good and bad. These other observers, myself included, are intrigued by an additional hypothetical explanation. Could a massive and monolithic interest have encouraged that lumping together, and could that interest have discouraged the kind of coexistence of the two orientations to public administration held out by Simon? Speculate about a narrowly political issue that had an unknown but probably significant impact. Directly, many observers came to the conclusion that a Phase III concept probably was "the single greatest threat to the continuing dominion of political science over public administration."[46]

These may seem surprising words, but two points are clear. Most public administration programs then were, and still are, located in departments of political science, a discipline that did, and still does, "dominate [public administration] intellectually as well as institutionally."[47] Moreover, in Phases I and II, public administration was tied to political science via two major conceptual linkages, in that the two areas of scholarly activity focused on more or less overlapping stages of the formulation and implementation of the same public policies or programs. Phase III threatened both these linkages. As formulation of policy and its implementation were differentiated, that is, so also would be weakened the conceptual ties between the two areas of study. And if "administration is administration," this would challenge the basic ties forged between political science and public administration through common programs.

Relatedly, separate schools and strong relations with business schools would become more appropriate for public administration.

A serious threat was plain to many observers, whether they were concerned about public administration's being swallowed by schools of business or generic administration, or simply about the various signs of independence or secession of public administration from political science. Recall—and many people are suprised by its lateness—that the American Society for Public Administration (ASPA) was not founded until 1939, as a reference group that was more specific than the long-standing American Political Science Association and yet not so narrowly focused as the American Public Works Association. Donald C. Stone vividly remembers some of the major dynamics at ASPA's birth: "Questions of loyalty, sedition, intrigue, separatism, and schism kindled emotions."[48] The fractioning off of ASPA, of course, was a by-product of the excitement of the development of "big government" in Roosevelt's New Deal, as well as an expression of the felt needs of the burgeoning graduates and faculty of suddenly virile programs in public administration. So much was at stake, practically as well as intellectually.

Preserving the "dominion of political science over public administration" was a great concern during the period after World War II, that much is clear. And Phase III won few admirers among those who saw it as a threat to the linkages of political science and public administration. The gravity of the issue was impressed on me as a young man. I announced my departure from a department of government to join a business school faculty and soon thereafter received this note from a political scientist of some note: "You, sir," the note minced no words, "are a TRAITOR."

Why the linkage of public administration with political science, or the domination of the former by the latter, was of such concern after World War II can only be speculated about, but the speculations have a compelling quality. Clearly, political science had come upon hard days immediately after World War II.[49] Professionally, as by the National Science Foundation, the discipline was considered a distinctly junior member of the social sciences. Organizationally, specialists in at least public administration and international relations were generating some real steam for secession. Financially, also, the American Political Science Association was experiencing a significant and prolonged challenge to its healthy existence. In sum, the Phase III concept of public administration would have had to offer tremendous advantages to gain wide acceptance at any time, and particularly so after World War II. The advantages of Phase III, however, were anything but clear at that time.

Phase III could not win for losing, in any case. It was widely seen as sharing a number of features with Phase II, such as the separation of politics from administration. Such sharing—sometimes real, sometimes not—encouraged censure. At the same time, where Phase III work differed fundamentally from

Phase II, that also was considered censurable. That is, Phase III emphasized the universality of administration, which distinguished it sharply from Phase II's territorial definition of *public* administration. Moreover, all Phase III work often was perceived (and sometime misperceived) as neglecting vast areas of interest to students of public affairs, while it urged commitment to a science whose efficacy was then questionable. This uncomfortable duality invited rejection.

Phase IV: Public-Policy Approach

Whatever the full catalog of reasons, many students moved toward a Phase IV concept of the boundaries of public administration, toward what is generally called the "public-policy approach." The emphasis can be dated accurately enough as a post-World War II phenomenon, and it was led by prestigious scholars from public administration and political science.[50] Phase IV was built upon two basic themes:[51] (1) the interpenetration of politics and administration at all or many levels, and (2) the programmatic character of all administration. In sum, these themes directed attention in public administration toward *political* or *policy-making* processes, as well as toward specific *public* programs.

Phase IV is definitely not monolithic.[52] Two varieties of the genus require early distinguishing, and four varieties of "public policy" will be distinguished in Chapter 3. For present purposes, note only that the immediate discussion focuses on a gentle concept of "public policy," a kind of loose metaphor for a broad community of interest that many students share. Some later attention is also given to public policy as a focus for scientific inquiry, for many purposes a different notion altogether.

To hazard a conclusion by way of introduction, Phase IV had multiple attractions. At the risk of further confusing a complex analysis, we shall distinguish two historical waves of concern: the periods 1945-1960 and 1960-1975. Each period highlighted distinct but reinforcing attractions of the public-policy approach.

Manifest Early Attractions, 1945-1960

Very early in the game, Phase IV had a number of attractions, especially to those eager to improve on the simplism of concrete politics/administration or to blunt the impact of Phase III. Conceptually, that is, Phase IV reasserted the ties between political science and public administration in two ways: via emphasis on a common locus through the programmatic aspects of administration and via stress on the interpenetration of politics and administration. Such an emphasis consequently highlighted the role of values in public administration, an emphasis congenial to almost all political scientists. At the same time, the emphasis also patently was not "mechanical" as was Scientific Management, an orientation so often criticized by political scientists and such a major brand of Phase III work. In effect, Phase IV undercut the rationale for pairing public administration with business administration, both in substance and in spirit. Administration was not administration, in sum.

Evolving Later Attractions, 1960-1975

This early exuberance was heightened by major developments in the late 1950s and early 1960s. Perhaps two factors contributed most to the growing attractiveness of Phase IV. Both political science and public administration had moved into a "postbehavioral era,"[53] after two or three decades of preoccupation with behavioralism. For present purposes, behavioralism in political science can be roughly characterized as follows:

- It is *descriptive* in its approach to political policies, processes, and institutions, which encourages an emphasis on what exists, on equilibrium.

- It is *interdisciplinary* in the sense that it "was widely felt that the study of political behavior required that a political scientist must first be a psychologist or sociologist"[54] and master *their* research methods and technologies.

- It is *value-free* in the sense that only a narrow range of "scientific values"[55] was to be admitted to analysis.

- It is often[56] associated with a philosophically *"liberal" position* placing an emphasis on "freedom, equality, and the dignity of man," typically expressed as an *ethical relativism* that defines the "good political life" as a resultant of the pushes and pulls of various groups or interests.

These characteristics of behavioralism ill suited *the* issue of the turbulent 1960s: ". . . in all the stress and disequilibrium, governments had failed to perform as fully and predictably as we had grown to expect."[57] The effects were dramatic. From one perspective, Lowi reports, "government in all its complexity became a series of variables rather than one undifferentiated constant" as it more or less seemed to be for the preceding thirty years. Moreover, to rely on Lowi again: "Suddenly there were thousands of students who were screaming against current political science courses and in favor of 'relevance.' Political science was, justifiably, accused of defending establishments."[58]

One scrambling first approximation of the postbehavioral era was essentially a countermanifesto. Thus, the avant-garde in both political science and public administration gave substantial attention in the 1960s to developing an approach that had the following characteristics:

- It was *prescriptive* as to the content of political policies, processes, and institutions, which implies the need to raise again and answer such traditional questions as, "What is the just state?"

- It was *intradisciplinary* in the sense that it redirected attention to what Lowi calls macro-politics: "the nature, composition, and functioning of the political system," with emphasis on "political theory, public law, institutional economics, and old-fashioned political institutions"[59]

- It was *value-loaded* in pervasive senses, in that values are explicitly admitted at all or many stages of analysis, even encouraged

- It was *philosophically nonparochial,* as in admitting *radical* values aimed at destroying the existing order as a prelude to building some new political order, as well as *conservative* values aimed at reforming the existing order

The "policy orientation" well suited these evolving emphases, for reasons that can be sketched only briefly here. The goodness of fit had at least four components. First, and no doubt primarily, the focus on policy had the effect on both political science and public administration of emphasizing their common and distinctive "political" content. As Kelley noted: "Most generally, the dispute of politics concerns matters of policy, not grand ethical principles."[60] Greater relevance for both public administration and political science, then, would result from addressing the burning questions of the 1960s and 1970s. In this view, the ultimate questions involved justice, equity, and the good civic life—that is, the major preoccupions of the prebehavioral political science.[61] For Lowi, the most important questions were the following:[62]

- What is the policy as a policy, defined not as an isolated individual decision but as part of a "long line of intention" of government?

- What is the policy as a law, that is to say, what is the specific type of coercion behind any policy?

- What is the impact of the policy on the political system? For example: How will different kinds of policy and coercion affect the long-run capacity to govern? How do current policies affect the access of all publics to the political system? How and to what degree do current policies and types of coercion provide defenses against bad policies?

And Lowi advises asking these questions, as is, no matter how imprecise the tools of analysis. Better tools are to be worked toward, to be sure. But the central questions cannot be postponed until those tools become available.

Second, the emphasis on public policy would reduce the time and effort devoted to mastering interdisciplinary technologies and knowledge and hence permit increased attention to unique disciplinary concerns, especially for beginning students. The underlying motivation can be diverse. Thus, some are concerned that many or all students of political science or public administration can do no more than dabble in other disciplines, that their efforts at best will induce only paternalistic condescension among real specialists. Moreover, some observers are at least dubious that interdisciplinary linkages can be developed in the proximate future, especially given the macro-character of the central concerns in political science and the micro-emphasis in much of sociology, psychology, and economics. More narrowly protectionist sentiments also may be at work.

Third, political scientists had long maintained that "theirs is *the* policy science." Some observers were pleased to see political scientsist now doing something to deserve that claim,[63] and others announced that "it may turn out that the sister disciplines have more to learn from political science than the other way around."[64]

Fourth, as Dye put it so straightforwardly, the emphasis on policy analysis is the "thinking man's response to demands for relevance." As was true in many disciplines, to provide brief background, both political science and public administration were rocked by forms of the political activism so prevalent in the late 1960s. The new major thrust was that professional relevance required drastic reshaping of how scholars approached their work and obligations. Commonly, this reshaping threatened academic values about objectivity, dispassionate analysis, the nature and use of "truth," and so on. Dye and others saw policy analysis as slipping between the horns of the dilemma, of permitting greater relevance while preserving academic values. He explains that

> political science can be "relevant" ... without abandoning its commitment to scientific inquiry; that social relevance does not require us to reject systematic analysis in favor of rhetoric, polemics, or activism; that knowledge about the forces shaping public policy and the consequences of policy decisions is socially relevant.[65]

Preliminary Concerns about Going Too Far

Concerning both politics/administration and behavioralism, the postwar support for Phase IV implied valid claims. But moderation was not the order of the day. For example, whereas Lasswell urged empirical science in the service of democratic values in his Phase IV definition, many others took the stress on values or policy to be rather more of a dance on the grave of Phase III administrative science.[66] Moreover, leading Phase IV definitions argued the unreality of naïve politics/administration. However, the general run of interpretatons stampeded beyond such reasonableness. All limits of real locus and analytical focus tended to be swept aside by many Phase IV definitions of the scope of the disciplines.[67]

Also expansively, Phase IV attempts to establish the linkages between political science and public administration often turned into exercises that conceptually implied the congruence of the two areas of study. That is, most variants of Phase IV build around variations on this theme: "... as a study, public administration examines every aspect of government's efforts to discharge the laws and give effect to public policy...."[68]

Certainly there is no mistaking the contrast between Phase IV and Phase I or III. In surveying concepts of the scope of the field of public administration, for example, Landau sees the sharpest differences between the definitions of the 1930s and those of the 1950s. Indeed, except for transdisciplinary ambitions, Phase IV is the end of the line. Landau puts the point sharply: "The field of public administration is neither a subfield of political science, nor does it comprehend it; it simply becomes a synonym."[69] That conclusion need not be tentative. Thus Waldo cites the "current view" that "a theory of public administration means in our time a theory of politics also."[70]

These considerations permit a general conclusion here, although a full demonstration will require the more specific analysis provided by Chapter 3. Overall, many students of public administration opted for Phase IV, an action that was consistent with their common training and identification with political science. In addition, some students may have been merely running scared. Political science was in delicate financial and professional condition following World War II, and it also was rocked by threats of secession. A public-policy definition of public administration apparently served to reinforce ties in jeopardy. Such a surmise helps explain the swift and widespread acceptance of Phase IV, which essentially rolled back some four or five decades of history, during which political science and public administration to a degree had become differentiated and yet related.

Notes and References

1. This chapter closely follows Robert T. Golembiewski, "Public Administration as a Field: Four Developmental Phases," *Georgia Political Science Association Journal* 2 (Spring 1974): 21-49.

2. Woodrow Wilson published "The Study of Administration" in 1887. It is reprinted in *Political Science Quarterly* 56 (December 1941): 486-506.

3. Luther Gulick and Lyndall Urwick, eds., *Papers on the Science of Administration* (New York: Kelley, 1969), p. v. The volume was initially published in 1937 by the Institute of Public Administration.

4. Frederick C. Mosher, "Research in Public Administration," *Public Administration Review* 16 (Summer 1956): 171.

5. Martin Landau, "The Concept of Decision-Making in the Field of Public Administration," in *Concepts and Issues in Administrative Behavior*, ed. Sidney Mailick and Eward H. Van Ness (Englewood Cliffs, N.J.: Prentice-Hall, 1962), p. 2.

6. Mosher, "Research in Public Administration," p. 171.

7. Dwight Waldo, *Perspectives on Administration* (University, Ala.: University of Alabama Press, 1956).

8. Dwight Waldo, "Scope of the Theory of Public Administration," in *Theory and Practice of Public Administration,* ed. James C. Charlesworth (Philadelphia: American Academy of Political and Social Science, 1968), p. 5.

9. Robert Aaron Gordon and James E. Howell, *Higher Education for Business* (New York: Columbia University Press, 1959); and Frank Pierson, *The Education of American Businessmen* (New York: Carnegie Corporation, 1959).

10. Committee for the Advancement of Teaching, American Political Science Association, *Goals for Political Science* (New York: Sloane, 1951).

11. Albert Somit and Joseph Tanenhaus, *The Development of Political Science* (Boston: Allyn & Bacon, 1967), p. 188.

12. For one sign, see Paul Buchanan, ed., *An Approach to Executive Development in Government* (Washington, D.C.: National Academy of Public Administration, 1973).

13. See Frank Marini, ed., *A New Public Administration: The Minnowbrook Perspective* (Scranton, Pa.: Chandler, 1971).

14. John M. Pfiffner and Robert V. Presthus, *Public Administration* (New York: Ronald Press, 1967), p. 5.

15. Frank Goodnow, *Politics and Administration* (New York: Macmillan, 1900), especially pp. 10, 11, 18, and 85.

16. Landau, "The Concept of Decision-Making in the Field of Public Administration," in Mailick and Van Ness, *Concepts and Issues in Administrative Behavior,* p. 17.

17. William F. Willoughby, *Government of Modern States* (New York: Appleton-Century, 1936), 219-221.

18. For massive evidence of the timing of the self-scrutiny that led to this major takeoff in schools of business and industrial administration, see Gordon and Howell, *Higher Education for Business*; and Pierson, *The Education of American Businessmen.*

19. Paul Appleby, *Policy and Administration* (University, Ala.: University of Alabama Press, 1949), p. 3.

20. Dwight Waldo, *The Administrative State* (New York: Ronald Press, 1948), pp. 32-33.

21. See Duane Lockard's reaction to a request by a young black official who advised that political scientists could make their greatest contribution to governing a large city by finding "some ways to break the civil service stranglehold." Lockard noted: "His request is not an ill-conceived one by any means. ... It is worth remembering how large a role political scientists played in helping create the civil service system; perhaps more attention should now be paid to means for correcting the overdose." "Value, Theory and Research in State and Local Politics" (Paper delivered at the Annual Convention of the American Political Science Association, Los Angeles, Calif., 1970).

22. Herbert A. Simon introduced the schema in *Administrative Behavior*
     (New York: Macmillan, 1947), but specific derivative research products
     took more than a decade to develop. By that time, Phase III's fate had
     long been decided. Moreover, Simon's technology was beyond that of
     most public administration scholars, though it had a substantial audience
     in business schools, in generic management programs, and in industrial
     administration.

        Simon's influence still persists, but more outside political science
     and public administration than within. Significantly, Simon's *Adminis-
     trative Behavior* has only recently gone into a third edition, with the
     essential argument remaining the same, even identical.

23. Robert T. Golembiewski, *Renewing Organizations* (Itasca, Ill.: F. E.
     Peacock, 1972).

24. For a useful introduction to technological contexts, see Charles Prerrow,
     Organizational Analysis: A Sociological View (Belmont, Calif.: Wads-
     worth, 1970).

25. For a full development of the point, see Marshall E. Dimock, *A Philosophy
     of Administration* (New York: Harper, 1958).

26. This essential argument was made to a political science audience by
     Norman M. Pearson, who sought to describe the limits of Taylorism
     while arguing for the broader usefulness of a Generic Management variety
     of Phase III. See "Fayolism as a Necessary Complement to Taylorism,"
     American Political Science Review 39 (February 1945): 68-85.

        Selecting examples of Phase III work must be arbitrary, but the
     following sources illustrate the broader family: Chester I. Barnard, *The
     Functions of the Executive* (Cambridge, Mass.: Harvard University Press,
     1938); Simon, *Administrative Behavior*; Peter Drucker, *The Practice of
     Management* (New York: Harper, 1954); Marshall E. Dimock, *Adminis-
     trative Vitality* (New York: Harper, 1959); Robert T. Golembiewski,
     Men, Management and Morality (New York: McGraw-Hill, 1964); Herbert
     Kaufman, *The Limits of Organizational Change* (University, Ala.: Univer-
     sity of Alabama Press, 1971); and Golembiewski, *Renewing Organizations*.

27. Lyndall Urwick, "Organization as A Technical Problem," in Gulick and
     Urwick, *Papers on the Science of Administration*, p. 49.

28. This superiority of public administration is a dominant emphasis in such
     sources as Gordon and Howell, *Higher Education for Business*, especially
     pp. 379-393.

29. Roscoe Martin, "Political Science and Public Administration," *American
     Political Science Review* 46 (September 1952): 667.

30. Herbert A. Simon, "A Comment on 'The Science of Public Administra-
     tion,'" *Public Administration Review* 7 (Summer 1974): 202.

31. Landau, "The Concept of Decision-Making in the Field of Public Adminis-
     tration," in Mailick and Van Ness, *Concepts and Issues in Administrative
     Behavior*, p. 15.

32. Herbert A. Simon, *Administrative Behavior,* 2nd ed. (New York: Macmillan, 1957), especially pp. 45-50.

33. Ibid., pp. 4-5.

34. Herbert A. Simon, *Administrative Behavior,* 3rd ed. (New York: The Free Press, 1976), p. 57.

35. Simon, *Administrative Behavior,* 2nd ed., p. 58.

36. Ibid., pp. 56-57.

37. The mnemonic represents planning, organizing, staffing, directing, coordinating, reporting, and budgeting and long remained the essential skeletal structure for teaching and writing in public administration. Thus Luther Gulick asks: "What is the work of a chief executive? What does he do?" He replies: "The answer is POSDCORB." "Notes on A Theory of Organization," in Gulick and Urwick, *Papers on the Science of Administration,* p. 13.

38. Herbert A. Simon, "A Comment on 'The Science of Public Administration,' " *Public Administration Review* 7 (Winter 1947): 202.

39. "Premises of Public Administration," *Public Administration Review* 17 (Spring 1958): 194. Generic Management is far from dead, of course, and many public administration programs are included in schools devoted to it. For example, see Michael A. Murray, "Comparing Public and Private Management: An Exploratory View," *Public Administration Review* 35 (July 1975): 364-371.

40. See notes 9 and 10 above.

41. Somit and Tanenhaus, *The Development of Political Science,* pp. 42-48.

42. Dwight Waldo, "Public Administration," in *Political Science,* ed. Marion D. Irish (Englewood Cliffs, N.J.: Prentice-Hall, 1968), p. 154.

43. Simon, *Administrative Behavior,* 2nd ed., pp. 55-58.

44. Herbert A. Simon, "The Proverbs of Administration," *Public Administration Review* 6 (Winter 1946): 53-67.

45. Simon, "A Comment on 'The Science of Public Administration,' " p. 202. A similar distinction is made by Luther Gulick, "Science, Values and Public Administration," in Gulick and Urwick, *Papers on the Science of Administration,* especially pp. 191-192.

46. Martin, "Political Science and Public Administration," p. 665.

47. Nicholas Henry, "Paradigms of Public Administration," *Public Administration Review* 35 (July 1975): 384.

48. Donald C. Stone, "Birth of ASPA—A Collective Effort in Institution Building," *Public Administration Review* 35 (January 1975): 87. More generally, see Martin, "Political Science and Public Administration," especially pp. 665-666; and Mosher, "Research in Public Administration," pp. 175-176.

49. Somit and Tanenhaus, *The Development of Political Science,* especially pp. 147-149, 153, and 167-170.

50. Phase IV may be roughly dated by Appleby's *Policy and Administration,* published in 1949. See also Daniel Lerner and Harold D. Lasswell, eds., *The Policy Sciences* (Stanford, Calif.: Stanford University Press, 1951); and Austin Ranney, ed., *Political Science and Public Policy* (Chicago: Markham, 1968).

51. Harold Stein, "Preparation of Case Studies," *American Political Science Review* 45 (June 1951): 479-487. Relatedly, Martin, "Political Science and Public Administration," p. 669, argued that administration must have roots to have meaning, and these roots rest in the soil of specific programs. In contrast to the Generic Management approach of Phase III, he urged that: "The administrator does not administer only: he administers *something,* and what he administers is of basic importance. . . ."

52. This section closely follows Robert T. Golembiewski, "Public Administration and Public Policy," in Robert N. Spadaro, Thomas R. Dye, Robert T. Golembiewski, Murray S. Stedman, and L. Harmon Zeigler, *The Policy Vacuum* (Lexington, Mass.: Lexington Books, 1975), pp. 79-82.

53. George J. Graham, Jr., and George W. Carey, *The Post-Behavioral Era: Perspectives on Political Science* (New York: McKay, 1972).

54. Theodore J. Lowi, "What Political Scientists Don't Need to Ask About Policy Analysis," *Policy Studies Journal* 2 (Autumn 1973): 62.

55. The point caused some monumental and momentous conflict. In some approaches, as in some versions of logical positivism, values were variously defined as out of bounds. Other interpretations tried to distinguish types of theories as well as stages within a single type where value concerns were appropriate and necessary. On the latter approach, see Robert T. Golembiewski, *Behavior and Organization* (Chicago: Rand McNally, 1962), especially pp. 48-60 and 69-79.

56. George W. Carey notes: ". . . by all outward evidences most behavioralists accept liberalism, and most liberals accept behavioralism." "Beyond Parochialism in Political Science," in Graham and Carey, *The Post-Behavioral Era,* p. 45.

57. Lowi, "What Political Scientists Don't Need to Ask About Policy Analysis," p. 64.

58. Ibid., pp. 64-65.

59. Ibid., pp. 66 and 65.

60. E. W. Kelley, "Political Science as Science and Common Sense," in Graham and Carey, *The Post-Behavioral Era,* p. 206.

61. Christian Bay, "Thoughts on the Purposes of Political Science Education," in Graham and Carey, *The Post-Behavioral Era,* pp. 88-102.

62. Lowi, "What Political Scientists Don't Need to Ask About Policy Analysis," pp. 66-67.

63. Philip O. Foss, "Policy Analysis and the Political Science Profession," *Policy Studies Journal* 2 (Autumn 1973): 68.

64. Lowi, "What Political Scientists Don't Need to Ask About Policy Analysis," p. 62.

65. Thomas R. Dye, *Understanding Public Policy* (Englewood Cliffs, N.J.: Prentice-Hall, 1972), p. xi.

66. Compare Lerner and Lasswell, *The Policy Sciences,* with Herbert Storing, ed., *Essays on the Scientific Study of Politics* (New York, Holt, Rinehart & Winston, 1962). especially pp. 65-116.

67. See note 50. Similarly, a recent text—Ira Sharkansky's *Public Administration* (Chicago: Markham, 1970)—comes close to defining public administration as a kind of derivative or resultant category. The volume's "principal roots are in political science," the reader is told (p. ix.), "and it seeks to bring together that information about administration that is most relevant to understanding of the larger political process. Of necessity, much of this information concerns *public* administration." For a similar but somewhat modified treatment, see John Rehfuss, *Public Administration as Political Process* (New York: Scribner's, 1973).

68. Marshall E. Dimock, Gladys O. Dimock, and Louis W. Koenig, *Public Administration* (New York: Rinehart, 1953), p. 12.

69. Landau, "The Concept of Decision-Making in the Field of Public Administration," in Mailick and Van Ness, *Concepts and Issues in Administrative Behavior,* p. 9.

70. Dwight Waldo, "Scope of the Theory of Public Administration," in Charlesworth, *Theory and Practice of Public Administration,* p. 14, attributes the quote to John Gaus.

Chapter 2

PUBLIC ADMINISTRATION AS A FIELD
Three Comprehensive Paradigms

There is another way of explaining how public administration came to its present predicament. Thought in the field has been guided by three successive "paradigms," or broad concepts of the scope, mission, and role of the field. Just as was the case with the four phases reviewed in Chapter 1, each paradigm can be shown to pose major problems for the development of public administration.

This chapter proposes to deal with a raw nerve, and in ways that cannot be soothing. The approach here is critical of three comprehensive sets of leading ideas in a field of inquiry that has felt its intellectual grip slipping. Hence the prognosis is better than even that this chapter will raise the blood pressure of some persons, whatever its quality.

Of Paradigms and Developmental Predicaments

The prognosis just made is especially certain because this chapter goes against the grain of most recent thought in public administration. There, paradigmatic change is seen as *the* answer to the developmental predicaments of public administration. The usual approach is: paradigm$_N$ is dead, long live paradigm $_{N+1}$. Chapter 6 will look at this usual approach in some detail. But this chapter on its own provides support for the proposition that the three paradigms reviewed here are not up to the task of resolving the field's predicaments.

Present purposes require only a thumbnail sketch of the "paradigm" in public administration. Here note only that, despite a notable looseness in usage,[1]

35

most public administrationists follow the lead of Kuhn,[2] who emphasizes an "essential characteristic of normal science," the general agreement among students of a "basic theoretical paradigm or framework." The criticality of such a paradigm is patent, in Ostrom's terms, because its

> basic concepts establish the essential elements of analysis; and relational postulates and axioms specify the essential rules of reason. These rules of reason enable members of an intellectual community to pursue a structure of inferential reasoning where the work of one can be added to the work of others. Frontiers of knowledge can be extended with reference to the understanding shared by all members of the community.[3]

Every so often, goes this version of scientific progress, a paradigm somehow proves inadequate in providing needed answers. Further scientific understanding then requires the development of a more comprehensive and more widely applicable paradigm. The processes of this development can trigger a burst in the accumulation of knowledge; or they may induce despondency as false leads frustrate scientists. Only one effect is certain: The period of transition between paradigms is typically unsettling, as comfortable ideas and associated skills become unhinged, as successor paradigms are proposed and evaluated.

Kuhn's approach implies both diagnosis and remedy. The current malaise in public administration is usually attributed to the failure of the current paradigm to lead to necessary truths by asking the required questions in useful ways. Hence, the common prescription is to develop a new and comprehensive paradigm that will do the job, immediately.

This chapter shares neither the common diagnosis nor the usual prescription. First of all, it is only in a vague sense—if at all—that science can be said to proceed by leapfrogging from one comprehensive paradigmatic formulation to another (the common diagnosis).[4] As Chapter 6 will demonstrate in detail, matters are far more complicated than conventional wisdom allows. Moreover, public administration is not yet ready to support a comprehensive paradigm (the usual prescription). The determined search for such a paradigm thus will at best be unrewarding and indeed may constitute an evasion of the central business at this phase of the discipline's development, and at this stage of the methodological awareness of students of public administration. As the analysis of three successive paradigms in public administration will show, the historical track record is convincing in this regard.

Five Preliminary Stipulations

The argument that follows will be complicated enough to encourage five simplifying stipulations at the outset. Readers may accept or reject them, of course. But the following argument rests on them nonetheless.

Classes of Target Phenomena

However "public administration" eventually will be circumscribed as an area of inquiry by some comprehensive paradigm, it is now possible to specify at least five classes of phenomena with which the student must cope:

1. *Internal processes* of any public administrative system, which encompass behavioral and rational-technical features

2. *Output measures,* as they relate to client choices and satisfaction as well as to employee performance

3. *Transactions with other systems,* whether public or not

4. The *environmental envelope* of any public administrative system, which includes such contextual features as specific public programs or policies; the character of the institutions within which the public system exists; the applicable laws, traditions, culture

5. A range of *value* or *normative* criteria that are necessary to evaluate the quality of the relationships, outputs, and institutions implied by items 1 through 4.

Interfaces with Political Science

The classes of target phenomena imply much common ground between public administration and political science. For example, classes 3 thorugh 5 in the list just presented patently involve issues variously central to political science. In contrast, competence in phenomena of class 1 may or may not be associated with training or identification with political science, and probably is not. Two rules of thumb can be suggested. Anyone doing teaching or research in public administration with a class 1 orientation should be employable in a school of business or management. Anyone doing class 3 or 4 teaching or research patently should be employable in a department of political science.

Two Central Challenges

This argument stipulates two major challenges in any area of scholarly concern such as public administration—"task" and "maintenance." Despite the need to respond to both as challenges over the long run, the basic thrust in the following discussion is that an emphasis on "task" is not only useful, but should get definite priority at this point in the development of public administration.

A rationale for this position begins with a rough distinction between the two central goals of public adminstration,[5] first maintenance and then task.

The first goal emphasizes the development of a sense of "inside" and "outside." This requires identifying the analytical "us" as contrasted with "them," as well as specifying the character and quality of the relationships between the "us" and the heterogeneous "them." Most central in this subtle process has been the academic speciality of political science, which both parentally and practically is home base for the bulk of the public administration writing crowd. Significantly, the historical search has been for a guiding concept that at once defines meaningful domains for both political science and public administration, and yet also specifies significant common conceptual territory with which many members of both categoric groups can identify. Politics/ administration was the first in a series of concepts, with public-policy analysis being the most contemporary of them.

The second central goal emphasizes comprehending what's going on in management—the development of tools and skills for description, analysis, and action.

The first goal may be labeled "maintenance," and the second "task." The key questions associated with the first goal are:

- Who am I professionally and, to at least some degree, who am I as a person?
- Whom do I associate with in seeking and applying knowledge?
- With what scholarly discipline(s) or field(s) do I identify?

The key questions associated with the second goal are:

- What is my legitimate domain for study?
- What concepts or tools should I use?
- What are my criteria of reality or truth?
- What are the broad goals or values that my contributions to knowledge or truth should serve?

No universal priority is given to either goal. Ideally, in fact, the movement toward increasingly precise questions and answers should be interactive. That is, maintenance and task activities should be critical complementarities. And if one really perseveres, it makes no difference which set of questions is emphasized initially.

In practice, the point of departure is critical, because maintenance and task activities are often seriously at cross-purposes. Identification, for example, can be such a pressing concern that students will only gently address their task. To illustrate, many public employees whose jobs involve finding the venereally diseased seek identification with medical doctors and other professionals, for reasons of prestige, the aura of expertise, and so forth. For many such employees, however, the fact is that these maintenance needs often seriously get in the way of task effectiveness: finding and getting treatment to those with venereal disease. Up to a point, an emphasis on task would encourage venereal-disease inspectors to identify primarily with those afflicted—to better know who the diseased are likely to be, how and where they might be found, and what resistances to, or feelings about, treatment characterize those afflicted, who may not consider themselves "patients" in the medical sense and hence might not seek treatment.

The awkward linkages between task and maintenance also can be suggested more generally. Maintenance activities can provide crucial support for collaboration and stimulation, but they also can be so limiting and protectionist that task activities suffer. Relatedly, so much attention can be devoted to task that relationships between academic specialties deteriorate, no sense of common mission exists, subareas become susceptible to poaching by other academic specialties, and so on. Some delicate fine tuning is clearly required.

This fine tuning will not be simple, for at least three reasons. First, maintenance historically has received priority in concepts defining public administration. The reason so much energy was devoted to developing concepts that tied together public administration and political science may be variously explained.[6] Most elementally, establishing a solid conceptual integration with political science is not surprising, dealing as that challenge does with developing a comfortable interface with one's esteemed fellow professionals who also typically constitute the overwhelming majority of the membership of the political science academic departments in which perhaps 75 percent of the public administration literati have prime residence. This motivating factor applies powerfully even today, and it was critical in earlier days when the new specialty might have succumbed except for the nurturance it received within political science.

Second, the concern over maintenance historically featured public administration in the role of tail to political science's dog.[7] That is, leading concepts of public administration tended to be more sensitive to developments in political science than to the character and texture of its own target phenomena and concerns. At one critical juncture, for example, Roscoe Martin articulated this prime characteristic of an acceptable state of the relationship: "the continuing dominion of political science over public administration."[8]

Patently, it is strategically perverse for public administrationists to settle on a comprehensive paradigm or guiding metaphor that is stronger on maintenance than on task. This is the case whether the outcome is intended, or whether it just occurs as a by-product of reasonable desires to preserve historical identifications and associations.

Third, there is only a slight possibility that any reasonably comprehensive paradigm or guiding metaphor can today satisfactorily meet both task and maintenance challenges. The point can be suggested from two perspectives, from that of general principle as well as of specific practice. As to the former, at least five possible mode of task/maintenance interaction are possible:

- The development of any specific comfortable guiding concept might be seen as enriching both political science and public administration, not only in maintenance terms, but also in effectively dealing with their respective areas of inquiry.

- The guiding concept might be seen as more or less irrelevant to task.

- A mutually acceptable guiding concept might be seen at one time as serving both the maintenance needs and task needs of political science and public administration, while that same concept could later become dysfunctional in both senses.

- A guiding concept might be seen as prescribing mutually acceptable relationships that complicate or severely hinder the analytic work of either political science or public administration, or both.

- A paradigm might emphasize task to the point of downplaying or disregarding maintenance needs.

As for specific practice, the historic record seems clear enough. On balance, the third and fourth modes in the list just cited most nearly describe the actual quality of task/maintenance interaction in leading approaches to public administration. For a relatively few people associated with public aministration, the fifth mode was dominant. See the Social-Psychological Paradigm described later for relevant detail.

Focus on Task

Despite the acknowledged long-run coprimacy of task and maintenance challenges, the emphasis in the discussion that follows is primarily on task. The underlying rationale has four emphases:

First, severe and growing dissatisfaction exists among public administrationists with what are here called task activities—that is, with their ability to develop, or at least use, powerful tools for analysis and action. This reflects a fast fall from grace. Through the 1940s, public administration was very much concerned with managerial matters, and specialists in this field were buoyantly confident that managerial answers to the critical problems were known or at least could be found.

Second, in my view, any developmental work toward a paradigm for public administration should give a clear preference to task rather than maintenance features, simply because the strong historical preference has been just the reverse. Witness Ostrom's quick disposition of Simon: "Simon challenged and his challenge stands. But having challenged, Simon returned to the world of bureaucratic organizations to pursue his work within the familiar constraints of a social universe dichotomized into the domains of politics and administration."[9]

Though it is easier said than done, the major criterion in judging a paradigm should be its value in helping students cope with the phenomena of public administration, rather than whether or not it challenges a prevailing concept of the relationship between public administration and political science. Thus the key question about Simon is not whether he returned to "familiar constraints," but how much he contributed to the development of managerial art and science in matters relevant to the historic concerns of public administration.

Although the point defies anything approaching proof, it is the viewpoint here that public administration literature generally emphasizes the wrong question about concepts for inquiry. The usual question strongly tended to be: What does this approach do to our maintenance activities, especially with reference to political science? The contrasting task-oriented question is: What does this approach do to help or hinder understanding of target phenomena? No great wonder, then, that major discontent does exist about public administration's track record in generating "correct answers," or at least useful directions for inquiry.[10]

Note that public administrationists clearly do not hold the patent on such apparent obtuseness. For perhaps fifty years, to illustrate, physical scientists searched for a "magic bullet" to kill all germs. To them the first priority seemed natural enough—develop a pure germ culture on which "magic bullet" candidates could do their thing, so as to permit conclusive test of any "bullet's" efficacy. The search was frustrating. Germ cultures often became "contaminated," sometimes by a curious mold, and scientists laboriously had to start over again. Suddenly, and simultaneously, a large number of researchers had the same insight—the mold was *a* solution rather than *the* problem. In short order, a whole spectrum of antibactericidal agents were developed, relatives of the curious mold penicillin.

The third reason for emphasis on task is that it is possible to contribute meaningfully to an enriched understanding of public management without much or any attention to "maintenance." This implies no cry for a radical separatism. That is to say, however the public administration turf is circumscribed, there will be many critical points of articulation with political science.

Fourth, and finally, some substantial untidiness concerning maintenance features is appropriate because of the diverse classes of phenomena that must be included in any viable concept of "public administration."

The implied case for a substantial untidiness regarding maintenance issues may be illustrated conveniently in terms of the five classes of phenomena relevant to public administration that were introduced earlier. Consider the politics/administration distinction. For most practical purposes, even a very strict separation would not be very troublesome in public administration effort focusing on class 1 above, that is on internal agency processes. And there is no doubt that much valuable work has been accomplished within a class 1 focus.

The literature tends far more toward a blanket rejection of politics/administration than toward a recognition of the valuable work that has been done under its guidance.

This is no argument for politics/administration as concrete locus, because such a procrustean concept would cut off public administration from most or all class 4 phenomena, for example. Simplistic views of scientism as rigidly setting fact apart from value—which often were part of the politics/administration vocabulary—would exclude class 5 phenomena.

These notions reject the kind of conceptual true believership that is so much in the fabric of the literature. Put positively, any viable paradigm is not likely to be one based on simple and clear distinctions, except at the cost of excluding or undervaluing some central phenomena in the five classes listed earlier. Moreover, it is most unlikely that we are today anywhere near the doorstep of a comprehensive paradigm.

Bias against Paradigmatic Closure

This argument urges against early closure toward any comprehensive paradigm because the prevailing mind set in the literature is awkward. To explain, the mind set appropriate to the development of paradigms is intellectual and self-correcting. In contrast, today's basic concern in public administration is seen here as more emotional than intellectual, as more concerned with who identifies with which discipline than with what specific problems should be analyzed and how. The needs are more will and skill than intellectual vision. As I noted elsewhere:

> progress in some areas of public administration will only be hindered by waiting for closure about its interfaces with other academic specialties. Indeed, in many areas, I am convinced that there is no intellectual crisis in public administration. The crisis is simply a failure to do more of what patently needs doing, and a failure to aggressively seek those skills necessary for the doing.[11]

Under existing conditions, in short, early closure most probably is unwise.

The focus in the following discussion will aggressively seek to argue against closing toward a comprehensive paradigm via an introduction and analysis of three paradigms in public administration. In overview, each of those paradigms has significant enough inadequacies as to imply pessimism about any comprehensive resolution in the foreseeable future. If major scientific advance is a matter of standing on the shoulders of conceptual giants, public administration has substantial growing to do before it can serve to support the last few steps toward a comprehensive paradigm.

In sharp contrast to electioneering for a comprehensive paradigm, the broad recommendation here urges the aggressive development of numerous sub-paradigmatic approaches that variously relate or integrate the several classes of public administration target phenomena described earlier, as well as draw on aspects of three public administration paradigms that historically have been supported by influential observers.

Three Comprehensive Paradigms in Public Administration

That history argues against closing on a comprehensive paradigm must be demonstrated in detail. At least three times over the last half-century or so, in fact, students of public administration have heralded the coming of a comprehensive paradigm, here understood as key orientations toward objects of concern and analysis.[12] Each of these paradigms will be sketched in a separate table and briefly discussed. The paradigms do not explicitly succeed and eliminate one another. Although dominant attention did shift from one to another, the paradigms are best seen as variably powerful conditioning influences on the work of individual scholars and practitioners.

Traditional Paradigm

Observers agree that the early history of public administration was based on a set of leading ideas like those in Table 2.1, despite some dispute about intellectual pedigree. Thus most scholars essentially see in Table 2.1 the imprint of the German theoretician Max Weber, the major contributor to what has come to be known as the "theory of bureaucracy." Others see the Traditional Paradigm as more of a product of the ideas of Woodrow Wilson, whose "The Study of Administration" is universally acknowledged to be a kind of birth certificate for public administration.

As Structure for Organizing Work

The Traditional Paradigm appears in many guises, but no doubt the most common one is the picture of an organization structure that most people carry around in their heads,[14] which picture also appears on most formal organization charts. Figure 2.1 sketches this skeletal structure for activities A, B, and C that contribute to products 1, 2, and 3. The "principles of public administration,"

TABLE 2.1 Traditional Paradigm

Guiding political philosophy	Centralized model: power is more responsible and responsive to the degree that it is unified and directed from a single center
Focal unit of analysis	Formal or legal structuring of individual jobs[13] and their aggregation into complex authority/responsibility networks for accomplishing broad purposes, with jobs being viewed as "building blocks" of larger and static organizational structures
Central emphasis	Emphasis on *a* collectivity that magnifies the impact of separate individuals, permitting several to accomplish what even the most skillful or powerful individual cannot do
Central concepts	Legitimate authority and responsibility
Implied metaphor of "organization"	A "trickle down" metaphor: there is a single dominant center of power, with absolute or substantial sovereignty and legitimate authority, whose members have little or no control or influence over it
Guiding principle	Perfection in hierarchical ordering so as to achieve economy and efficiency
Central focus	Prescriptively intraorganizational: the focus is on how authority and responsibility in organizations should be structured so as to be internally efficient, effective, and even orderly, reinforced by sharp distinctions between "politics" and "administration"
	The focus is on developing processes and structure for internal control in organizations, with the goal of heightening efficiency and production
Model for motivating and controlling behavior	Within public agencies: command-obey model, a vertical linkage of organizational superiors to subordinates
	Between an agency and its clients: basically through the ballot box, which impacts on elected officials and, through them, on high-level political appointees
	This pairing of representative democracy in political life with autocracy in administrative life may seem anomalous or even contradictory, but the pairing reflects the intended superiority of political mandates and also implies the complementary concept of administration as technical, as narrow implementation, and as value-neutral
Dominant role for officials	The responsible technocrat, whose tenure and competence are protected by public employ in exchange for neutral and equal service to all policies and to all administrative superiors

or the traditional theory of organization, prescribe a generic structure that is consistent with certain axioms or assumptions, among the most important of which are the following:

- Authority is a vertical, or hierarchical, relation.

- Only a relatively small number of subordinates should report to any one superior.

- Work should be departmentalized in terms of "like" activities, typically called "functions" at high levels of organization and "tasks" or "processes" at low levels.

Some Major Problems

The overall sense of Table 2.1 and Figure 2.1 should be relatively straightforward and, if not, lengthy critical analyses are available elsewhere.[15] So we need here pause only to detail some major limitations of the paradigm. Four emphases will do the job.

First, Table 2.1 fixates on prescription, on how the public administrator's world should be. This encourages two charges. First of all, the paradigm often has been shown to be variously wide of the mark in describing what actually exists, even though such demonstrations are often interpreted only as providing further proof that reality should be organized as the Traditional Paradigm prescribes. Relatedly, and far more seriously, because its prescriptions are not based on knowledge of empirical regularities, the paradigm is vulnerable to demonstrations that administrative efficiency does not necessarily result when the conditions it prescribes actually exist. These demonstrations came regularly, typically first in the form of some blockbuster like the Hawthorne studies, or

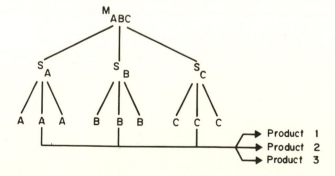

Fig. 2.1 A structure patterned after the "principles of public administration."

Blau's later work, seminal efforts that were followed by numerous variations on their general theme.[16]

Second, the Traditional Paradigm emphasizes formal and technical uniformity, as contrasted with human diversity. This leaves it vulnerable to charges by those with a humanist orientation that organization analysis is interested only in finding round pegs for round holes, that "the organization" not only comes first but that its demands are exclusive and preemptive.

Third, Table 2.1 implies a curious internal contradiction. Its sanctions representative government in political life, yet prescribes a patent autocratic sovereignty in organizational life. That contradiction bothers many observers, who worry that incautious emphasis on the "theory of unitary sovereignty" in the Traditional Paradigm can unbalance the basic institutional arrangements of our political life, which rest on a more complex theory of multiple or concurrent sovereignty. For example, the forty-year expansion of the presidency—blunted somewhat in recent days by Watergate, but perhaps only temporarily—implies just such an imbalance with respect to the Congress.[17]

Fourth, the Traditional Paradigm suffers grievously because of its association with politics/administration. The argument is a complex one. But to make a long story very short, the distinction as an *analytic* one has much to recommend it, at least in maintenance terms. It describes separate domains for political science and public administration, while also providing a stout umbilical between the two areas of inquiry. But many made too much of a convenient notion.[18] They bowdlerized the analytic distinction into the patently false notion that politics and administration each had a *concrete locus*, administration in the bureaucracy and politics in the executive branch and legislature.

Why this change in usage occurred is elusive, but it is at least clear that early proponents of politics/administration did not specify a concrete locus. Consider Ostrom's view that "Wilson and his associates" argued for a sharp distinction between politics and administration. That point has not always been that clear to all.[19] At least five interpretations of Wilson have been made, and each has some support:

1. Wilson explicitly urged a sharp distinction between politics and administration.

2. Wilson shrank from making a sharp distinction, although he often talked around it and even sometimes approached it.

3. Politics and administration for Wilson commingle at some hierarchical levels and are relatively distinct at others.

4. Wilson was really interested in morality in government, with some vagueness on politics/administration being useful in legitimating the

kinds of behavior in which Wilson was really interested, that is, behavior related to the delicate balance of making "public opinion efficient without suffering it to be meddlesome."

5. There are common problems, processes, and dynamics in all or most administrative activities, in all polities and businesses, and an emphasis on "generic administration" is therefore a more convenient early target than is politics, whose patterns clearly vary in kaleidoscopic ways in different regimes.

My view is that Wilson and other early students like Goodnow are most conveniently read as reflecting combinations of alternatives 2, 3, 4, and 5.

But conceptual care was hardly the order of the day. And right or wrong, concrete locus came to be associated with the politics/administration notion, almost inevitably so both in the past and now.

Social-Psychological Paradigm

Beginning with the World War II period, more or less, a new paradigm began to influence significantly the literature of public administration. Conveniently, this new set of leading ideas is here called the Social-Psychological Paradigm, and is sketched in Table 2.2. It differs markedly from the Traditional Paradigm, especially in three senses that deserve highlighting.

First, the Social-Psychological Paradigm emphasizes description, while the Traditional Paradigm is essentially prescriptive. The contrast can be established in two ways, one direct and the other more subtle. The direct way of establishing the contrast is through a comparison of early public administration texts with the Hawthorne studies,[20] that exemplar of work in the tradition of the second paradigm. In sum, the thrust of much work in the Social-Psychological Paradigm can be characterized in these terms:

- Such work often establishes that the conditions prescribed by the Traditional Paradigm do not in fact exist.

- Such work sometimes establishes that, even when the conditions prescribed by the Traditional Paradigm do in fact exist, the predicted consequences do not occur in many or most cases.

A more subtle approach to demonstrating the prescriptive character of the Traditional Paradigm illustrates at the same time the descriptive character of the Social-Psychological Paradigm. Basically, observers like Douglas McGregor began to stress that the "principles" consistent with the Traditional Paradigm were only logical derivations from a set of implicit axioms or assumptions,

TABLE 2.2   Social-Psychological Paradigm

Guiding political philosophy	Pluralist model: power is more responsible and responsive to the degree that it is exerted by multiple collectivities, both large[21] and small[22]
Focal unit of analysis	"Informal" collectivities such as the small group are seen as key elements in large productive or social organizations; indeed, the abreaction to the formal or legalistic approach is so complete that much derivative work can be characterized as focusing on "people without organizations"[23]
Central emphasis	Emphasis on several collectivities or "reference groups," in whose incomplete congruence individuals variously find freedom and fear, security and anomie, emotional support and oppressive conformity[24]
Central concepts	Cohesiveness, group climate or atmosphere, leadership, and so forth
Implied metaphor or "organization"	A "percolate up" metaphor: authority and sovereignty are seen at least as two-way streets, with some formulations like that of Barnard even arguing that: "Authority is the character of a communication (order) in a formal organization by virtue of which it is accepted by a contributor to or 'members' of the organization as governing the action he contributes.... Therefore under this definition the decision as to whether an order has authority or not lies with the persons to whom it is addressed, and does not reside in 'persons of authority' or those who issue these orders."[25]
Guiding principle	Increasing the congruence among the demands of formal organizations, the personality needs of organization members, and the characteristics of the reference groups of members[26]
Central focus	Descriptively intraorganizational: on how organizations and their members actually behave, especially as contrasted with formal prescriptions, with two themes being dominant: (1) that formal authority is not adequate to describe or prescribe relationships in effective organizations;[27] and (2) that "politics" and "administration" are not sharply differentiated
	Moreover, such descriptive work increasingly begins to generate prescriptions about how to increase the integration of organizations and their employees, with the goals

TABLE 2.2   (Continued)

Central focus (continued)	of heightening production *and* employee satisfaction.[28] In part, these prescriptions are technique-oriented and deal with decentralized delegation, greater employee participation, and so on. In larger part, these prescriptions are ends-oriented and thus argue for the replacement of the Traditional Paradigm with models of man that rest on such formulations as Theory Y, on Maslow's self-actualizing man, on Argyris's dimensions for individual growth, or Herzberg's concept of motivators versus satisfiers, and so on.[29]
Model for motivating and controlling behavior	Within public agencies: emphasis on how employee participation and group decision making can complement and to a degree supplement the command-obey model[30]
	Between agency and its clients: emphasis on describing how the control of "politics" over "administration" is limited,[31] as by: (1) short tenure and inexperience of top-level political appointees; (2) the social and emotional identifications of career employees with specific programs or policies, with respect to which they are not neutral even though they might be neutral toward specific political parties or candidates; and (3) the impact of interest groups on the development and implementation of public policy
Dominant role for officials	The representative civil servant who variously influences policy in its development or implementation, and who often identifies with a specific public program and hence is not neutral,[32] but who—because of lateral entrance and the open character of our public personnel systems—reflects the needs and aspirations of the broader citizenry.
	Administrators are no longer seen as solely controlled by their political neutrality and responsiveness to elected officials; they are administratively responsible because they are representative, in vaguely defined senses[33]

rather than universally valid prescriptions, as most had long imagined. Table 2.3 depicts one popular way of expressing the assumptions and axioms form which the "principles" are said to derive by the critics of the Traditional Paradigm, using McGregor's terminology. It is fair to say that McGregor's approach came

TABLE 2.3   Assumptions of Axioms Underlying "Principles"[a]

Explicit Propositions or "Principles"	Underlying Assumptions or Axioms
1. A well-defined chain of command that vertically channels formal interaction	1. Work is inherently distasteful to most people
2. A system of procedures and rules for dealing with all contingencies at work, which reinforces the reporting insularity of each bureau and functionary	2. Most people prefer to be directed and have little desire for responsibility in developing and maintaining a social system
3. A division of labor based upon specialization by major function or process that vertically fragments a flow of work	3. Most people have little capacity for creativity in work or in developing values or norms to guide behavior
4. Promotion and selection based on technical competence defined consistently with 1-3 above	4. Motivation occurs only (or mostly) at an elemental stimulus-response level
5. Impersonality in relations between organization members and between them and their clients	5. Therefore, people in organizations must be closely controlled and directed, and often coerced

[a] Based on Douglas McGregor, *The Human Side of Enterprise* (New York: McGraw-Hill, 1960), especially 33-58.

to characterize a generation of work in organizational analysis, and so compelling was his argument that today his name is accorded the highest level of recognition by students and practitioners of management.

McGregor's formulation was used by critics of the "principles of organization" in two basic ways. That is, critics took pains to make the central points that the axioms or assumptions taken to underlay the Traditional Paradigm and the diverse forms in which it has been expressed (1) either did not appear to be consistent with reality and/or (2) are not normatively attractive in any case. Thus the "bureaucratic ethos" associated with the Traditional Paradigm was attacked on both empirical and normative grounds.

As Structure for Organizing Work

Based especially on empirical grounds, but also to some extent on what seemed to many to be more desirable conditions at work, alternative models for organizing work began to evolve during the hegemony of the Social-Psychological

Paradigm. The terms describing these alternative models differ widely. Thus one may refer to "product organization," "flow of work," "decentralized management," "discrete subassemblies," "autonomous teams," and "matrix overlays"—among many other variants—and the basic referent is quite similar or even identical. That is to say, the common underlying model of such diverse designators is of the generic form sketched in Figure 2.2; and the several variants of that generic form also rest on axioms or assumptions similar to those detailed there.

The simple structure in Figure 2.2 could support wide-ranging description and analysis, but only three points about the "alternative structure" for organizing work will be made here.

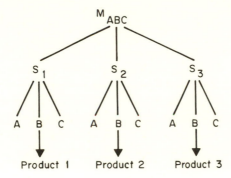

Fig. 2.2 An alternative structure for organizing work, with associated assumptions or axioms.

Explicit propositions:

- Authoritative relations occur up, down, and across an organization.
- Under appropriate conditions, many subordinates can report to a single superior.
- Work should be departmentalized in terms of *related* activities necessary to a flow of work.

Underlying assumptions or axioms:

- Work can be attractive to most people.
- Most people prefer substantial autonomy at work and can be responsible.
- Motivation occurs at complex social and psychological levels, as well as at an elemental stimulus → response level.

First, there is no need here to detail the behavioral probabilities associated with the structure in Figure 2.2, as contrasted with Figure 2.1. It is enough here to suggest the nature of the contrast, while directing inquisitive readers elsewhere.[34] I concluded a lengthy comparison of the two structures in these words:

> the model ... organizes around integrative departments, that is, it groups together activities that are related in a total flow of work. This integrative thrust at the departmental level also can be extended to operators, as through job rotation and job enlargement. In addition, the model seeks the minimum control that is consistent with end-item quality and quantity. The multiple opportunities for self-discipline and self-control built into the model, for example, reduce the need for external repression in tying individual needs to organization goals. The key factors are teams which control a flow of work whose performance is easily and meaningfully comparable.[35]

There is both advantage and disadvantage in this descriptive bias of work reflecting the Social-Psychological Paradigm. Illustratively, such work at its best provides a picture of what administrative reality is; and it can also generate a growing awareness of the conditions necessary to support desirable existential states. However, such work at its worst also can encourage some convenient but dangerous assumptions. These assumptions include two central ones: (1) that what is, also should be; or (2) that any differences between what is and should be are of no concern in the scientific study of management. Much of the dispute about Phase III's science of public administration, in fact, hinged on just such central issues. Consider many Phase III variants of the mission and role of public administration, for example, which emphasized their value-free character. Many public administrationists were concerned that many administrative scientists were all too willing to make one or both of the two central assumptions about values detailed above. And many, probably most, public administrationists would not accept those assumptions and were willing to wage major academic war over the issue.

Second and relatedly, the new paradigm is behavior-oriented, whereas the Traditional Paradigm emphasizes legitimacy, structure, and authority. Crudely, the organization comes first in the Traditional Paradigm, and people must adapt to it or be discarded. In the Social-Psychological Paradigm, in contrast, the priorities accorded to organization and individual are certainly not reversed, but their relative weights clearly shift in major ways. For example, the essence of two of its major themes—"participation" and "group decision making"—is that people and their needs matter, even in organizations and perhaps especially in organizations. These two themes, of course, are major derivations from the descriptive research encouraged by the Social-Psychological Paradigm.

Third, the Social-Psychological Paradigm is not rooted "out there" in a kind of font of sovereignty, but has a definite if complex locus in the behavior of members of an organization. This bias is reflected most dramatically in the definition of authority as residing not in those who issue orders, but in those who are the targets of the orders. To be sure, not all observers were willing to go as far as Simon certainly did go, or as far as Barnard may have gone, in this critical definition. But the Social-Psychological Paradigm clearly provides encouragement for assigning real importance to the receivers of orders. The Traditional Paradigm emphasizes the order giver, in contrast, and encourages a view of order receivers as "the hands," a revealing measure of their status in the paradigm.

Some Attractions and Repulsions

This second paradigm has proved to be a source of major contention in public administration. In sum, the paradigm has induced a number of double binds, if not multiple binds, for public administrationists. For example, the paradigm was at the heart of the debate (some call it warfare) between the "behavioralists" and the "traditionalists" or "institutionalists."

Four examples illustrate the depth and diversity of the complex set of attractions and repulsions generated by the Social-Psychological Paradigm. First, the paradigm directs attention to "the organization" as a kind of abstracted singularity. For a minority of public administration specialists, this simplification of reality promised an opportunity to develop a real science, or at least a chance to add substantially to our knowledge of what administration is really like. However, "the organization" poses a barrier for most of those associated with public administration, as well as for many political scientists, for two major reasons. "The organization" often seems too tidy and discrete a target for those whose training and interests are rooted in complex levels of institutions,[36] such as international, federal, state, or local. In addition, the focus on an "abstracted singularity" seems simplistic to those accustomed to thinking in terms of diverse "political cultures" or "national characters." For such students, the Social-Psychological Paradigm adequately serves neither task nor maintenance needs.

Second, the paradigm encourages early attention to lower levels of "the organization."[37] The micro-focus is not attractive to many in public administration, the bulk of whom were more or less enthusiastic supporters of a burgeoning presidency and were little attracted to the worm's-eye view of the bird.[38] Less directly but no less certainly, the micro-focus of the Social-Psychological Paradigm is seen as providing comfort to—if not actually opting for—a Politics/Administration distinction, which notion has been vigorously rejected since World War II by political scientists and public administrationists alike. This micro-focus also threatens a popular approach to establishing a sturdy conceptual tie between public administration and political science via "public policy."[39]

Whatever its task-related virtues, then, the Social-Psychological Paradigm threatened major maintenance efforts to tie together political science and public administration conceptually, and at a crucial time.[40] This fact encouraged many to reject the paradigm enthusiastically.

Third, the Social-Psychological Paradigm is often seen as neglecting values, or even as forcefully rejecting them. There are many imprecisions in the bundling together of such notions as "science," "value-free," "behavioralism," and so on. But the bundling was often engaged in as enthusiastically by proponent as by opponent of this second and aggressively scientific paradigm. In this particular, many persons identified with public administration and political science decided that there was too little in that paradigm that was relevant to their traditional concerns. In their view, it threatened maintenance needs without facilitating important aspects of task.

Fourth, the second paradigm is transitional, and consequently it was open to bombardment from all sides. Consider the flurry of attention to "participative management," an early product of the study of behavior in organizations consistent with the Social-Psychological Paradigm. Proponents of the Traditional Paradigm attack such work as subverting the concepts of sovereignty and authority underlying that paradigm. Other observers attack group decision making from an opposite perspective. Thus, some highlight the manipulative quality of some early approaches to participative management, as in the "cow sociology" whose goal was to increase production by dealing with the symptoms of worker discontent by means of "talking therapies" or "walking counselors," without ever dealing with the causes of discontent. Behavioral scientists of this genre sometimes became "servants of power" who sought only to make more palatable a technical system that is designed around nonhuman or antihuman properties. Many other political scientists and public administrationists saw "participative management" as merely being naïve politics/administration in another (if clever) guise, and hence a fit target for rejection. To be fair about it, major exemplars of the Social-Psychological Paradigm like Herbert Simon sometimes seemed to embrace just such a distinction,[41] and hence they encouraged the rejection of their broader systems of thought.

Humanist/Systemic Paradigm

The very designation of this third paradigm implies the magnitude of the intellectual dilemmas for which it seeks resolution. The goal is nothing less than integration of that which commonly stands in contraposition, if not in stark opposition. The scholarly pedigrees of the two orientations stitched together by the third paradigm can be illustrated briefly.

Some Humanist Sources

To begin, the third paradigm is called "humanist" because it places far stronger emphasis on the needs of the sovereign individual than does the Social-Psychological model which, however, did much to start that conceptual ball rolling. Dvorin and Simmons mince no words in their version of "radical humanism." They assert "that the ends of man *are* the ends of bureaucracy." Most of the literature puts it the other way around. To a great extent, other humanistic proponents join Dvorin and Simmons in noting that they are "not willing to compromise . . . human values on any grounds."[42]

Only general agreement exists about what specific "ends of man" are at issue, but the usual emphasis is on some set of human needs or goals whose satisfaction, the available evidence suggests, is closely tied to mature personal development. No doubt, the most well known set of these growth goals is Maslow's "hierarchy of needs."[43] Similary, Argyris argues that the growing personality needs to move rightward on continua as the following:

Passivity ⎯⎯⎯⎯⎯⎯→ Increasing activity

Dependence ⎯⎯⎯⎯⎯→ Growing independence and inter-
dependence

Limited behaviors ⎯⎯⎯⎯→ Widening behaviors

Short perspective ⎯⎯⎯⎯→ Lengthening time perspectives

Lack of awareness and control ⎯⎯→ Growing awareness and control

When an individual is prevented from moving further rightward, and even moreso when he or she is forced to move leftward, a need-depriving situation exists, whose prime organizational consequences include decreased satisfaction and output.[45] To avoid such consequences, the Argyrian version of organizational humanism prescribes that managerial systems should be constituted so as to permit (even encourage) rightward movement on the continua above, as by creating conditions under which the organization member can:

- Experience the totality of the organization
- Increase self-responsibility, self-discipline, and self-motivation
- Decrease compulsive and defensive behaviors
- Increase control over immediate work environment
- Utilize a broadening range of abilities, especially cognitive and inter-personal ones
- Increase time perspective

Although the argument has been made at length elsewhere, it is important to note here that such prescriptions are direct opposites of those implied by the Traditional Paradigm, as it is reflected in Figure 2.1. For example, that figure prescribes specialization by function or process, as contrasted with a total flow of work. That is, the traditional organization of work requires limiting employee behavior, which is exactly what the Argyrian approach proscribes. Oppositely, the Argyrian needs fit nicely with the structure sketched in Figure 2.2, which rests upon the descriptive work inspired by the Social-Psychological Paradigm.

At its best, then, the humanist component of the Humanist/Systemic Paradigm seeks to put in the explicit service of man the kind of research inspired by the Social-Psychological Paradigm. In this sense, it is a value-sensitive use of behavioral science.

Some Systemic Sources

The second basic orientation in the third paradigm is called "systemic" because it proposes to utilize tools and models for analysis that are oriented toward maximizing some sort of broad social utility based on rigorous analysis of the most comprehensive possible set of social priorities and objectives.

"System" as concept intruded in major ways on the consciousness of scholars and practitioners in the 1950s,[46] but its most obvious and impressive impact on public adminsitration came with PPBS, or planning-programming-budgeting system. As Mosher and Harr note: PPBS "broke over the Pentgon building in 1951 and is beating on other agencies today...."[47] And "system" was its watchword, in diverse meanings. PPBS emphasized "system" in such diverse senses as the following:

- A "systematic" linkage encompassing broad social and political objectives as well as plans, then detailed programs, and finally operating budgets
- A planning "system" that projects (perhaps) five years beyond a current budget year
- "Systematic" comparisons of various possible alternative combinations of inputs and outputs in terms of costs and benefits
- The use of skilled "systems analysts" to make such comparisons
- Reliance on techniques and computational technologies to make such "systemic" comparisons
- A strong sense of "system" as a hierarchy of objectives or goals, with quite strict subordination of some objectives to others

The second component of the Humanist/Systemic Paradigm also draws support from another popular approach to Public Administration, through what is commonly called "public choice" or sometimes "political economy."[48] Work in this tradition is an extension of classical economic thought, and is characterized by the intensive and intentionally rational analysis of assumptions or propositions about man, his nature, and his collective relationships. Chapter 5 will analyze in detail one influential variant of this kind of analysis. Some sense of the typical line of argument can be suggested here by Downs's analysis of bureaucracy. All bureaucratic agents, he explains, are "assumed to be *utility maximizers*," a concept that in its economics meaning refers to "a sort of mental currency that decision makers use in arriving at choices among things that have no 'lowest common denominator.' " Because "utility maximization really means the rational pursuit of one's goals," Downs goes on, he finds it necessary to distinguish a variety of "general motives" and "individual goals" that he assumes operate according to a "self-interest axiom." Thus Downs observes: "Whenever we speak of rational behavior, we mean rational behavior directed at least partly toward ends that serve the self-interests of the actors concerned." From such building blocks, Downs goes on to derive a set of types of bureaucratic officials and to develop logical ways in which various types should behave so as to maximize their utility.[49]

In its general line of argument—the logical development of assumptions and axioms to develop a rational model—the second basic aspect of the Humanist/Systemic Paradigm shares significant common ground with the Traditional Paradigm. The difference is that the third paradigm more exuberantly defines "system" rather than "organization" as its unit of analysis.

The Humanist/Systemic Paradigm, then, is one huge conceptual suture seeking to bring together much that has been practically disparate, if not ineluctably separate.

Table 2.4 details this third paradigm, which derives from many sources. The major explicit expressions consistent with this paradigm, however, are in the literature of the new public administration and in Ostrom's *The Intellectual Crisis in American Public Administration*.

Five Major Characteristics

Several major characteristics of the Humanist/Systemic Paradigm deserve discussion. First, like the Traditional Paradigm, the third paradigm is strongly prescriptive. The point is perhaps most easily made in terms of the role demands on public managers that have been derived from the general world view of the third paradigm. Ross Clayson and Ron Gilbert provide an especially comprehensive and artful example of this genre, parts of which are illustrated in Table 2.5[55]

Table 2.5 takes some liberties with the presentation of Clayton and Gilbert, but it should not violate the spirit of their work. In effect these two students prescribe two ideals in some detail: how the public manager should view self; and how the public manager should view the recipients of public services. These ideal views contrast sharply, depending upon whether the public manager operates within the framework of the Traditional Paradigm or that of

TABLE 2.4   Humanist/Systemic Paradigm[a]

Guiding political philosophy	Market model: power is responsible and responsive to the degree that it is divided among multiple wielders who can and do limit and control one another
	This prescription is based on: (1) observations as to how large organizations, both public and business, tend to serve their own internal needs at the expense of the needs of their clients or customers, of how they tend to misread or neglect feedback from clients or customers;[50] (2) observations as to how supposedly countervailing organizations can in fact collude to submerge or distort the needs of common clients or customers, as in "sweetheart contracts" between "labor" and "management"; and (3) conclusions as to the ineffectiveness of *the* classic tool of popular control, voting in elections, given new tools for inducing and managing public opinion
Focal unit of analysis	Individuals as sovereign consumers with market power, which power is enhanced by the deliberate fragmentation of authority within any one jurisdiction or organization, as well as between several of them[51]
Central emphasis	Emphasis on unmediated response to needs and aspirations of individuals, which implies minimal control or interference by government or other large bureaucracies
Central concepts	Costs/benefits, congruence between social objectives and allocations of resources
Implied metaphor of "organization"	A systems metaphor: any organizational system is seen as one of a nest of systems of increasing comprehensiveness, with an ultimate system specifying the priorities or social objectives against which the processes and outputs of all less comprehensive systems are to be judged[52]
Guiding principle	Equity in the service of social justice
Central focus	Prescriptively intersystemic: the focus is on an organization *and* its multiple interfaces with clients *as well as* with other organizations in its total environment[53]
	For example, the emphasis is on the delivery of services which implies, at least, an interface between: (1) efficient internal agency processes; (2) employees who are highly motivated to be responsive to clients, and who are also willing and able to change as well as to integrate diverse specialties at the point of delivery; and (3) con-

TABLE 2.4   (Continued)

	sumer demands as to when, where, and how agency services are desired
	Consistently, distinctions between "politics" and "administration" are blurred or disappear; and determining what is internal to an organization and what is external becomes more come chancy and arbitrary
	The focus is on the kind and character of distribution and consumption, with the goal of heightening and balancing satisfaction both for users of an organization's goods and services, as well as for employees through the quality of the organizational life they experience
Model for motivating and controlling behavior	Within an agency—as well as between an agency, its clients, and other competing or collaborating organizations—many models are potential alternatives to hierarchy, to the ballot box, and to various forms of employee participation, including bargaining, exchange, competition, nonviolent demonstration and confrontation, and, perhaps, violent demonstration and confrontation
Dominant role for officials	The responsive administrator, a proficient advocate who can be a pleader for a cause dictated by social equity while applying technical or programmatic expertise to the pursuit of that cause
	Any deviations from equity "always should be in the direction of providing more and better services to those in lower social, economic, and political circumstances"[54]

[a]This paradigm draws several emphases from Vincent Ostrom, *The Intellectual Crisis in American Public Administration* (University, Ala.: University of Alabama Press, 1973), especially pp. 111-112.

the Humanist/Systemic Paradigm. Only part of the Clayton/Gilbert prescription is presented in Table 2.5, that dealing with the public manager's concept of his own role. Even that part, however, illustrates how work consistent with the Humanist/Systemic Paradigm implies both significant and different effects than the two earlier paradigms, and especially different from the Traditional Paradigm.

Second, the Humanist/Systemic Paradigm seeks to transcend the limitations of its predecessors by assimilating them. That is, its system component owes much to the Traditional Paradigm, as has been suggested in the section

TABLE 2.5   The Public Manager, Ideal View of Self, and Two Paradigms[a]

Perceptions of Public Managers in Relation to:	Ideal View of Self	
	In Traditional Paradigm	In Humanist/Systemic Paradigm
Projects	An administrator of	A champion of
Policy	A policy implementer	A policy maker
Perception of political authority	Organizationally centered—vertical	Community centered—horizontal
Effectiveness criteria criteria	Commited to economic and efficient government	Commited to social and economic justice
Change	An adaptor who copes	An advocate who influences

[a]Based on Ron Clayton and Ron Gilbert, "Perspectives of Public Managers: Their Implications for Public Service Delivery Systems," *Public Management,* vol. 53 (November 1971), especially p. 10.

above dealing with some systemic sources of the third paradigm. In addition, its humanist component derives from the research and though in the Social-Psychological Paradigm, as well as from such predecessors as many Phase III variants. For example, note that the Humanist/Systemic Paradigm tends to blur the distinction between public and business organizations, between what is external and what is internal in an organization's comings and goings. The third paradigm is very attractive from this point of view, for compelling theoretical and practical reasons urge such an integration.[56]

Third, the Humanist/Systemic Paradigm rests on substantial bodies of theories and technologies related to both humanist and systemic components. These theories and technologies can only be sketched here, but even a sketch suggests the conceptual range encompassed by the third paradigm. More specifically:

- On the humanist side,[57] the third paradigm rests on (1) several "growth psychologies," which share a model of the person as having relatively specific needs qua human, the satisfaction of which needs constitutes a kind of ontological goal for human development; and (2) technologies for individual and organization change, such as those deriving from the "laboratory approach."

- On the systemic side, the third paradigm rests on (1) models for the comprehensive analysis of complex exchanges or input/output transactions, such as cost/benefit study and systems analysis; and (2) technologies for quantitative analysis and decision making, such as linear programming, queueing theory, and so forth, whose use really began with World War II and has rapidly expanded since then.

Critically, also, these theories and technologies are but recently and incompletely developed. This elemental fact is a source of substantial mischief. For example, public administrationists can espouse the third paradigm in broad principle, as it were, yet lack an appreciation of the existing mechanisms to activate the paradigm or even an empathic understanding of the implications of that paradigm and its evolving methodologies for various definitions of the scope of public administration.

Fourth, the Humanist/Systemic Paradigm variously and radically seeks to expand the field of vision of the two other paradigms. Thus the behavioral focus of the Social-Psychological Paradigm often neglects system features; and the intraorganizational focus of the Traditional Paradigm encourages the neglect of relationships between organizations, which is also a weakness of the Social-Psychological Paradigm. The Humanist/Systemic Paradigm proposes to include the perspectives of the other two paradigms, as well as to improve on them by stressing systemic interrelations.

Fifth, the third paradigm is an attractive candidate for the new paradigm in public administration, in some part at least because of its maintenance features. For example, the paradigm is quite compatible with the public-policy approach, which implies a more or less common conceptual base for political science and public administration. Relatedly, the paradigm is consistent with major recent efforts to shift attention to an economic model from the psychological and especially sociological orientations prevalent in public administration and political science literature since World War II.[58] Finally, the third paradigm is consistent with broad desires for advocacy rather than neutral description, toward social relevance rather than knowledge gathering.

Five Major Problems and Concerns

Given this expansive characterization—which implies an amalgam of "can do" and "hope for"—it is no wonder that the third paradigm implies problems as well as promise for guiding work in public administration. Five concerns are most prominent. First, the prescriptive quality of the paradigm raises momentous questions about whether the world can actually become enough like what the paradigm prescribes that it should be. The point is not a quibble. For the paradigm proposes at once that power be systematically dispersed enough so that consumers of public services have meaningful market power. Yet it also requires that power be concentrated enough to permit the development and enforcement of comprehensive social objectives and priorities. Both individual and comprehensive systemic needs are to be met in the process. The aim is certainly a commendable one; but the required balancing and fine tuning pose formidable challenges.

Two points, especially, exacerbate the present concern that the prescriptive vision of the Humanist/Systemic Paradigm may be so attractive as to discourage facing monumental practical problems. There is as yet no technology or representational system capable of inducing the required paradigmatic blend of individual and systemic needs. Some relevant theory and experience has been provided by a technology having similar goals for learning in small groups that has been transferred into large organizations, but no easy extrapolation to broad social systems seems possible. Indeed, that technology is only now beginning to raise the kind of ethical and practical questions that bear on its usefulness for inducing and maintaining appropriate social systems in even relatively small units.[59]

Moreover, the history of unattainable prescriptive systems has been a bad one. Consider the excesses committed in behalf of the apocalyptic vision of Marxism, or of the missionary zeal to create "one world in Christ" by "bringing Christianity to the heathen." Specifically, if the ultimate vision seems attractive enough, it can tempt humans to convenient judgments about the end justifying the means. The human capacity for tragic even if temporary delusion in this regard is a large one, indeed, to judge from our inglorious history.

Second, at a more practical level, the Humanist/Systemic Paradigm prescribes blending two sets of technologies that rest on different, even opposed, world views. Broadly, the third paradigm calls for an integration between what may be called organizational humanists and organizational rationalists. The former emphasize behavior, inductive logic, experience, and the broad range of values relating to effectiveness; and the latter emphasize technical systems, deductive or formal logic, and efficiency. Two orientations could powerfully reinforce each other, but generally do not.

More specifically, the Humanist/Systemic Paradigm proposes to unite two approaches to administrative phenomena that have stubbornly resisted assimilation or integration. They are:

- The *rationalists* whose contributions to administrative thought and practice have tended to emphasize technical analysis and quantitative methods, as in (1) Scientific Management, as manifested in time-and-methods work and micro-motion analysis; (2) mathematical and statistical technologies for decision making or problem solving; and (3) systems analysis associated with PPBS, as in cost-benefit analysis, and so forth

- The *humanists* whose contributions to administrative thought and practice have tended to emphasize social integration and behavioral methods, as in (1) the Organization Behavior literature which, in general, establishes the importance of meeting human developmental needs at work; and (2) the Organization Development literature which, in general proposes a set of learning designs to facilitate the development of organizational arrangements that will be growthful for humans by meeting their developmental needs

There is no easy and satisfactory way to explain the usual contraposition of the rationalists and humanists, but adherents of the two orientations find themselves on different sides of many fences.[60] Sometimes, that explanation is easy enough. At least some rationalist thought assumes the world view consistent with the Traditional Paradigm, a more or less unvarnished Theory X view of the world. And the humanist preoccupation is very likely to be with some variant of growth psychology, one relatively straightforward version of which is the Theory Y world view, parts of which were introduced earlier. A simplified contrast of the Theory X and Y world views is sketched in Table 2.6. Such explanations permit easy, and cheap, victories of the humanists over the rationalists. Thus the rationalists can be rightly accused of ignoring the motivational and emotive aspects of human behavior, and of building upon the shifting

TABLE 2.6   Two Sets of Organizationally-Relevant Assumptions and Beliefs

Theory X World View	Theory Y World View
Work is inherently distasteful to most people.	Most people can find work as natural as play.
Most people prefer to be directed and have little desire for responsibility in developing and maintaining a social system.	Most people prefer to be self-controlling in the pursuit of organization objectives and can develop and maintain appropriate social systems.
Most people have little capacity for creativity in work or in developing values or norms to guide behavior.	Most people can exercise significant creativity in organizational problem solving and in developing values or norms to guide behavior.
Motivation occurs only (or mostly) at an elemental stimulus-response level.	Motivation often occurs in response to opportunities for personal and group development, as well as in response to opportunities to control the work environment.
Therefore, people in organizations must be closely controlled and directed, and often coerced.	Therefore, most people can be allowed substantial initiative for self-control, self-direction, and self-motivation.

sands of assumptions that humans need be considered only as "rational man" or "economic man."

Such an easy explanation often does not apply, however, and so the analyst has no alternative but to try harder. Thus, the rationalist orientation emphasizes administrative reality *as it should be,* given assumptions built into various mathematical and statistical models, whereas the humanist orientation emphasizes administrative reality *as it can be,* given the central concept of humans as growth-oriented beings whose full range of needs must be met at work, thereby motivating involved, committed, and even eager participants in increasingly complex and rapidly changing productive systems. No wonder, then, that the two pervasive orientations do not integrate easily.

The common intensity of rationalist-humanist interaction suggests that such differences coexist with powerful similarities, which is the case. For example, both rationalists and humanists are likely to disparage work *as it is.* Rationalists are likely to see existing work as a jerry-built and inefficient set of nonsystemic compromises; and humanists are likely to see existing work as built around assumptions that—if they are not in fact positively repressive of the human spirit—at least do little or nothing to encourage the growth experience at work that will result in more satisfied and productive organization members. Disparaging work as it is can serve as a significant bonding agent, of course. The rub is that what to the humanist may reflect a release of the human spirit often appears to the rationalist as merely another nonsystemic compromise.

This second perspective helps, but there is still much to be explained about why adherents of rationalist and humanist orientations are often at odds. More of this unexplained variance, perhaps much of it, can be accounted for in another way. Most often, perhaps, the difference between rationalists and humanists is a matter of degree rather than high principle. Thus, rationalists may provide for motivational and emotional materials, but they usually assign them a lesser importance than humanists are comfortable with. Similarly, humanists may give too little effective attention to systemic or technical concerns to satisfy the rationalists.

Such differences in degree easily can become polarized when the chips are down. Specifically, adherents of the two persuasions are likely to differ in their orientations to action taking. One wag caught much of the sense of this difference in observing that the issues between rationalists and humanists are differences between "pushers and shovers" and "touchers and feelers," differences that can easily escalate into polarities. Oversimply, perhaps, emphasis on individual needs can be seen as implying major difficulties for meeting systemic needs. Hence, providing more room for the "touchers and feelers" can make life more untidy for the "pushers and shovers," and vice versa.

A good sense of this mutual potential for escalation is inherent in the obvious point that all institutions are today experiencing profound change in the needs and motives that individuals are increasingly expressing. Two observers note: "Extrinsic rewards such as pay, job security, fringe benefits, and conditions of work are no longer so attractive. Younger people are demanding intrinsic job satisfactions as well. They are less likely to accept the notion of deferring gratifications in the interests of some distant career."[61] Changes in motives and needs seem to underlie such effects. "In most organizations today," these observers conclude, "the dominant motives of members are the higher-order ego and social motives—particularly those for personal gratification, independence, self-expression, power, and self-actualization. . . ." These newly aroused motives can take a variety of forms, many of them already familiar. For example:

- The emphasis on self-expression and self-determination, as in "doing your own thing"

- The emphasis on growth and self-actualization, as in the "growth center" movement or in sensitivity training

- The unleashing of power drives, as in revolutionary movements

- A combinatory effect, the rejection of established values as repressive and exploitative, which sometimes involves rejection by revolution

There is no easy management of such forces, once unleashed. The difficulty of fine tuning is manifest in these concluding comments by the same two observers:

> With the need for self-expression goes the ideology of the importance of spontaneity; of the wholeness of human experience; the reliance upon emotions; and the attack upon the fragmentation, the depersonalization, and the restrictions of the present social forms. It contributes to the anti-intellectualism of the student movement and is reminiscent of the romanticism of an older period in which Wordsworth spoke of the intellect as that false secondary power which multiplies delusions. Rationality is regarded as rationalization.[62]

This second point is a simple one, although its development has been long and complex. The Humanist/Systemic Paradigm implies a real challenge in prescribing the integration of two approaches to administrative phenomena that often have been at sixes and sevens, and no doubt usually will continue to be. A few notable exceptions permit some optimism that at least partially reconcilable needs are involved, however.[63]

Third, given these formidable barriers to achieving the balance prescribed by the Humanist/Systemic Paradigm, the root concern is whether an organizational equivalent of Gresham's Law might not be expected. Gresham's Law holds that bad money drives out the good. The organizational equivalent maintains that if both individual and systemic needs cannot be met, or do not seem attainable, preoccupation with systemic needs will be dominant. Even further, some argue that even for relatively small organizations, that is the way it will be *whether or not* individual needs can be met or seem attainable. Consider this portion of a response to a letter in which Carl Rogers stressed that an increased concern with human relationships was perhaps *the* prerequisite for managing our institutions. The letter writer was of two minds: he fervently hoped that Rogers would be listened to, while doubting it profoundly. He explained:

> out of experiences working in and with cities, it is clear that in the basic decision making that takes place, the values Dr. Rogers and I hold so dear have an extremely low priority. Indeed, the old-fashioned concerns with power, prestige, money and profit so far outdistance the concerns for human warmth and love and concern that many people consider the latter extremely irrelevant in the basic decision making. Sadly, it is my feeling that they will continue to do so.[64]

If this concern exists for relatively small organizations, so much greater should that concern be at the broad social level addressed by the Humanist/Systemic Paradigm.

Fourth, even granted that there is too much bureaucratic bigness in government and business, it is almost certainly the case that even determined efforts at disaggregation will leave us with still huge units of organization long after passing the point of a reasonably economic smallest-size of operations. For example, one could argue that the thirteen major oil companies control a very large share of their market and hence are too "big." But a single modern refinery still costs $50-100 million. And even that implies a "large" organization, even if it were economic to limit each oil compnay to a single refinery, which it most definitely is not. Similarly, many public programs are inherently massive as was (and is) the NASA space program.

Fifth, given the short-run maintenance attractions of the Humanist/Systemic Paradigm, I see relatively little effort in public administration or political science to gear up for the task features of that paradigm. Directly, that paradigm implies a complex of skills and technologies that are rare among political scientists or public administrationists. Earnestness about accepting the third paradigm, patently, both in principle and in practice requires major tooling up.

So far, however, most observers seem content to accept the third paradigm as a kind of gentle metaphor,[65] as Chapter 3 will take some pains to establish in detail.

Without anticipating the argument of Chapter 3, one implication here requires stating. Emphasis on the third paradigm, without a corresponding emphasis on appropriate tools and technologies for research and application, implies that the short-run maintenance features of the Humanist/Systemic Paradigm are most attractive to many. If true, this might complicate the development of the tools and technologies necessary to exploit the potential of that paradigm for defining the area of inquiry for public administration.

Such facts constitute major objective dilemmas for the third paradigm and imply major limitations on approaching its philosophical ideal.

Toward an Antiparadigmatic Approach

The analysis just presented is seen as variously supporting, or at least being related to, an approach that for the present avoids closure regarding *a* comprehensive paradigm for public administration. A brief interpretive summary may provide needed order for the complex issues raised earlier. Two major points are emphasized.

First, this analysis is not intended as a kind of King Canute commanding the waters of the Humanist/Systemic Paradigm to stop rising. If that paradigm is viable over the long run, for example, this analysis will little harm its development and may even usefully steer it some. Similarly, if that paradigm is fated to pass, more powerful forces than this essay will do the job.

Second, the preceding analysis patently shows that each of the three paradigms has distinctive strengths but even more compelling weaknesses that are likely to withstand even herculean efforts at resolution in any proximate future. This book will extend the implied antiparadigmatic thrust in many detailed ways, and it will also sketch guidelines for the kind of miniparadigms that offer immediate developmental opportunities for public administration. A second, complementary volume will illustrate and analyze one of these useful miniparadigms, the laboratory approach to organization development.

Generally, "public administration" deals with such a diversity of phenomena that I value several conceptual qualities above others. These include a certain acceptance of conceptual untidiness and resistance to the superficial allures of comprehensive paradigms, a substantial tolerance for differences in approaches as well as for ambiguities, and a major commitment to hold things together while matters jell a good bit more.

More specifically, the following chapters will both argue for primary emphasis on what may be called subparadigms or miniparadigms; and a second volume will provide an in-depth illustration of one of them. The purpose is transparent: to move beyond the present anguish about identity or intellectual crises in public administration, and to do so in constructive ways that will highlight specific skills and technologies for both research and application. Only in this way, this argument proposes, is progress in public administration likely to occur. The extreme alternatives are unattractive: to continue to flounder; or to have such high expectations about developing a comprehensive paradigm, and soon, that public administrationists will keep the debate at such a general and abstract level that the uncharitable will charge that the zeal for comprehensive newness can be written off as a search for new ways of legitimating old approaches to standard topics.

Notes and References

1. Over twenty distinct uses of the term "paradigm" are isolated by Margaret Masterman, "The Nature of A Paradigm," in *Growth of Knowledge,* ed. Manfred Kochen (New York: Wiley, 1967), pp. 383-394.

2. Thomas S. Kuhn, *The Structure of Scientific Revolutions* (Chicago: University of Chicago Press, 1970).

3. Vincent Ostrom, *The Intellectual Crisis in American Public Administration* (University, Ala.: University of Alabama Press, 1973), p. 13.

4. Stephen S. Toulmin, *Human Understanding* (Princeton, N.J.: Princeton University Press, 1972).

5. The immediate argument closely follows Robert T. Golembiewski, " 'Maintenance' and 'Task' as Central Challenges in Public Administration," *Public Administration Review* 32 (March 1974): 168-169.

6. See Robert T. Golembiewski, "Public Administration as a Field: Four Developmental Phases," *Georgia Journal of Political Science* 2 (Spring 1974): 22-49.

7. Dwight Waldo, "Public Administration," in *Political Science,* ed. Marion D. Irish, (Englewood Cliffs, N.J.: Prentice-Hall, 1968), especially pp. 153-155.

8. Roscoe Martin, "Political Science and Public Administration," *American Political Science Review* 46 (September 1952): 665.

9. Ostrom, *The Intellectual Crisis in American Public Administration,* p. 47.

10. Thus Robert L. Peabody and Francis O'Rourke reflect on the less-developed character of the literautre dealing with public bureaucracies. See their "Public Bureaucracies," in *Handbook of Organizations,* ed. James G. March (Chicago: Rand McNally, 1965), p. 802.

11. Golembiewski, " 'Maintenance' and 'Task' as Central Challenges in Public Administration," p. 174.

12. An earlier version of this section appeared in Robert T. Golembiewski, "Public Administration and Public Policy: An Analysis of Developmental Phases," in Robert N. Spadaro, Thomas R. Dye, Robert T. Golembiewski, Murray S. Stedman, L. Harman Zeigler, *The Policy Vacuum* (Lexington, Mass.: Lexington Books, 1975), pp. 102-117.

13. The formal treatment of jobs is exemplified by Frederick W. Taylor's work, as reported in *The Principles of Scientific Management* (New York: Harper, 1911).

14. Herbert Wilcox, "The Culture Trait of Hierarchy in Middle-Class Children," *Public Administration Review* 28 (May 1968): 222-235.

15. The internal logical contradictions of the "principles" were pointed up by numerous authors, both early and late. To anchor the critical literature by an early example as well as a more contemporary critique, see Francis W. Coker, "Dogmas of Administrative Reform," *American Political Science Review* 16 (August 1922): 399-411; and Herbert A. Simon, "Proverbs of Administration," *Public Administration Review* 6 (Winter 1946): 53-67. Pointing up the multiple inconsistencies of the "principles" with the growing empirical literature on organization behavior was the essential objective of Robert T. Golembiewski, *Men, Management and Morality* (New York: McGraw-Hill, 1965).

16. Fritz J. Roethlisberger and William J. Dickson, *Management and the Worker* (Cambridge, Mass.: Harvard University Press, 1939); and Peter M. Blau, *Bureaucracy in Modern Society* (New York: Random House, 1959). For a useful summary statement of the impact of such work on public administration, see Emmette S. Redford, *Democracy in the Administrative State* (New York: Oxford University Press, 1969).

17. For a recent critique, see Ostrom, *The Intellectual Crisis in American Public Administration,* pp. 109-129.

18. Golembiewski, "Public Administration as A Field," especially pp. 25-29.

19. Richard J. Stillman, II, "Woodrow Wilson and the Study of Administration," *American Political Science Review* 67 (June 1973): 582-588.

20. Roethlisberger and Dickson, *Management and the Worker.*

21. The classical macro-level statement of "interest-group liberalism" is provided by John Kenneth Galbraith, *American Capitalism: The Concept of Countervailing Power* (Boston: Houghton Mifflin, 1952).

22. For an influential summary statement at the micro-level, see Edward A. Shils, "The Study of the Primary Group," pp. 44-69, in *The Policy Sciences,* ed. Daniel Lerner and Harold D. Lasswell (Stanford, Calif.: Stanford University Press, 1951).

23. The characterization comes from Warren G. Bennis, "Leadership Theory and Administrative Behavior: The Problem of Authority," *Administrative Science Quarterly* 4 (December 1959): 259-301.

   Examples of the emphasis on "informal organization" or "groups" or "cliques" are everywhere in the literature. Witness Sayle's conclusion: "The individual's most immediate and meaningful experiences of work are obtained in the context of the work group and his work associates. The larger organization is experienced by indirection, but membership in the small group contributes directly to the shaping of attitudes and behavior toward the entire world of work." Leonard R. Sayles, "Work Group Behavior and the Larger Organization," in *Organizations: Structure and Behavior,* ed. Joseph A. Litterer (New York: Wiley, 1963), p. 163.

24. For an early expression of this point of view, see Emile Durkheim's seminal *La division du travail social.* He wrote around the turn of the century. The work cited here was translated as *The Division of Labor in Society* (Glencoe, Ill.: Free Press, 1949).

25. Chester I. Barnard, *The Functions of the Executive* (Cambridge, Mass.: Harvard University Press, 1964), p. 163.

26. Such an orientation has been reflected diversely, as in the interest in sociometry, in group dynamics, and most broadly in the "third force" or humanist approach in the behavioral sciences, in psychology especially. See A. H. Maslow, *The Farther Reaches of Human Nature* (New York: Viking Press, 1971).

27. Illustratively, see Blau, *Bureaucracy in Modern Society*; and Michael Crozier, *The Bureaucratic Phenomenon* (Chicago: University of Chicago Press, 1964).

28. Robert T. Golembiewski, *Behavior and Organization* (Chicago: Rand McNally, 1962), pp. 87-210, provides one detailed approach to these two goals.

29. For a summary treatment, see Robert T. Golembiewski, *Men, Management, and Morality* (New York: McGraw-Hill, 1965), especially pp. 161-202.

30. The classic demonstration is by Lester Coch and John R. P. French, Jr., "Overcoming Resistance to Change," *Human Relations* 1 (1948): 512-532.

31. See Joseph Harris, *Congressional Control of Administration* (Washington, D.C.: Brookings Institution, 1964); and Dean E. Mann, "The Selection of Federal Political Executives," *American Political Science Review* 58 (March 1964): 81-99.

32. "For it is in the crucible of administrative politics today that public policy is mainly hammered out, through bargaining, negotiation, and conflict among appointed rather than elected officials. The bureaucratization of policy process is particularly pronounced in defense and foreign affairs, but it reaches into domestic politics as well." Francis E. Rourke, *Bureaucracy, Politics, and Public Policy* (Boston: Little, Brown, 1969), p. vii.

33. The central term "administrative responsibility" was introduced by J. Donald Kingsley in his book of that title (Yellow Springs, Ohio: Antioch Press, 1944). Samuel Krislov notes that the "late development" of the concept "is hardly surprising," because it could come only after the significant role of the bureaucracy became manifest and after the inadequacy of viewing public officials as a kind of netural instrument became clear. See Samuel Krislov, *The Negro in Federal Employment* (Minneapolis: University of Minnesota Press, 1967), especially pp. 48-49. Kingsley was convinced that "administrative responsibility" could derive from personnel who were recruited from all social classes, but he was

equally convinced that employees were in fact not broadly representative of American citizenry.

For an insightful analysis of this central and slippery concept, see Frank J. Thompson, "Types of Representative Bureaucracy and Their Linkage," in *Public Administration,* ed. Robert T. Golembiewski, Frank Gibson, and Geoffrey Y. Cornog (Chicago: Rand McNally, 1976), pp. 576-601.

34. Golembiewski, *Men, Management and Morality.*

35. Robert T. Golembiewski, *Renewing Organizations* (Itasca, Ill.: F. E. Peacock, 1972), p. 510.

36. This deficiency triggers Ostrom's rhetorical question: "Can we best understand the structure, conduct, performance of the American system of higher education ... by reference to a bureaucratic chain of command accountable to a central chief executive or by reference to a relatively open but constrained rivalry among a diversity of collective enterprises?" *The Intellectual Crisis in American Public Administration,* p. 20.

37. That the micro-focus can also be useful at the very top of complex organizations was late in being established, as by Chris Argyris, "T-Groups for Organization Effectiveness," *Harvard Business Review* 42 (April 1964): especially 60-62; and Irving Janis, *Victims of Groupthink* (Boston: Houghton Mifflin, 1972).

38. Hence the rarity of studies of day-to-day public management such as Victor Thompson's *The Regulatory Process in OPA Rationing* (New York: King's Crown Press, 1950).

39. The headwaters of this approach may be traced to Paul Appleby's *Policy and Administration* (University, Ala.: University of Alabama Press, 1949).

40. See Golembiewski, "Public Administration as a Field," especially pp. 37-40.

41. Herbert A. Simon, *Administrative Behavior* (New York: Macmillan, 1957), p. 54.

42. Eugene P. Dvorin and Robert H. Simmons, *From Amoral to Humane Bureaucracy* (San Francisco, Calif: Canfield Press, 1972), pp. 60, 61.

43. Abraham H. Maslow, *Motivation and Personality* (New York: Harper & Row, 1954).

44. Chris Argyris, *Personality and Organization* (New York: Harper & Bros., 1957), especially pp. 49-53.

45. For a detailed specification of such consequences, see Robert T. Golembiewski, *Behavior and Organization* (Chicago: Rand McNally, 1962), especially pp. 130-138.

46. In political science, the concept of "system" first got prominent attention from David Easton, as in *A Framework for Political Analysis* (Englewood Cliffs, N.J.: Prentice-Hall, 1965).

47.   Frederick C. Mosher and John E. Harr, *Programming Systems and Foreign Affairs Leadership* (New York: Harper & Row, 1957); and James M. Buchanan and Gordon Tullock, *The Calculus of Consent: Logical Foundation of Constitutional Democracy* (Ann Arbor, Mich.: University of Michigan Press, 1962).

48.   See Ostrom, *The Intellectual Crisis in American Public Administration.*

49.   Anthony Downs, *Inside Bureaucracy* (Boston: Little, Brown, 1967), especially pp. 81-91.

50.   The charge was a common one against monopolies and other forms of "giant business," as in our trust-busting era or in the muckraking literature. It is only recently that such a charge has been commonly directed against "big government," especially by liberals against the federal government. Illustratively, Theodore J. Lowi, *The End of Liberalism* (New York: Norton, 1969), p. xiii, phrased the new guiding insight in revealing terms: "government itself is the problem."

51.   For example, Alan Altshuler has called for more *popular* decisions and greater *market* influence on decisions to counteract the effects of large public and business bureaucracies that variously shape and modify client or customer needs or opinions. Generally, he urges us "to think more systematically about the virtues of disaggregation vs. integration, pluralism vs. coordination, and the free market vs. regulation in social life." "New Institutions to Serve the Individual," in William R. Ewald, Jr., *Environment and Policy* (Bloomington: Indiana University Press, 1968), p. 425.

52.   PPBS is the most refined, if often the most maligned, expression of this point of view. For a telling critique, see Ida R. Hoos, *Systems Analysis in Public Policy* Copyright © 1972 by the Regents of the University of California; reprinted by permission of the University of California Press.

53.   The general neglect of environmental forces was characteristic of much research in both public administration and political science, in large part due to the dominant "behavioral" orientation in both fields. Thomas R. Dye explains: "Political Science has been so preoccupied with describing political institutions, behaviors, and processes, that it has frequently overlooked the overriding importance of environmental forces in shaping public policy." *Understanding Public Policy* (Englewood Cliffs, N.J.: Prentice-Hall, 1972), p. 23.

      In the study of large productive organizations, a similar reorientation was expressed in such theoretical statements as that of S. E. Emery and E. L. Trist, "The Causal Texture of Organizational Environments," *Human Relations* 18 (February 1965): 21-31.

      The neglect of environmental differences also was highlighted by the inapplicability in "developing countries" of generalizations derived from the American experience. See A. Dunsire, *Administration* (New York: Halsted Press, 1973), especially pp. 134-152.

54.   H. George Frederickson, "Creating Tomorrow's Public Administration," *Public Management* 53 (November 1971): especially 2-3.

55. Ross Clayton and Ron Gilbert, "Perspectives of Public Managers: Their Implications for Public Service Delivery Systems," *Public Management* 53 (November 1971): 9-12.

56. In the U.S. Department of State, for example, proponents of a PPBS-like system perceived that adoption of that rational-technical system required broad organizational and personal change via a humanist approach in Project ACORD. The effort had mixed consequences, and its history is still being written. For some clues as to the logic that paired a humanist technology for change with a rational-technical system, see Mosher and Harr, *Programming Systems and Foreign Affairs Leadership.*

57. Stephen R. Chitwood and Michael M. Harmon, "New Public Administration, Humanism, and Organizational Behavior," *Public Management* 53 (November 1971): 13-22.

58. Among the earliest efforts of this kind was William C. Mitchell, *Public Choice in America* (Chicago: Markham, 1971).

59. See, for example, Robert T. Golembiewski, *Renewing Organizations* (Itasca, Ill.: F. E. Peacock, 1972).

60. For example, see the recent debate in *Public Administration Review* featuring Chris Argyris and Herbert Simon. Consult Herbert A. Simon, "Organization Man: Rational or Self-Actualizing?" 4 (July 1973): 346-353; Chris Argyris, "Organization Man: Rational *and* Self-Actualizing?" 4 (July 1973): 354-357; and Simon's letter, 4 (September 1973): 484-485.

61. Daniel Katz and Basil S. Georgopoulous "Organizations in a Changing World," *Journal of Applied Behavioral Science* 7 (May 1971): 350.

62. Ibid., p. 351.

63. For the detailed development of one rationalist-humanist interface, see Arthur C. Beck, Jr., and Ellis D. Hillmar, *A Practical Approach to Organization Development Through MBO* (Reading, Mass.: Addison-Wesley, 1972).

64. Quoted in Warren G. Bennis, "A Funny Thing Happened on the Way to the Future," *American Psychologist* 25 (July 1970): 601-602.

65. For a relatively rare exception, see Thomas R. Dye who argues that development of his concept of the public-policy approach will require "an expansion of the traditional boundaries of political science well beyond any previous definition of these boundaries." "Policy Analysis and the Urban Crisis," mimeographed, n.d.

     Similarly, Ostrom, *The Intellectual Crisis in American Public Administration,* argues for the application of the tools and technologies of "political economy."

SECTION 2

WHERE PUBLIC ADMINISTRATION IS
Evaluations of the Present

Chapter 3

THE PUBLIC-POLICY APPROACH
Gentle Metaphor or Major Transformation?

The preceding two chapters have painted with a broad brush, concluding that the development of public administration faces major conceptual problems. The conclusion is the same, whether the approach is through developmental phases or guiding paradigms.

This chapter and the two following provide further support for the same conclusion, reflecting as they do major concerns about three contemporary ways of approaching public administration. The final chapter of this trinity seeks a critical assessment of Vincent Ostrom's "democratic administration," which is so much with us these days. The second chapter will deal with the "new public administration," which created quite a stir a few years ago. Immediate attention will be given to a more specific analysis of the "public-policy" approach. The approach was introduced earlier as Phase IV in the development of public administration.

The several varieties of public policy considered in this chapter support three summary conclusions. First, all limits of real locus and analytical focus are swept aside by some Phase IV definitions of the scope of the public administration. Second, more limited public-policy concepts add much richness to the analysis of governmental activities. Third, no variety provides the comprehensive concept or paradigm so much sought after in public administration. This is the case despite the attractions of public policy as a gentle metaphor, as well as some features of more robust versions of public policy.

Public Policy As Medium

Before getting into specific varieties of public policy—the "message" in McLuhan's terms—it is useful to talk about the "medium" in which the approach has evolved. The "medium" is critical in this case, as in many others: The global emphasis on public policy at once nourishes and feeds upon a massive reevaluation of this age's leading ideas. That reevaluation takes many forms, both bizarre and reasonable, some at the heart of major analytical problems and some so much dilettantish embroidery. At the broadest social level, this generation's writer of songs caught the essential spirit in a few words: "The times they are a-changin'." More specifically, political scientists have directed attention to a new and still-emerging Weltanschauung, a new orientation to the world of scholarly inquiry. And students of public administration, relatedly, have heralded the coming of a new paradigm, a different way of conceiving and structuring their priorities for concern and analysis.

Let us get more specific about public policy's "medium," beginning with major concerns at the frontiers of today's political science. These concerns center around an apparent change in disciplinary focus that may imply a new Weltanschauung, or world view, a replacement for the leading ideas that have defined the leading edge of political science over the last two or three decades.[1] Van Dyke distinguishes the two analytic world views at the level of first approximation.[2] The first is concerned with the *form,* or *processes,* of public policy. It shares much conceptual ground with what was described in Chapter 2 as the "behavioral approach" to political science and public administration. The second analytic world view stresses the *content* of public policy, and it is consistent with major emphases in the "postbehavioral approach" also sketched later in this chapter. Table 3.1 attempts to add substance to Van Dyke's basic distinction, at the risk of overdrawing the differing emphases.

The times during which old world views get toppled are, almost by definition, exciting and frightening in varying degrees. Hence, balance and perspective are likely to be in short supply. So note here that any guiding concept is only a tether, no more and no less; and that is its strength and its weakness. At different times, the balance of benefits over costs will vary. At its best, one world view can provide researchers with a valuable map to significant analytic territory. At its worst, that same Weltanschauung may enmesh researchers in a set of sentiments that its subscribers sense only dimly or not at all, a "metaphysical pathos of ideas" that misdirects their attention from the relevant to the comfortable and accepted. As Gouldner develops the point:

> commitment to a theory often occurs by a process other than the one which its proponents believe and it is usually more consequential than they realize. A commitment to a theory may be made because the theory is congruent with the mood or deep-lying

TABLE 3.1   Two Alternative World Views for Political Science[a]

Old *Weltanschauung*: Form or Process	New *Weltanschauung*: Content
1. Emphasis on developing general knowledge, theory, and science	1. Emphasis on promoting human welfare
2. Emphasis on value-free findings	2. Emphasis on values, goals, moral judgments
3. Emphasis on overall patterns of activity and behavior, on general and enduring features of governmental processes	3. Emphasis on specific, even if transient, features of the content of public policies or issues
4. Emphasis on those processes considered presently susceptible to scientific analysis	4. Emphasis on structure, dynamics, or policies that are considered relevant to public welfare, their susceptibility to specific analysis being a lesser concern
5. Emphasis on large groups, institutions, aggregates	5. Emphasis on feelings, attitudes, and motivations of individuals
6. Emphasis on the individual as a type, an aggregate statistic, a role player subject to massive determinative forces that are largely uncontrollable	6. Emphasis on the individual as a valuing, deciding, and choosing organism who can and should define his environment in significant ways
7. Emphasis on nonrational and irrational behavior and upon the situational factors inducing them	7. Emphasis on purposive behavior by individuals who reason or act in support of, or opposition to, specific policies
8. Tendency to be action-distant, not of direct relevance to the policy maker	8. Desire to be action-proximate, of direct relevance to the policy maker

[a]From Jean A. La Ponce and Paul Smoker, eds., *Experimentation and Simulation in Political Science* (Toronto: University of Toronto Press, 1972), p. 371.

sentiments of its adherents, rather than merely because it has been cerebrally inspected and found valid. This is as true for the rigorous prose of social science as it is for the more lucid metaphor of creative literature, for each has its own silent appeal and its own metaphysical pathos.[3]

The World Is Not Either/Or

The starkness of Table 3.1 may imply more than it intends, if it is read as providing only this choice: column one or column two? Like the menu in the apochryphal Chinese restaurant, some from column one and some from two is the more fulfilling choice for the student. Unfortunately, too much of the literature implies just such a forced choice between the "old" and the "new" public administration, between the "Traditional Paradigm" and the "revolutionary world view."

It is easiest to deal with the point in personal terms. I see myself as having a foot in both camps represented in Table 3.1. Most of my work is consistent with the new Weltanschauung in major particulars;[4] and yet there are significant reasons to resist the conclusion that that's where it's all at. Basically, the emphases of the new world view in Table 3.1 are necessary reactions against extreme extensions of its predecessor. However, history urges caution in such cases. At an extreme, for example, the new world view might encourage a neglect of a man's collective experiences and needs. It might even curtail the development of an expanding science. At the very least, lack of caution might exacerbate an inherent potential for conflict. Such win-lose competition concerning world views can engage powerful needs, whose expression and maintenance can absorb more energy than goes into comprehending reality. These needs are pressing and intensely personal, and hence can prove very difficult to manage. For example, they involve the bittersweet succession of one scholarly generation by another, bitter for those who feel themselves being deposed before the fullness of time and only temporarily sweet for the new Turks. These needs also can include reasonable if self-defeating efforts to preserve one's self-worth, which is often variously rooted in skills and formal status whose days are done.

Sometimes alternative world views are so inherently disparate that a fight is unavoidable, as was the case in Galileo's time. But such is not the case in today's political science and public administration, because the two world views contain notions of complementary value that need not be sacrificed. Efforts to displace one Weltanschauung by the other may be satisfying to zealots, but this requires sacrificing of some perspectives of value. Relatedly, the either/or choice is a highly abstract and generalized one, so much so that it is seldom apparent what revisionists are really for even when it is more or less obvious what they are against. Moreover, the consequences of most such either/or choices are far from clear, both with regard to long-run and short-run development of public administration, as well as with regard to task and maintenance aspects. The task, then, is to integrate the two world views, an integration that is likely to be most successful and least conflictful when it is attempted in bits and pieces, as specific research or action issues are dealt with in terms of specific technology or skills.

The potential for integration is patent in Table 3.1. Consider item eight, for example. It is likely that proponents of a "pure" rather than an "applied" orientation to any area of inquiry will end up struggling for supremacy, given the historical track record. However, it is also clear that some integration of the two orientations is ideal. Conveniently, the easiest integration of that kind occurs in the minds of individual students. Short of that ideal, persons with different mixes of "pure" and "applied" needs can be as mutually stimulating as they often are competitive in zero-sum senses. Similarly, the issue never really can be fact or value? Of course, much energy has been expended in just such illusory tussles, from the times of Bacon and Machiavelli even unto our own. The more useful issues relate to blending empirical and normative concerns, to when and how that is to be done.

This Medium Is Not *That* Message

We are in a very real sense now all proponents of the new Weltanschauung in Table 3.1. This is comforting enough to encourage neglect of a prime reality. It is important, even crucial, to realize that the broad orientation reflected there is neither sufficiently explicit nor precise enough to define useful areas of specialization, and much less is that orientation able to define how useful research and application should proceed most expeditiously. More or less, Table 3.1 defines a general approach to all of reality. This is at once its strength and its weakness. And that is the meaning of the cryptic subhead above this section: *This* medium (in Table 3.1) is not *that* message (a workable definition of the scope of public administration).

It will require the remainder of this book and all of the companion volume to demonstrate that central point. The demonstration will have two thrusts, in its broadest compass. The remaining four chapters of this volume, essentially, will be *critical* of typical ways of approaching the task of circumscribing the boundaries of public administration. The eight chapters of the second volume will seek to be *constructive* in two ways: (1) by sketching some useful guidelines for one specific approach for developing the field, and (2) by illustrating in detail one approach that respects those guidelines.

Public Policy as Message

Two broad conclusions get us underway in this analysis of the multichannel message encoded in the convenient label "public policy." The immediate focus is on the task and maintenance features of that major contender for defining the scope of public administration, the public-policy approach. Chapter 1 provides general perspective on Phase IV in the development of public administration. The goal here is greater specificity, as befits an approach that is so up-front in the consciousness of both political scientists and public administrationists. Moreover, what follows may be outspoken, but the simple fact is that there is no way to tell whether "public policy" is the conceptual end of the road for public administration. Observers of goodwill also can disagree about even its short-run usefulness.

Indeed, only four points seem beyond any reasonable dispute. First, the tide for public policy is running full and strong. As Dye notes: "Today the focus of political science is shifting to public policy—to the description and explanation of the causes and consequences of government activity."[5] Second, a critical perspective is difficult to sustain while maintaining credibility. Simply everybody is into policy analysis, whatever it means. Third, the wide adoption of a Phase IV concept raises many issues of locus and focus. Fourth, there are several more or less distinct public-policy approaches, and these have characteristics and probable consequences that differ profoundly, at both task and maintenance levels.

This chapter distinguishes three major varieties of the public-policy approach and speculates about their impacts on public administration. Public policy has been conceived as:

- A guiding metaphor that expresses a broad and diffuse scholarly community of interest
- "Descriptive policy analysis," after the fashion popularized in political science
- "Prescriptive policy analysis," after the pattern of an applied blend of the social sciences with technologies for choice and decision making whose ultimate vision is some kind of superdiscipline or suprafield

As Gentle Metaphor

This first usage—that of public policy as a convenient shorthand for a broad scholarly community of interest—has long been with us, and usefully so, up to a point. To put the matter in the boldest terms, the public-policy orientation was initially offered as an integrative concept reinforcing ties between political science and public administration. In the vocabulary of Chapter 2, maintenance features of public policy as a metaphor loomed very large.

Some elemental but basic points introduce this analysis. Overall, most varieties of public policy as organizing metaphor contributed little to task activities in public administration. Rather, common varieties provided a kind of benign and broad academic anchorage within which scholars could keep doing what they had long been doing, safe from the gales of uncertain change and comforted by the notion that their work fitted in the context of the most modern concept of the field.[6] A few public-policy approaches suggest real progress on task, but they also imply major challenges to time-honored maintenance activities. That is, some Phase IV varieties contribute to fragmentation between political science and public administration, as well as to confusion within public administration. It is also likely that things will get worse.

These summary conclusions will be developed in terms of three developmental themes in the history of public policy as a guiding metaphor. In turn, emphasis will be given to:[7]

- Early public-policy usage, which emphasized case studies
- Frameworks for structuring the rigorous analysis of public policymaking and policies
- Public policy as defining the field of inquiry for public administration and political science

By way of introduction, the first two themes imply a gentle reliance on public policy as a guiding metaphor, whose products often are useful aids to analysis and discussion of governmental activities. The third theme is seen as less benign, as more mischievous.

Early Usage in Case Studies

Case studies reflect an early reliance on Phase IV as a general organizing concept in their focus on the formulation and implementation of specific public policies. The case-study approach—whose use has been common in policy research in political science generally—received its biggest boost in the seminal volume edited by the late Harold Stein. In *Public Administration and Policy Development* (1952), Stein left little to the imagination about where he stood with respect to Phase II and early varieties of work in Phase III. He looked at case studies as both *process* and as *politics*. The former has basic reference "only to the internal functioning of a public agency," as in the act of bringing "to bear on a decision all the relevant intellectual resources" by using hierarchy to integrate appropriate specialties. "Politics," in Stein's view, basically refers to an administrator's "understanding and pursuit of his objectives and his relations with the social environment outside his agency. . . ." To be sure, politics in this sense exists to a degree in all organizations, as when businesses give conscious thought to their several constituencies. But politics is at least in degree more prevalent in public administration, and it is politics that Stein emphasizes when he has a choice. He explains that "public administrators" generally stand apart from "private administrators" in one crucial particular: They are "far more deeply affected . . . by large, complex, often vaguely defined, social objectives and by the need for adjusting effectively to a highly complex environment composed of many forces, frequently conflicting—individuals, private associations and the government itself."[8] The sources of these centrifugal pressures are diverse and deeply set, in the "Constitution, our customs and traditions, the size and complexity of our land and our society." Consequently, Stein notes:

> Every executive agency, and many of its top administrators, have responsibilities to or toward the President, to a variety of control agencies either only partially or not at all under the President's discretionary supervision; ordinarily to at least four congressional committees, to Congress more generally, and to an indeterminate number of individual Congressmen and Senators; to the organized and unorganized constituencies of the agency; to pressure groups, public and private, local and national, powerful or merely persistent; frequently to the courts, and occasionally to a political party.

"It is in this atmosphere," Stein concludes, "that the administrator makes his decisions."

Beyond such general emphases, case studies can be characterized as often massive chronicles that seek to "tell it like it was." They are careful historical accounts, told from the standpoint of the more or less neutral observer who assiduously seeks to develop a narrative after exhausting available documents and sources. The historical sequence of events in time normally provides the structure for organizing the case narrative. Beyond that critical assumption, early case studies eschew explicit theory or interpretation or even reject them.[9]

The associated public-policy concept was a general one, fittingly, for Stein and many others. Note that Stein does not even attempt to define "policy," even though it is prominent in his volume's title. Policy is more illustrated than it is defined, in fact. Stein was in good company in this regard. For example, Appleby—who is by any measure the father of "public policy"— uses the term hundreds of times without being concerned with more than a general specification of the concept. In Appleby's view:

- "Policymaking is . . . the exercise of discretion."
- "The matter involves value-judgment, hence policymaking."
- "At every level, the answer to the question 'What is my judgment about this which I have to decide, or about this on which I need to have a judgment?' is a policy question."[10]

As in such general definitions, the acceptance of public policy as a broad metaphor is also implicit in other early conceptual fuzziness. To illustrate, administration for Appleby is one of the eight political processes, whose totality may be said to be coextensive with "government." Although "all administration is political," in Dunsire's words, "some [administration] is more political than other."[11] Moreover, Appleby also proposes two "scales for distinguishing between kinds of administration." One scale runs from "more political" to "less political," and the second distinguishes the kind of administration that involves more policymaking from the kind that requires less. Throughout, however, the terms "politics" and "policy" are only vaguely distinguished, and are all but equated. Witness statements by Appleby such as the following, which suggest and perhaps even require an equivalence: "Thus, the long attempts [in Phase II] to make sharp and real the separation of powers, the separation of policymaking and administration and politics and administration have been undergoing abandonment."[12]

The total sense of public policy as case studies is broad and amorphous, with integrating tendencies. The point can be supported from three perspectives: practical, technical, and conceptual.

Practically, in my view the concept was imprecisely drawn so as to provide an acceptable definition of mission and role for many scholars and practitioners. Proponents of the case-study approach, in any case, were more eager to enlist converts than they were to make enemies by being doctrinaire.

Technically, the case-study approach relied on the classical tools of historical analysis, despite the major impact of psychobehavioral thoughtways on fiction, history, and social commentary. Hence it is entirely fitting—and perhaps even intended—that the late Harold Stein was an unreconstructed specialist in English and was defiantly proud of it. Of course, Stein was the most central figure in the burgeoning of the case-study approach in public administration following World War II.

Conceptually, the looseness with which the term "policy" is used seems appropriate to the maintenance emphasis I attribute to the policy orientation. Notice the fulsome integrative challenge in Jones's contrast of a "policy approach" with an "institutional approach." Jones explains that the latter emphasizes developing generalizations about a single institution. He notes: "Questions to be answered include the following: What is the function of this institution (e.g., Congress) in the overall political process? How is this function achieved: How does the behavior of specific actors contribute to the function of the institution?" In contrast, the bias of leading questions necessary to ask about substantive public problems is pervasive and integrative. Jones explains that such an emphasis requires considering cross-institutional relationships in asking: "How is this problem acted on in government? To respond intelligently, you must see where the problem takes you rather than limit yourself to one institution in government."[13]

The case-study approach to the interpenetration of politics and administration held center stage for a decade or so, and its net result was strongly to reinforce ties between political science and public administration. Consider how case studies required an integration of empirical and value concerns, as via the notion of "public interest." The complex relationships between interest groups, legislatures, and administrative agencies were highlighted on a case-by-case basis;

the fact-value mix was inescapably demonstrated by tying concern with "public interest" to specific administrative ways of seeking the good civic life; and the subtle interplay of policy development and implementation was established by the ebb and flow of real-time narratives. Moreover, the case-study approach also encouraged a variety of interdisciplinary work, as through the obvious relevance of the developing literature on decision making as well as through various interdisciplinary forays such as that dealing with the role of groups in administration.[14]

Many other illustrative approaches could be taken here to establish the characteristic impacts of the case-study approach. But their common essence is one of a complex commingling or separation of various specialties in political science, public administration, and other relevant disciplines and perspectives. These impacts also came to be similarly evaluated over time. Case studies were particularistic and did not lead to the scientific generalizations that were so attractive to so many in the decade of the 1950s. Hence the need to variously augment the common case-study approach to public policy, one variety of which will be of immediate concern.

Structured Analysis of Public Policies

More recently, diverse attempts have been made to structure the analysis of specific public policies, again often using case-by-case analysis. The goals of such structuring of analysis are direct. They seek to:

- Emphasize description of what exists, as contrasted with prescription of what should exist
- Highlight the impacts of specific public policies
- Engage in a rigorous search for the causes and consequences of classes or types of public policies
- Develop and test general propositions about which causes and consequences tend to occur under which circumstances in various policy arenas, whose accumulating product will be research findings of general relevance

These goals are tethered short in one sense, and expansive in another. The emphasis on accumulating descriptive propositions is rooted in paucity. "Social scientists," Dye advises in italics, "simply do not know enough about individual and group behavior to be able to give reliable advice to policy makers." But that emphasis on description is also challenged by a broad vision of what needs doing, which only begins with a description of the content of public policy. Beyond that, public policy can be seen as a kind of dependent variable that varies with specific environmental forces, institutional arrangements, and political processes, as they are flavored by the spirit of the changing times. And further still, public policy also can be viewed as an independent variable. Thus policy can impact on the political system as well as on social and economic activities in expected or unexpected ways.[15]

In short, the four goals for structured analysis of public policy just sketched refer to a huge analytic domain. That domain is conveniently distinguishable into two categories, which are not exclusive but nonetheless are useful.

Policy and Impact Analysis. The more narrowly bounded approach to structuring the analysis of public policies focuses on their impact. Following Dye,[16] "impact" is understood in the sense of multidimensional effects or consequences of a policy on:

- Some specific target situation or group
- "Spillover effects" on situations or groups other than the target
- Future as well as immediate conditions
- Direct costs of relevant programs
- Indirect costs, including alternative programs on which resources might have been spent

The basic notions behind impact analysis or policy evaluation seem at once reasonable and straightforward. An Urban Institute publication put it directly. To make certain that public policies and management of their associated programs "meet the needs of society, it is necessary to analyze programs to determine their consequences—that is, to measure their successes and failures in meeting the nation's goals."[17] More specifically, it seems not only useful but necessary to know how things are going with respect to three critical levels in any management situation:

- Are policies and programs generating expected and desirable outcomes, on balance?
- Are organizations accomplishing their mission and role with efficiency?
- Are specific individuals within any organization performing well or poorly?

Given the lack of a market for many governmental goods and services, moreover, the significance of impact or evaluation at these three levels seems especially relevant, as contrasted with a business organization in a truly competitive situation.[18]

However, the fact is that the study of impact and evaluation in public administration has been seriously neglected. The evidence can only be sampled here, but even a brief review demonstrates this clearly. For example, Poland concludes that "our literature, teaching, and research have not been overly concerned with" the assessment of individual or organization performance.[19]

And a major study of fifteen federal programs observes flatly that "the whole federal machinery for making policy and budget decisions suffers from a crucial weakness: it lacks a comprehensive system for measuring program effectiveness."[20] The same may be said of administration at all levels of government.[21] Individual pieces of research fare no better. Thus Wholey and co-workers note that "few significant" impact/evaluation studies have been undertaken. "Most of those carried out have been poorly executed," they continue, "with such lack of uniformity of design and objective that the results rarely are comparable or responsive to the questions facing policy makers."[22]

Why this condition of neglect exists cannot be explained definitively here, or perhaps anywhere. But three major contributors to that condition may be detailed with some confidence. These contributors are (1) the complexity and subtlety of impact/evaluation, (2) the range and early stage of development of methods of analysis, and (3) the preeminence of nonresearch considerations in the process of policy development and implementation.

The complexity and subtlety of policy impact and evaluation no doubt account for much of the sorry research record. To explain, the focus in impact analysis is on policy as an independent variable, as it were. Derivative questions for analysis take this form: Does a specific public policy do what is intended, and with what unexpected consequences? This is a disarmingly simple question. But such questions typically are in reality highly complex, both in terms of methods necessary for more or less conclusive analysis as well as in terms of the tendency for every effect to be related to ever-widening ripples of effects.

It is possible economically to suggest the complexity and sublety of impact/evaluation studies, while simultaneously indicating how seriously short the available literature falls. Consider Logan's review of one hundred empirical studies that sought to evaluate the impact of juvenile institutions on their clientele.[23] Logan proposes six criteria in terms of which he rates those studies. Specifically, Logan proposes that an "adequate" piece of impact analysis *should, at a minimum,* do the following:

- Provide an adequate definition or description of the program or techniques whose impact is being tested

- Provide assurance that the program or techniques can be learned and applied by others

- Divide the study population into "treatment" and "control" groups, preferably on a random basis so as to wash out as many confounding variables as possible

- Establish that the "treatment" group is in fact being exposed to the intended program or techniques and, moreover, that the "control" group is not being so exposed

- Provide before and after measures of the behavior targeted for change

- Establish definitions of "success" or "failure" that provide valid standards for assessing the outcomes of the treatment

Applying these minimal methodological criteria to the pool of one hundred studies, Logan concludes that *not one* of them is "adequate." In fact, application of only two criteria—those for distinguishing treatment versus control populations and for defining successful treatment—eliminate ninety-seven of the one hundred studies. There is obviously much room for improvement.

Logan's conclusions are not a scholarly fluke. Using a similar approach, for example, Fischer generates similar conclusions.[24] Relatedly, Gibson and Prather illustrate the poverty of available research by surveying a number of policy issue areas, all about equally inconclusive and inadequate.[25]

The quality of the research record also derives from the range of analytic methods required for sensitive anlaysis, as well as from the early stage of development of the methods and the lack of experience with them. For example, the appropriate methods range from elementary face-to-face efforts to learn which policy shoes pinch and which please, all the way to mathematical and statistical exotica for whose minimal appreciation advanced training is an absolute prerequisite. Illustratively, Tufte falls somewhere in between. He uses a range of statistical techniques to answer questions relevant to politics and policy. For example: Do automobile safety inspections save lives? The reader is encouraged to play that analytic game with Tufte himself, who makes a skillful beginning on a critical approach to public policy.[26]

Tufte's analysis also illustrates how the policy analyst's world is often terribly complicated, with everything being related to everything else. For our illustrative purposes here, consider only some superficial aspects of the wide use of DDT in Asia after World War II. The realized and intended consequences included the alleviation of human suffering, as by virtually eliminating such scourges of mankind as malaria. But the balance of nature is not to be trifled with. In this case, in the longer run, DDT had a major and largely unexpected impact on population growth. More recently, famines in parts of the world can be traced in some degree to the well-intended efforts after World War II by organizations such as the UN's World Health Organization. Alleviating one kind of human suffering contributed to a different kind of suffering, about which consequence sensitive policy analysis might have provided some early warning.

Primarily, perhaps, the quality of available impact/evaluation efforts stems from a related set of considerations centering around the nonresearch character of policy development and implementation. Four of these considerations will be sketched here.

First, impact/evaluation often suffers because of the probable conflict between two grossly defined roles—that of evaluator and administrator. Gibson and Prather go to the heart of the point. They note: "The demands of applied treatment and the demands of scientific inquiry are often in automatic conflict." They explain that the evaluator, "if he is objective, must assume a challenging, skeptical attitude toward any findings, whereas the administrator of a program is often put in a position of trying rather desperately to come up with positive findings."[27] Major motivation for administrators may derive from the fact that they often depend for funding upon some external organization that requires evidence of the worthwhileness of the program. Hence the tendency, as Campbell notes, for specific programs or reforms to be "advocated as though they were certain to be successful."[28] Moreover, such an optimistic approach might be essential to foster the early development of morale and momentum among implementors that is required to give a program a fighting chance of achieving desired results.

Second, public policies are often initiated in response to a demand, especially by some potent interest group, to do something fast, even when the consequences of that specific something may be obscure. It is easy enough to parody such efforts. But it is no more just to do so than to parody the efforts of the captain of a ship on storm-tossed seas whose only goal is to stay afloat, so that it might later be possible to make expeditious progress toward the intended destination. The measure of such a captain is not that the ship expended too much fuel, or that it was too far behind schedule. Keeping the ship afloat is sometimes, perhaps often, the most that can be reasonably expected.

The goals of specific public policies can be both significant and enormous, and the pressure to do something can be strong and unremitting, and yet even the wisest heads might be puzzled and troubled about what to do and how. Hence Gibson and Prather conclude that "it is not surprising that administrators of [such] programs were not highly in favor of evaluations."[29] Who needs the additional trouble?

Third, public policy is seldom initiated or implemented by those with a research background. In this particular, administrators are far more equal than evaluators in what gets said and how. As Campbell concludes: "Ambiguity, lack of truly comparable comparison bases, and lack of concrete evidence all work to increase the administrator's control over what gets said, or at least to reduce the bite of criticism in the case of actual failure."[30]

Fourth, evaluators may join in telling the varnished truth, for reasons extending all the way from blatant self-interest to ardent advocacy. The most extreme case in point is probably the turmoil in Soviet genetics, where the fear of imprisonment and death often shaped the behavior of participants.[31] Many other garden varieties of the tendency also may be found in the literature, especially in the case of ardent advocates of particular programs or treatments.[32]

These complex particulars devolve to a straightforward conclusion. Although narrowly bounded in one sense, then, impact analysis of even a very specific policy with clear objectives can spiral out to overwhelming complexity in terms both of methods for analysis and of a complex rippling of effects. To suggest the compound point, analyses of the impact of the policies of the U.S. Selective Service System as carried out during the recent past require poking in the very guts of our social and educational institutions.[33] Similarly, efforts to assess the impact of such programs as Head Start soon find analysts wrestling with the complexities of child-rearing practices or of cultural mores in the home and immediate neighborhood.

Given the lack of attention to public policy as an independent variable, it comes as no surprise that human history shows little evidence of systematic learning from policy experience. As Dror concludes: "Very few evaluations of the real outcome of complex issues are made, and there are even fewer on which improvement of future policymaking can be based."[34] To put it another way, even determined analysts typically lack major parts of the puzzle of estimating policy impact. Specifically:

- The major objectives may not be defined precisely, or they might be conflicting or even contradictory.
- Due to their complexity, the principal outputs may not permit even gross estimation, let alone "precise measurement."
- It may not be possible to identify the inputs of required resources, especially "indirect" or social costs, so that they can be estimated and aggregated.
- It may be difficult to compare alternative combinations of inputs and outputs.
- It may be practically difficult and politically impossible to really compare programs for alternative uses of the same resources.

In sum, the public-policy analyst often will not have available the kind of data required by PPBS and other similar approaches to estimating costs and benefits.[35]

Policy and More Ambitious Analysis.   Far broader in ultimate intent is the search for policy-related generalizations. The focus in not on individual policies. Rather, the concern is with the classes of policies, as well as with the generic processes that may commonly underlay several classes of policies. At least six approaches to structuring the analysis of public policy in this more ambitious sense can be distinguished. Whereas impact analysis is particularistic and tied to implementation of quite specific policies, the following six varieties of analytic effort seek to move from broad comparisons toward the development of generalizations and the conditions under which they are likely to hold. Moreover, these six varieties aspire to greater rigor in testing for associations and relationships. Some would call these varieties "more scientific" than impact analysis. They patently are more ambitious.

First, some students have sought to differentiate kinds or types of policies, to facilitate the search for generalizations about differences between types. These can include differences in sources of support or opposition to various classes of policies, roles that are played in various phases of policymaking by diverse elites or segments of the population, how various types of policies come to be enacted or rejected, and so forth. For example, the Mitchells distinguish six kinds of problems that have social or political significance:[36]

Resource mobilization	Controls
Distribution of benefits	Adaptability and stabilization
Allocation of costs	Division of labor and role allocation

Substantial literature has developed around such efforts at classification, with the goal of providing a kind of fine tuning for analyses of public policy. When approached rigorously, major problems of method and substance become apparent in this literature.[37] But their general purpose is straightforward—to provide subclasses of policy that can, however preliminarily, help structure the search for similarities or differences between classes. For example, it may be useful—for some purposes, even critical—to know that (hypothetically) policies concerning resource mobilization involve different publics and key actors than do policies relating to division of labor and role allocation. Those different publics and key actors, to make the obvious point, will somehow have to be brought together in any successful policy sequence.

Second, numerous attempts have been made to structure analysis by detailing the steps in, or the functions of, the generic process of policymaking. For example, Jones suggests ten "functional activities in the policy process," while urging the reader to understand that they are "tentative and undogmatic." He identifies:[38]

1. Perception	6. Legitimation
2. Definition	7. Application and administration
3. Aggregation and organization	8. Reaction
4. Representation	9. Evaluation and appraisal
5. Formulation	10. Resolution and termination

Illustratively, such lists can help in both the description and evaluation of policymaking. Descriptively, they encourage attention to the fullness of activities involved in policymaking and consequently underscore the need for integrative analysis. For example, the perception of a policy issue might occur basically in an interest group or trade association; the formulation and legitimation of a policy response often would be accomplished in various congressional and executive offices; application and administration of that policy might be delegated far down the hierarchy in some public agency; and so forth. Moreover, evaluatively, such lists also can help in judging the adequacy of particular policy-making sequences. For example, evaluation and appraisal have long been neglected aspects of policymaking processes, even though they are critical ones. Lists like the one just given highlight such neglect and can remind both the formulators and analysts of public policy to touch all the bases.

Third, other students have attempted to structure the analysis of public policy by using various theoretical or interpretive models for analyzing policy-making sequences. Guidance has been sought at both macro- and micro-levels. Thus Brinton's broad theory of social revolutions has been used as a conceptual framework for describing administrative reorganizations.[39] Similarly, small-group theory also has been used to enrich the analysis of a standard case study in public administration.[40] And Allison applies three conceptual models to the same event—the blockade of Cuba by American forces during the missile crisis during the Kennedy Administration.[41] Similarly, other scholars have attempted to use case studies or analysis of policy areas in novel ways. Sundquist attempts to explain the cyclical character of our political and governmental systems in order to add perspective on why periods of intense activity and relative quiet seems to alternate.[42] He makes liberal use of mini-case studies. Moreover, Mosher has sought to analyze a batch of case studies to help determine, among other aims, the degree of direct applicability in large organizations of the sociological and psychological research on such concepts as "participation."[43] The latter research was often rigorous, but its findings were largely developed from observations of small groups. Mosher's goal, then, was to assess the applicability of a kind of micro-analysis in much larger organizations.

These structuring perspectives or models need not be imports, as it were. Thus Dye illustrates the usefulness in analyzing public policy of six models that had variously gained significant attention in political science and public adminis-tration.[44] These models include:

Systems model	Rational model
Elite-mass model	Incremental model
Group model	Institutional model

In permitting such illustrations of the simultaneous applicability of observa-tional or interpretive perspectives that already had gained some currency, such versions of policy analysis build on the past, as well as suggest that higher-order integration may be possible in the future.

Fourth, other analysts emphasize the actors in policymaking sequences and focus on the kind and quality of relationships that exist between sets of actors. For example, Lindblom focuses on four kinds of actors: (1) citizens; (2) voters especially as they effect competition between political parties; (3) interest-group leaders; and (4) the "proximate policymakers," or those "closest" to the actual making of relevant decisions. Lindblom also seeks to characterize the policy-making "game" as a play of power that basically involves a process of cooperation among specialists who seek to resolve policy issues by complex mixtures of analysis and political pragmatics. Lindblom sees the process as being gamelike, for the most part proceeding by rule and precedent.[45]

Fifth, other scholars have sought to do wide-ranging analyses of broad policy areas, such as water resource development[46] on the environment.[47] The approach has one prime consequence. It avoids the particularism of individual case studies or, to say much the same thing, roots the analysis in an evolving context of law, precedent, and the working resolution of major issues in contention over time. The analysis of broad policy areas in this sense, that is to say, helps emphasize the full sense of the "political" in political science.[48]

Sixth, a related approach seeks to define "arenas" or "subsystems" of policymaking, but not in terms of institutional categories such as agriculture policy, military policy, and so on. The most well known example is Lowi's classification of policies into four arenas of power—redistributive, distributive, constituent, and regulatory.[49] A number of others have developed generically similar approaches,[50] which Henry characterizes as "neo-institutionalism" because they are concerned "chiefly with political institutions, but with an eye toward generating theoretical predictions about how policy types relate to the branches of government and the polity generally."[51]

These six major kinds of approaches to structuring the description or discussion of policymaking processes are more illustrative than exhaustive, but they have common features that fill important needs. They all direct attention to the kind and quality of the policy products that are being generated by our governmental institutions and processes. Any derivative insight is most helpful, given the widespread concern, if not disillusionment, with public policies today. Relatedly, such multiple efforts to structure reality can be revealing because they provide reinforcing perspective. As we all know, where one sits determines what one sees. The use of several interpretive or analytic structures for viewing the same policymaking process thus can enrich understanding and control. Finally, such structuring devices contribute to systematic analysis of public policy. This orientation is often seen as a good in itself, as developing an "increased concern for social relevance of potential study,' and also as helping focus attention on the possibility of informed and meaningful choice, both for policymakers and for citizens. As Jones explains:

> Why not ... attempt to analyze in such a way that teachers, students, and policy makers can determine the social value of what is being learned? This is not to say that you or I should become advisers to those who are governing, though some of us shall. It is rather to suggest that students of politics should begin to employ

their increasingly sophisticated tools of analysis so as to contribute more directly to social action.[52]

Public Policy As Defining a
Field of Inquiry

Another class of public-policy concepts has a less benign potential. Examples will be relied on heavily to illustrate the point here, which is global in extent but elusive in content. That is, the focus here is on versions of public policy as a broad conceptual umbrella for encompassing a field of study, as contrasted with its use as a guide for analysis.

The broadest usage of public policy clearly has some major paradoxical consequences, four of which deserve especial emphasis. First, consider a significant if delicate point. It is but a small step from arguing that, if specific public programs policies are so central, the reasonable thing to do is to spin off an organizational array of "administrations" that have so far made more or less strong claims for attention. These include development administration, comparative administration, criminal justice administration, ecological administration, environmental administration, urban administration, transportation administration, welfare administration, and others. There is fragmenting potential aplenty in such a possibility.

Care is appropriate on this point, in the sense of affirming and denying. To affirm: Such policy-oriented efforts as that of Price on science[53] or Caldwell on the environment[54] are patently central in public administration. That is to say, public policy can clearly and properly be *one* of the several secondary or tertiary organizing foci for public administration. To deny: Having made such an affirmation, the position here rejects the capacity of any policy orientation to provide *the* stable primary organizing focus. To the contrary, if anything, such an orientation is perhaps inherently fragmenting as a primary organizing focus, unless two conditions hold. First, students of public administration must be willing to settle for relatively superficial acquaintance with a number of policy areas, as a concession to the complex historical, institutional, procedural, and personality detail involved in relative mastery of any one policy area. Second, students of public administration must be able to develop detailed acquaintance with several policy areas, despite the complex historical, institutional, procedural, and personality detail involved in relative mastery of any one policy area.

The two conditions hold out little promise for public administrationists, however. The first condition is undesirable; and the second is unlikely.[55]

The probable effect of reliance on public policy as a primary organizing focus is to spin off a variety of "administrations,"[56] then, and the view here is that such fragmentation is counterproductive at this state of the development of public administration. The rationale is straightforward. Basically, there is ample generic content common to the several administrations, which probably would not be attended to if the primary rubric for organizing is the particularistic policy area. To be sure, some policy-oriented schools—such as those of education—can be large enough to provide resources necessary for treating the several generic aspects of administration or management relevant to that one policy area. But such fragmentation is not practical now in public administration, given existing resources and knowledge, and given that a very substantial critical mass of both is necessary to trigger concerted effort in any single discipline or field, however it is defined. In any case, public policy now poorly serves those interested in defining mission and role for public administration to the degree that its basic thrust is to induce numerous mini-administrations.

Second, based on its record so far, Phase IV probably cannot avoid or manage such fragmentation. Ironically, to put the matter in bold terms, the public-policy orientation was initially offered as an integrative concept reinforcing ties between political science and public administration. However, Phase IV has contributed both to a fragmentation between political science and public administration, as well as to confusion within public administration.

Historically, that is, Phase IV applications have developed in such ways that too much has been made of a good thing, and all evidence suggests a broad movement to make even more of that once useful emphasis. Consider that early Phase IV work was characterized by emphasis on "public interest." The net result of such an approach to policy/administration interpenetration strongly reinforced ties between political science and public administration and resulted in such interdisciplinary empirical research as that on groups.[57] The overall impression of work consistent with the public-interest theme is the complex commingling or separation of various specialties in political science and public administration. Consider also, however, that later varieties of Phase IV work have less sanguine potential. Overall, to illustrate, the dominant trend in available textbooks is toward integration by assimilation of public administration into political science.[58] For example, Rehfuss notes that his goal is to restore "politics to center stage as the driving-force behind most administrative behavior."[59] Other recent Phase IV usages come close to defining public administration as a kind of derivative or resultant category. Readers of one book are told that its "principal roots are in political science, and it seeks to bring together that information about administration that is most relevant to *an understanding of the larger political process.* Of necessity, much of this information concerns public administration."[60]

Third, to make the point more explicit, many later Phase IV variants are so general and inclusive as to be useless, and perhaps even dangerous.[61] For example, Landau stresses that the public-policy definition of the scope of public administration "challenges the integrity of the 'field.' " The "rigidities of the politics-administration dichotomy" needed correction, he observed, but supporters of the public-policy orientation provided the correction only by defining away the problem. A Phase IV concept, Landau continued, is "so extensive as to provide little meaning." Indeed, he notes, those who argue for a public-policy approach "make it virtually impossible to specify an area of [governmental] activity that cannot be considered within [their] scope." The Phase IV definition of the field, that is, fails two primary tests: (1) It does not designate clearly the phenomenal field of interest; and (2) its locus is as wide as all of political science. Landau pushes the point even further: "In the effort to define the field," he concludes, "the field evaporates."[62]

Landau seems to have a firm grasp on important features of reality.[63] Consider Mosher's response to the central question of whether public administration is a discipline. He concludes:

> Public administration cannot debark any subcontinent as its exclusive province—unless it consists of such mundane matters as classifying budget expenditures, drawing organization charts, and mapping procedures. In fact, it would appear that any definition of this field would be either so encompassing as to call forth the wrath of ridicule of others, or so limiting as to stultify its own discipline. Perhaps it is best that it not be defined. It is more an area of interest than a discipline, more a focus than a separate science.[64]

If directly given, this response implies significant costs for public administration as a distinct area of inquiry. Rather than being a proud area of specialization, public administration must somehow find its "chief satisfaction in providing a way of looking at government." This offers only a vague opportunity, if it is not a death rattle.

Similarly, even Waldo's notable effort to define scope and method for public administration ends in substantial pessimism. To be specific, Waldo seems to agree with Mosher that, rather than being a proud area of specialization, public administration must somehow find its "chief satisfaction in providing a way of looking at government." He goes much further, in fact. "What I propose," he notes, "is that we try to act as a profession without the hope or intention of being one in any strict sense." Waldo observes: "Frankly, it took some courage to say that, as it is patently open to ridicule."[65]

Fourth, and finally, public-policy usages broader than a loose metaphor for expressing a scholarly community of interest are troubling because they typically do not emphasize the technologies and skills that will be required to do the job. And even when explicit emphasis is given, the required retooling seldom gets reflected in specific courses and curricula.

The total sense of it is that many Phase IV usages not only want their cake while they eat it, but there is no rush to learn baking skills. The point can be illustrated by focusing on the insights of Thomas R. Dye concerning the inescapable demands that he sees deriving from his core-observation that "today the focus of political science is shifting to public policy—to the description and explanation of the causes and consequences of government activity."[66] Perhaps basically, the challenges for Dye inhere in the variety of conceptual models and approaches to public-policy research, approached scientifically. He emphasizes three:

- Case studies of the formulation and implementation of public policy, whose use has been "most common in policy research in political science generally"

- Public-choice models—including operations research, cost-benefit analysis, and so on—that "emphasize concepts of rationality and focus on the relation between values achieved and values sacrificed in public policy alternatives"

- Systems models, in which "public policy is viewed as an output of a political system which is acting in response to environmental forces and in which outputs themselves are viewed as having an independent feedback effect upon the environment in the political system"

Such diverse models and approaches imply very different technologies and tools, Dye advises. And the public-choice and systems models require technologies and skills uncommon in political science, which will have to be mastered if political scientists are really serious in urging comprehensive public-policy usages. Dye's choice is clear, but he also recognizes that political scientists differ radically as to the virtues of the required expansionism. Thus Dye explains:

> There is no doubt that policy analysis requires an expansion of the traditional boundaries of political science well beyond any previous definition of those boundaries. If public policy is to be the dependent variable in our research, we must be prepared to search for policy determinants among economic, social, cultural, historical, technological factors, as well as political forces. If public policy is to be the independent variable, we must be prepared to search for policy consequences which are economic, social, cultural, historical, and technological, as well as political.

And Dye also quotes Vernon Van Dyke's warning that political scientists pursuing such a public-policy concept "might soon find themselves shoulder to shoulder with professors and researchers of almost all other disciplines, trying to solve all kinds of problems . . . An all-out policy orientation would help take political scientists fully into the realm of normative problems and social engineering. The prospect is appalling. . . ."

Descriptive Policy Analysis

Not all public-policy variants rely on a global concept; nor do they all propose to redefine the boundaries of public administration. Beginning in the 1960s, that is, a number of political scientists began pioneering in the discrete analysis of quantified aspects of public policies, relying on newly available electronic data-processing equipment to manipulate large batches of data according to well-established statistical conventions, within the broad framework of "systems theory."[67] In this approach, to quote Dye: "Public policy is viewed as an output of a political system which is acting in response to environmental forces and in which outputs themselves are viewed as having an independent feedback effect upon the environment in the political system."[68] Such work is labeled "descriptive policy analysis," respecting the distinction suggested by Yehezkel Dror without employing his terminology.[69]

Descriptive policy analysis is straightforward in concept, but single studies can deal with a hundred variables and hence often are complicated. Essentially, the focus is on individual public policies—or more precisely, on narrow indicators of some characteristics or outcomes of the implementation of public decisions in selected issue areas—both as dependent variables and independent variables. The analyst then searches for differences among units at the same or similar level of government—often states, but not necessarily so—that covary with differences in quantifiable aspects of similar policies. For example, in a historically significant study, Dye analyzed the interaction between some "system characteristics" of our several states and differences in aspects of their public policies. His research design is schematized in Table 3.2. Contrary to the common wisdom, Dye reports that system characteristics have little impact on public-policy outcomes. He concludes:

> partial correlation analysis reveals that these system characteristics have relatively little *independent* effect on policy outcomes in the states. Economic development shapes both political systems and policy outcomes, and most of the association that occurs between system characteristics and policy outcomes can be attributed to the influence of economic development. Differences in the policy choices of states with different types of political systems turn out to be largely a product of differing socio-economic levels rather than a direct product of political variables.[70]

Descriptive policy analysis patently constitutes an important area of inquiry but, for a variety of reasons, it does not provide a viable mission and role for public administration. Moreover, the approach also implies major conceptual problems for political science and public administration.

TABLE 3.2   A Characteristic Research Design for Descriptive Policy Analysis

Independent Variables	Dependent Variables
Differences in SYSTEM CHARACTERISTICS $\Longrightarrow$ of American states, such as:	As they covary with differences in ASPECTS OF POLICIES of American states, such as:
Division of two-party vote Level of interplay competition Level of voter participation Degree of malapportionment in state legislatures	Educational policy, as measured by: Pupil/teacher ratios Per pupil expenditures Dropout rates and
	Welfare policy, as measured by: Per capital welfare expenditures Unemployment recipients
	Highway policy . . .

[a] Based on Thomas R. Dye, *Politics, Economics, and the Public: Policy Outcomes in the American States* (Chicago: Rand McNally, 1966).

Four Major Concerns

Four points support these conclusions. First, descriptive policy analysis gets double-barreled reproof for what it is as well as for what some of its adherents maintain it should become. The approach has been criticized because it fixates only on those narrow aspects of policy that have been quantified, which to some observers leaves much (and perhaps everything) to be desired. Thus, Jones states hopefully: "Perhaps Dye's analysis will be extended to consider the major determinants of policy outcomes that are less easily quantified—perhaps more significant to the polity."[71]

If descriptive policy analysis is too narrow for some, however, it also causes problems because some adherents argue that an adequate descriptive policy analysis in the longer run requires a profound redefinition of disciplinary territory. Thus, for Dye there "is no doubt" that the evolution of explanatory policy analysis "requires an expansion of the traditional boundaries of political science well beyond any previous definition of those boundaries."[72]

Second, some commentators have emphasized the critical differences between descriptive and prescriptive approaches to policy analysis. The following section attempts to describe the evolution of the prescriptive approach. For present purposes, the prescriptive approach seeks to bridge several related gulfs—that between "study" and "practice," as well as that between a "pure science" and an "applied science." The thrust toward application does not characterize descriptive policy analysis, which is steadfastly oriented toward analysis only. This simplification also constitutes a major limitation for public administration, which must bridge the gap between action and thought or research.

Several methodological concerns exacerbate this "analysis only" quality of descriptive policy analysis. For one thing, its most common statistical procedures—various forms of correlation analysis—are competent only to establish covariation, as distinguished from causality or interrelationship.[73] So it is necessary to be careful in interpreting such descriptions of what exists as those Dye offers, lest one fail to respect the limitations of the statistical technology. Consequently, the results of the typical piece of descriptive policy analysis can only be used cautiously, if at all, in formulating answers to the key questions with which policymakers must deal. Such a key question is: "If we vary variable X in a specific case, what will happen to variable Y?" At its best, descriptive policy analysis is better suited for making only tentative statements of this form: "If you look at variable X in a number of similar jurisdictions—like states or cities—we may find some nonrandom distribution of differences of variable Y." This is useful information, but it must be interpreted narrowly. Wade expresses the point elegantly:

> as Morss has pointed out, these studies in no way *explain* the manner in which community decisions get made; at most they enable one, within a more or less known margin of error, to predict what state expenditures will be, given knowledge of the variables (nonpolitical) which are related to expenditures.[74] This is clear enough. However, if prediction is what is sought, the wrong variables have been analyzed since the best predictor of a state's expenditures is probably the state's revenues. Another excellent predictor would be last year's expenditure, modified by whatever growth factor, if any, appears to be roughly constant.[75] Of course, neither revenues nor past expenditures, although very highly correlated with current expenditures, explain anything at all. They are aids to prediction, however, and are important for that reason.[76]

Moreover, the phenomenon of spurious correlations implies potentially significant questions about the real meaning of any such distribution of scores of Y and X.[77]

These methodological concerns may be expressed economically. Any descriptions of the covariates of policy—as dependent or independent variable—should be tentatively interpreted as long as nonexperimental research designs are employed. And this will be a very long time indeed, in the general case, given the enormous problems of formulating experimental designs that are policy relevant.[78] Time-series designs—observing the interaction of any variables X and Y over a long period of time—sometimes can help in this regard. But the passage of time typically sees major changes in environmental, cultural, legal, or demographic characteristics that complicate or even confound analysis.

Third, the units of analysis in descriptive policy analysis—typically states, cities, or regions that coincide with state boundaries—may be more convenient than they are realistic wholes that can be treated as entities. The issues are fiendishly complicated, and for now only one point is clear. Data gathering would be enormously more complicated if (for example) Sharkansky,[79] had not chosen to define regions as having boundaries coterminous with state lines. Convenient compilations typically classify data in terms of some legal jurisdiction such as a state, of course. It is not clear whether convenience distorts reality or just delightfully simplifies the task of analysis.[80]

Fourth, despite its substantial impact on research[81] and on contemporary leading ideas,[82] the literature of descriptive policy analysis has provoked some important second thoughts. Relevant revisionary themes relate both to broad concept and to interpretations of specific research findings. At the conceptual level, for example, Sharkansky and Hofferbert conclude: "We have been too simple-minded in our measurement of 'politics' and 'policy.' " Moreover, they note: "There is no single answer to the question: 'Is it politics or economics that has the greatest impact on public policy?' "[83] Wade adds an important qualification relevant to common interpretations of descriptive policy analysis as constituting a world view of the determinants of policy. He notes that it is undoubtedly correct to observe that "some political factors are not closely or even remotely associated with the determinants of public policy." But Wade also urges caution. For that undoubtedly correct observation is a "far cry" from the conclusion that "policy is produced largely or even principally by socio-economic factors in all, even most cases. [The] views which hold politics to be insignificant to policy [are exaggerated] ."[84]

Such ferment is encouraging from a scientific perspective, of course, but it also implies a need for caution. Descriptive policy analysis does provide a model for research with a self-correcting potential. But the work with correlates of aspects of policies is controversial in its implication of an economic determinism; and that work does raise methodological questions. Hence the area clearly can support scientific inquiry, and indeed requires it. Judgments about the adequacy of the world view implicit in much existing research are best delayed, however.

Prescriptive Policy Analysis

Other proponents—without doubt, presently the most influential proponents—of a public-policy concept make Dye's expansionism look puny in comparison. These proponents argue for an emerging field of policy sciences, which is here called "prescriptive policy analysis." Policy sciences do not define the scope of public administration, except to provide for its inclusion in a broad supradiscipline, one version of which was described by Bunker in these terms:

The creation in 1968 at the State University of New York at Buffalo of a new Doctoral Program in Policy Sciences recognized both the growing body of significant scientific work bearing upon an understanding of policy processes and the need to work toward its integration and its utilization in the improvement of practice. The Buffalo program is concerned with the development of the policy sciences as an interdisciplinary field bridging the social and decision sciences, and with the preparation of hybrid research-scientists/practitioners who can make the fruits of this new interdiscipline accessible to policy-making and social guidance elements in our society.[85]

There is no simple way to introduce the policy sciences, and probably no really satisfactory brief way. But we can try. At the broadest level, Lasswell provides useful guidance. "The policy sciences may be conceived," he notes, "as knowledge *of* the policy process and of the relevance of knowledge *in* the process."[86] This takes a very critical step beyond "descriptive policy analysis," in short, which focuses on knowledge of policy process only. That step is both awesome and difficult. As Bernstein notes, social science research has been "disappointing" in furnishing guidance for policymakers, and governments have therefore had to make policy decisions on the basis of scanty information about their probable effects. The policy sciences seek to fill this critical void—to fill an "informational vacuum" by approaching the analysis of social problems via "systematic frameworks which include the means for gauging changes in society's conditions through various policy interventions taking the form of either allocation or regulation."[87]

Lasswell argued for the same step in 1951, but developments since then add the force of major increases in technical sophistication to his argument. For one thing, the intervening years have witnessed the evolution of, and experience with, what Dye call "public choice models." They include operations research, cost-benefit analysis, and so on, and commonly "emphasize concepts of rationality and focus on the relation between values achieved and values sacrificed in public policy alternatives."[88]

The application of such models was given major impetus in the 1960s by a pressing need to decide between alternative courses of public action, given new and often unreconcilable demands for greater shares in public goods. At first, the need for policy analysis was most recognized in national security affairs, where "policy sciences first got named and flourished." When domestic problems were first considered, in Lewis's words, they "were largely macro-economic and were themselves associated with our emerging world role: Could we 'afford' our foreign policy?" Then came the 1960s. Lewis reminds us: "What is now termed the urban crisis was blasted into the forefront of public attention by the events of Watts, Hough, Detroit, Newark, and on and on, [and] actions were set in train which might ultimately cause substantial reallocation of resources to the internal problems of the nation that show their symptoms most dramatically in our cities."[89]

This combination of technology and experience in national security, plus urgent domestic need, has emboldened many to urge development of the policy sciences. Consider the visionary words of Dror, who stresses the need to establish "policy sciences as a new supradiscipline [which] involves a scientific revolution, requiring fargoing innovations in basic paradigms." Of particular significance are:[90]

- An interdisciplinary thrust, especially integrating the social sciences and analytical approaches to decision making

- Somehow reconciling "pure" and "applied" work or overcoming the "dichotomy" between them

- The recognition that "tacit knowledge" is a scientific resource

- Explicit development of interfaces between empirical regularities and values

- A lengthy time-frame, that is, a broad perspective both backward and forward in conventional time

- An emphasis on "metapolicies" or broad statements of goals

- A major commitment to improving the full policymaking process

- Major attention to extrarational or even irrational processes, including creativity

Conceptual and Practical Concerns

Without wishing to rain on anyone's parade, but risking that consequence nonetheless, two conclusions seem patent. First, the policy sciences clearly do not provide either an immediate conceptual or practical solution to the problem of defining mission and role for public administration. Second, this is particularly the case for those who find it strategic or politic to maintain strong ties with political science.

These two broad conclusions cannot be proved in any vigorous sense, but perspective on such a proof can be shared conveniently. It is necessary to be harshly selective, but two examples should serve to make the present point. One of these perspectives is conceputal, the other is practical.

First, a cluster of major conceputal concerns with prescriptive policy analysis may be distinguished. Essentially, granted that this may be only a temporary condition, it is fair enough to characterize the policy sciences as resting on optimistic assertions that they can or should avoid the inadequacies or awkward assumptions of predecessors, primarily systems analysis and systems engineering. This negative and hopeful mode of establishing the policy sciences as a new supradiscipline is reflected, for example, in Dror's "required innovations" just listed. Consider one commonly cited "unrealistic assumption" of the decision and analytic technologies associated with systems analysis, such as operations research. That is, these technologies admit only variables that can be quantified. To improve on such an inadequacy, Dror prescribes that the policy sciences should and perhaps can admit a far broader range of data dealing with institutional or political factors, or even with what Dror calls "tacit knowledge." Similarly, if many systems analysts accept "unrealistic assumptions" about "economic rationality," Dror prescribes that the policy sciences should and perhaps can provide satisfactory inclusion of "extrarational and irrational processes." This amounts to problem solving by verbal fiat; a kind of hopeful "can do" resting on "should be."

This negative and optimistic mode of establishing the policy sciences raises substantial concerns. Basically, the should/can gap seems an enormous one. To emphasize how a new supradiscipline should surpass its predecessors: It may have to rediscover objective dilemmas that remain as recalcitrant as they were when those very predecessors failed to resolve them; and the boosterism may be ungenerous and induce counterproductive competition. Hence Radnor's pleas "for unity in place of competition" in efforts that seek to establish the role of the policy sciences vis-à-vis the management sciences or systems analysis. Hence also Radnor's caution about the present developmental stage of the policy sciences and his conviction about what progress will inevitably mean. He urges that if the policy sciences do develop, they will do so only by developing their own "unrealistic assumptions." This being the case, Radnor prescribes a substantial suspicion of "any science and technology which purports to be *the* science or technology which eliminates once and for all the unrealistic assumptions and models of its predecessors." All scientific or systematic effort, he continues, cannot do other than "to model and approximate the systems that we wish to analyze." Radnor concludes: "There are no sciences without models, there are just sciences with better or poorer models. The development of useful and operational models will be a critical testing point for Policy Sciences."[91]

Among some political scientists at least, the emphasis on prescriptive policy analysis is suspect in this regard in a special sense. That is, some observers see policy sciences as simply providing a new front or legitimation for the very micro-analytic methods and technologies whose use was earlier inspired by the behavioral era in political science and public administration. Such observers question, or deny, the applicability of micro-phenomena to policy analysis.[92] Or such observers question or deny the applicability of the assumptions of the technologies of other disciplines. For example, Adams questions whether two assumptions of economics drawn from the private sector—the production model and evaluation by return on investment—make sense in the analysis of public policy.[93]

Moreover, it may even be that the should/can gap is simply insurmountable, period. Hence, Rittel and Webber argue that the "search for scientific bases for confronting problems of social policy is bound to fail," the best intentions and efforts of researchers notwithstanding. The reason lies in the "wicked" • nature of the problems of social policy. They explain:

> Policy problems cannot be definitively described. Moreover in a pluralistic society there is nothing like the undisputable public good; there is no objective definition of equity; policies that respond to social problems cannot be meaningfully correct or false; and it makes no sense to talk about "optimal solutions" to social problems unless severe qualifications are imposed first. Even worse, there are no "solutions" in the sense of definitive and objective answers.[94]

In contrast, the problems with which science has successfully coped are "tame"; they are analytical pussycats by comparison. One observer made that comparison in an interesting way. Electrons are easier to study, he noted, if only because they can neither read tomorrow's newspaper describing their behavior, nor opt to change that behavior on the basis of their reading.

It is probably premature to judge the degree to which Rittel and Weber are correct. It is certainly not too early to agree that many problems of public policy are truly wicked ones that are well beyond our present power to deal with scientifically.

A second perspective on the two conclusions that began this section involves a cluster of practical concerns that must be faced if prescriptive policy analysis is to provide conceptual guidance for public administration; these concerns must be faced especially by those who desire strong interfaces with political science. Paramountly, the policy sciences are proposed as a supra-discipline and—although all versions are developmental and no pattern can yet be called prototypical—their common organizational form is an interdisciplinary program or school.

Even this early evolutionary form implies several practical concerns. Primarily, at least in the short run, the interdisciplinary thrust raises the hoary issue of the complex relationships between individual scholars and practitioners, their several subject matter disciplines, and the matrix organization. In this sense, the policy sciences do not resolve the issue of mission and role for public administration or political science. Rather, it relocates the issue and brings to bear on it a new set of constraints and opportunities that probably will differ widely from case to case. Bunker implies relocation versus resolution in his discussion of prescriptive policy analysis as "an applied social science approach," while acknowledging that "the task of bridging between the form and content of the social sciences and policy problems is still far from complete." He sees social science as heuristic, as enriching "frames of appreciation," but as essentially a failure in helping decision makers deal with the problems they confront. Bunker acknowledges only a "partial exception to this indictment" in some areas of applied welfare economics. He concludes:

> Part of this strain between scientific and applied concerns derives from the fact that while scientific work tends toward specialization and the divergence of disciplines, policy problems don't present themselves as convenient packages suited to the prevailing styles of disciplinary research. There are many other facets of this problem. . . . It is enough for us to say here that our commitment, contrary to prevailing fashions in the social sciences, is toward interdisciplinary and problem-oriented approaches. This applies to both the research and practice aspects of the roles for which we prepare our graduates.[95]

Even given this indeterminancy, however, it is safe to say that a viable partnership for political science or public administration in any policy science supradiscipline will practically require that many, and perhaps most, adherents of those two disciplines who somehow join will bring with them substantial skills in the several relevant behavioral and analytical technologies. Bunker implies this need in his description of the Buffalo doctoral program, which rests on four basic orienting perspectives: (1) general systems theory with special attention to open systems; (2) the central concepts and propositions of welfare economics; (3) contemporary organization theory; and (4) the insights into human information processing provided by cognitive psychology. He explains:

> Each of these fields has its penumbra within which each of the others fall, yet each provides an essential and unique framework. General systems theory provides an intellectual stance that aids the perception of function and the ordering of complexity; welfare economics, a theory of choice and a framework for comparison of alternatives; cognitive psychology, a reminder that ideas are not given in nature and that varieties of percepts and images are infinite, lawfully determined, and extremely influential in policy transactions; and organization theory, a sense of the concrete setting of relationships, roles, and purposive assumptions, and normative judgments in which policy issues are embedded.[96]

Bunker notes that not all students are required to develop a working competence in operations research, or quantitative systems analysis, or whatever. But those students are required to become familiar "with the major applications and limitations of these methods, an acquaintance with the logic and intuitive mathematics underlying their use, and an ability to communicate and collaborate with quantitative analysts in project situations."[97]

There are substantial reasons to believe such a partnership will be a difficult one to achieve, if only for three reasons. First, in a practical sense, although a few exceptions exist, neither political science[98] for public administration[99] has provided a particularly congenial humus for the growth of the orientations and skills on which a partnership must rest. Second, in a power sense, moreover, Foss argues that political science "has the lowest professional status of any of the social sciences," which implies some obvious difficulties. For Foss, himself a political scientist, the low status has a solid existential base. He notes: ". . . our professional organizations have done little to serve their members or enhance the status of the profession; [and] political scientists have little knowledge and few skills that are of interest or value to anyone except other political scientists."[100] Third, reflections of the concerns just cited are not always subtle. Consider the reaction of Lowi on learning that the prevailing outlook of political scientists was not even included in the original plan for a symposium on "interdisciplinary approaches to policy study." He explains:

> This implied two things. It implied that an interdisciplinary approach to public policy had little to learn from political science. More significantly, it implied that if political scientists were now to interest themselves in policy studies, their primary obligation would be to learn how policy analysis is done from all the social science disciplines *except* political science. There is much we would need to know and are afraid to ask. In effect a political scientist who would be a policy analyst must also be a sociologist, or an economist, or a physical scientist, or an anthropologist, or a geographer, or some combination of these. And the members of those sister disciplines would not have to feel any obligation to become political scientists.[101]

To Lowi, this meant only a regression to the 1950s and the biases of its behavioral era, which he hoped had been left behind.

On the whole, then, policy science programs may imply some major political issues for those seeking viable reflections of the interests and concerns central to political science or public administration. Directly, those who see only the short-run maintenance features of Phase IV public policy may be put off by the longer-run task features. Some sense of the kind and quality of those longer-run issues is highlighted by this reaction of Vernon Van Dyke to the prospect of participation by political scientists and public administrationists in prescriptive policy analysis. These students, he warns:

> might soon find themselves shoulder to shoulder with professors and researchers of almost all other disciplines, trying to solve all kinds of problems. . . . An all-out policy orientation would help take political scientists fully into the realm of normative problems and social engineering. The prospect is appalling. . . .[102]

Other observers are less appalled than they are impressed by a kind of "mandarin delusion" underlying the desire to "get into the action"[103] that pervades prescriptive policy analysis. Horowitz is concerned that the desire is more or less doomed to frustration. The heart of it for Horowitz is this: "Social scientists engaged in governmental work are committed to an advocacy model defined by politicians. For the most part, they do not *establish* or even *verify* policy—only legitimize policy."[104] That is, Horowitz concludes that the usual heroic scenario of the policy sciences is substantially a myth. That usual scenario takes a form such as the following: Public officials become aware of a "need to know," but because existing knowledge is inadequate, public officials arrange grants or contracts so as to get appropriate aid from "outside knowledge factories." The resulting increase in knowledge then becomes the basis for some action by the originating public officials.

Horowitz proposes an alternative scenario, which he sees as "more nearly empirically verifiable." It begins with policies being decided, somewhere in government. The goals are some real or assumed need of a nongovernmental elite or a mass constituency, spurred along by some ambitious public administrators or legislators seeking "to define their uniqueness in the political heavens." Only then, Horowitz notes, is there generated "a frantic search for precedent in the past, justification in the present, and rationalization in the future." And it is only then, he adds, that "social scientists are called to do 'feasibility studies,' 'demonstration effects,' and 'simulation analyses' which prove beyond a shadow of a doubt the legitimacy of the course of decision-making accomplished [without] any reference to the empirical world."[105]

Notes and References

1. Albert Somit and Joseph Tanenhaus, *The Development of Political Science* (Boston: Allyn and Bacon, 1967), especially pp. 173-194.

2. Vernon Van Dyke, "Process and Policy as Focal Concepts in Political Research," in *Political Science and Public Policy,* ed. Austin Ranney (Chicago: Markham, 1968), pp. 23-39.

3. Alvin W. Gouldner, "Metaphysical Pathos and the Theory of Bureaucracy," *American Political Science Review* 44 (December 1955): 498.

4. Especially in Robert T. Golembiewski, *Renewing Organizations* (Itasca, Ill.: F. E. Peacock, 1972).

5. Thomas R. Dye, *Understanding Public Policy* (Englewood Cliffs, N.J.: Prentice-Hall, 1972), p. 3.

6. For a fine example of such usage, see Peter Woll, *Public Policy* (Cambridge, Mass.: Winthrop, 1974).

7. The argument here closely follows Robert T. Golembiewski, "Public Administration and Public Policy: An Analysis of Development of Developmental Phases," in Robert Spadaro, Thomas R. Dye, Robert T. Golembiewski, Murray S. Stedman, and L. Harmon Zeigler, *The Policy Vacuum* (Lexington, Mass.: Lexington Books, 1975), pp. 82-102.

8. Harold Stein, *Public Administration and Policy Development* (New York: Harcourt Brace Jovanovich, Inc., 1952), p. xv.

9. For statements regarding cases as they are and as they should be, see Edwin A. Bock, ed., *Essays on the Case Method in Public Administration* (New York: Inter University Case Program, 1962).
    Some critics trace a major liability of the case approach to this bias. Theodore J. Lowi takes such a position, and suggests an extrapolation. He notes: "broad-gauged theories of politics are not related, perhaps not relatable, to observable cases." "American Business, Public Policy, Case Studies, and Political Theory," *World Politics* 16 (July 1964): 687.

10. Paul Appleby, *Policy and Administration* (University, Ala.: University of Alabama Press, 1949), p. 156.

11. A. Dunsire, *Administration: The Word and the Science* (New York: Wiley, 1973), p. 156.

12. Appleby, *Policy and Administration*, p. 16.

13. Charles O. Jones, *An Introduction to the Study of Public Policy* (Belmont, Calif.: Wadsworth, 1970), p. 4.

14. Direct linkages may be drawn between interest-group literature such as David B. Truman, *The Governmental Process* (New York: Knopf, 1951), and such efforts as Robert T. Golembiewski, *The Small Group* (Chicago: University of Chicago Press, 1962).

15. Dye, *Understanding Public Policy*, pp. 3, 6, 13.

16. Ibid., p. 292.

17. Joseph S. Wholey et al., *Federal Evaluation Policy: Analyzing the Effects of Public Programs* (Washington, D.C.: Urban Insititue, 1971), p. 11.

18. For a powerful argument about the difficulties and importance of evaluating public agencies, see James D. Thompson, *Organizations in Action* (New York: McGraw-Hill, 1967).

19. Orville F. Poland, "Why Does Public Administration Ignore Evaluation?" *Public Administration Review* 31 (March 1971): 201-202.

20. Wholey, *Federal Evaluation Policy*, p. 23.

21. For a convenient summary, see Nicholas Henry, *Public Administration and Public Affairs* (Englewood Cliffs, N.J.: Prentice-Hall, 1975), especially Chap. IX.

22. Wholey, *Federal Evaluation Policy*, p. 15.

23. C. H. Logan, "Evaluation Research in Crime and Delinquency: A Reappraisal," *Journal of Criminal Law, Criminology, and Police Science* 63, 1 (1972): 379-381.

24. Joel Fischer, "Is Casework Effective?: A Review," *Social Work* 18 (January 1973): 5-19.

25. Frank K. Gibson and James E. Prather, "The Neutral Effects of Systemic Variables on Policy Outcomes" (Paper delivered at the Annual Meeting of the American Society for Public Administration, Syracuse, N.Y., 1974).

26. Edward R. Tufte, *Data Analysis for Politics and Policy* (Englewood Cliffs, N.J.: Prentice-Hall, 1974).

27. Gibson and Prather, "The Neutral Effects of Systemic Variables on Policy Outcomes," p. 3.

28. Donald T. Campbell, "Reforms as Experiments," *American Psychologist* 24 (April 1969): 409.

29. Gibson and Prather, "The Neutral Effects of Systemic Variables on Policy Outcomes," p. 4.

30. Campbell, "Reforms as Experiments," p. 409.

31. The reference is to the "Lysenko affair," which has been widely written about and analyzed.

32. Paul Lerman, "Evaluative Studies of Institutions for Delinquents: Implications for Research and Social Policy," *Social Work* 13 (July 1968): 62.

33. James W. Davis, Jr., and Kenneth M. Dolbeare, *Little Groups of Neighbors* (Chicago: Markham, 1968); and Gary L. Wamsley, *Selective Service and a Changing America* (Columbus, Ohio: Merrill, 1969).

34. Yehezkel Dror, *Public Policymaking Reexamined* (Chicago: Markham, 1968), p. 275.

35. Fremont J. Lyden and Ernest G. Miller, eds., *Planning Programming Budgeting: A Systems Approach to Management* (Chicago: Markham, 1967).

36. Joyce M. Mitchell and William C. Mitchell, *Political Analysis and Public Policy* (Chicago: Rand McNally, 1969), pp. 392ff.

37. For such an attempted analysis of "issue areas" and "community elites," see Robert T. Golembiewski, William Welsh, and William Crotty, *A Methodological Primer for Political Scientists* (Chicago: Rand McNally, 1967), pp. 149-190.

38. Jones, *An Introduction to the Study of Public Policy,* pp. 10-11.

39. Crane Brinton, *The Anatomy of Revolution* (New York: Harper, 1938).

40. Robert T. Golembiewski, *Behavior and Organization* (Chicago: Rand McNally, 1962).

41. Graham T. Allison, *Essence of Decision: Explaining the Cuban Missile Crisis* (Boston: Little, Brown, 1971). See also his "Conceptual Models and the Cuban Missile Crisis," *American Political Science Review* 63 (September 1969): 689-718.

42. James L. Sundquist, *Politics and Policy* (Washington, D.C.: The Brookings Institution, 1968).

43. Frederick C. Mosher, ed., *Governmental Reorganizations: Cases and Comments* (Indianapolis: Bobbs-Merrill, 1967).

44. Dye, *Understanding Public Policy*, especially pp. 17-35.

45. Charles E. Lindblom, *The Policy-Making Process* (Englewood Cliffs, N.J.: Prentice-Hall, 1968).

46. The prototypical book is Arthur Maass, *Muddy Waters* (Cambridge, Mass.: Harvard University Press, 1951).

47. Lynton Keith Caldwell, *Environment* (New York: Natural History Press, 1970).

48. E. W. Kelley, "Political Science as Science and Common Sense," p. 206, in *Post-Behavioral Era Perspectives on Political Science,* ed. George J. Graham and George W. Carrey (New York: McKay, 1972).

49. Theodore J. Lowi, "American Business, Public Policy, Case Studies, and Political Science."

50. For example, consult Randall B. Ripley, *Public Policies and Their Politics* (New York: Norton, 1966), especially pp. vii-xvii; and Robert Salisbury and John Heinz, "A Theory of Policy Analysis and Some Preliminary Applications," in *Policy Analysis in Political Science,* ed. Ira Sharkansky (Chicago: Markham, 1970), pp. 39-60.

51. Henry, *Public Administration and Public Affairs,* Chap. IX.

52. Jones, *An Introduction to the Study of Public Policy,* p. 5.

53. Don K. Price, *The Scientific Estate* (Cambridge, Mass.: Belknap Press, 1967); and Dean Schooler, Jr., *Science, Scientists, and Public Policy* (New York: Free Press, 1971).

54. Caldwell, *Environment.*

55. Unless I seriously misread between the lines, for example, I see signs of this tension in Don Allensworth, *Public Administration: The Execution of Public Policy* (Philadelphia: J. B. Lippincott, 1973).

56. Ibid., especially pp. 7-125, seems to reflect such a tendency. See also Henry, *Public Administration and Public Affairs.*

57. The link between Truman, *The Governmental Process,* and Golembiewski, *The Small Group,* was alluded to earlier.

58. See John B. Richard, "Politics In/And/Or/But Administration," *Public Administration Review* 35 (November 1975): especially 647-648; and Douglas M. Fox, "What's Public Administration?" *Administrative Science Quarterly* 21 (June 1976): 346-352.

59. John Rehfuss, *Public Administration as Political Process* (New York: Scribner's, 1973).

60. Ira Sharkansky, *Public Administration: Policy-making in Government Agencies* (Chicago: Markham, 1970), especially p. 9.

61. This conclusion clearly does not apply to all public-policy research, such as Thomas Dye's work on the correlates of policy outcomes. This line of work may be controversial in that it may imply an economic determinism or may involve methodological problems. But such work does provide a model for research with a self-correcting potential. See Thomas Dye, *Politics, Economics, and the Public: Policy Outcomes in the American States,* (Chicago: Rand McNally, 1966).

62. Martin Landau, "The Concept of Decision-Making in the Field of Public Administration," in *Concepts and Issues in Administrative Behavior,* ed. Sidney Mailick and Edward H. Van Ness (Englewood Cliffs, N.J.: Prentice-Hall, 1962), p. 9. See also Vincent Ostrom, *The Intellectual Crisis in American Public Administration* (University, Ala.: University of Alabama Press, 1973).

63. See also James C. Charlesworth, ed., *Theory and Practice of Public Administration* (Philadelphia: American Academy of Political and Social Science, 1968).

64. Frederick C. Mosher, "Research in Public Administration," *Public Administration Review* 16 (Summer 1956): 177.

65. Dwight Waldo, "Scope of the Theory of Public Administration," in Charlesworth, *Theory and Practice of Public Administration,* p. 10.

66. Thomas R. Dye, "Policy Analysis and the Urban Crisis," mimeographed, n.d.

67. David Easton, *A Framework of Political Analysis* (Englewood Cliffs, N.J.: Prentice-Hall, 1965).

68. Thomas R. Dye, "Policy Analysis and the Urban Crisis."

69. Yehezkel Dror, "Some Diverse Approaches to Policy Analysis," *Policy Studies Journal* 1 (Summer 1973): 258-260.

70. Thomas R. Dye, *Politics, Economics, and the Public,* p. 293. See also Richard I. Hofferbert, "The Relation Between Public Policy and Some Structural and Environmental Variables in the American States," *American Political Science Review* 60 (March 1966): 73-82; and R. Dawson and James Robinson, "Inter-Party Competition, Economic Variables, and Welfare Policies in the American States," *Journal of Politics* 25 (May 1963): 265-289.

71. Jones, *An Introduction to the Study of Public Policy,* p. 144.

72. Dye, "Policy Analysis and the Urban Crisis." See also Thomas R. Dye, "Political Science and Public Policy: Challenge to A Discipline," in Spadaro, Dye, Golembiewski, Stedman, and Zeigler, *The Policy Vacuum,* especially pp. 31-33.

73. Donald T. Campbell, "From Description to Experimentation," in *Problems in Measuring Change,* ed. Chester W. Harris (Madison: University of Wisconsin Press, 1963), pp. 212-242.

74. Larry L. Wade, *The Elements of Public Policy* (Columbus, Ohio: Charles E. Merrill Publishing, 1972), pp. 22-23.

75. See Ira Sharkansky, *Spending in the American States* (Chicago: Rand McNally, 1968).

76. Larry L. Wade, *The Elements of Public Policy* (Columbus, Ohio: Merrill, 1972), pp. 22-23.

77. Keith R. Billingsley et al., "Spurious Correlation in Aggregate Data Analysis Using Index Variables," *Georgia Political Science Association Journal* 1 (Fall 1973): 102-111.

78. Some policy choices have been the subject of experimental studies, of course, as in the case of the form of welfare payments in this country. See also Jean A. Le Ponce and Paul Smoker, eds., *Experimentation and Simulation in Political Science* (Toronto: University of Toronto Press, 1972), pp. 94-105.

79. Ira Sharkansky, *Regionalism in American Politics* (Indianapolis: Bobbs-Merrill, 1970), pp. 23-25.

80. For example, Daniel J. Elazar argues that more meaningful regions can be isolated if their borders are so defined that parts of some of the same states can be assigned to different regions, in contrast to Sharkansky's convention. See *American Federalism: A View from the States* (New York: Crowell, 1966).

81. John H. Fenton and Donald W. Chamberlayne, "The Literature Dealing with the Relationships Between Political Process, Socio-Economic Conditions and Public Policies in the American States: A Bibliographical Essay," *Polity* 1 (Spring 1969): 388-404.

82. Wade, *The Elements of Public Policy,* especially 24-41.

83. Ira Sharkansky and Richard I. Hofferbert, "Dimensions of State Politics, Economics, and Public Policy," *American Political Science Review* 63 (September 1969): 867, 878.

84. Wade, *The Elements of Public Policy,* p. 25. See also Dye, *Understanding Public Policy,* especially pp. 254-261.

85. Douglas R. Bunker, "A Doctoral Program in the Policy Sciences," reprinted from *Policy Sciences,* Vol. 2, No. 1 (1971), pp. 35, 36, and 39 (see esp. p. 35), with permission of Elsevier Scientific Publishing Company, Amsterdam.

86. Harold D. Lasswell, "The Emerging Conception of the Policy Sciences," *Policy Sciences* 1 (1970): 3.

87. Samuel J. Bernstein, "Toward a General Paradigm for Policy Analysis," *Policy Studies Journal* 1 (Autumn 1972): 49.

88. Dye, "Policy Analysis and the Urban Crisis."

89. Joseph H. Lewis, "Policy Sciences and the Market," *Policy Sciences* 2 (1972): 291, 293, 299.

91. Michael Radnor, "Management Sciences and the Policy Sciences," *Policy Sciences* 2 (1971): 447, 451.

92. Most prominently, see Lowi's "What Political Scientists Don't Need to Ask About Policy Analysis," *Policy Studies Journal* 2 (1973): 62-67.

93. Harold W. Adams, "On Economic Values in Policy Analysis," *Policy Sciences* 1 (1970): 207-215.

94. Horst W. J. Rittel and Melvin M. Webber, "Dilemmas in a General Theory of Planning," *Policy Sciences* 4 (1973): 155-169.

95. Bunker "A Doctoral Program in the Policy Sciences," pp. 33-42.

96. Ibid., p. 36.

97. Ibid., pp. 39-40.

98. For detailed efforts in political science to apply economic concepts and methods, see Robert L. Curry and Larry L. Wade, *A Theory of Political Change: Economic Reasoning in Political Analysis* (Englewood Cliffs, N.J.: Prentice-Hall, 1968); and Wade and Curry, *A Logic of Public Policy* (Belmont, Calif.: Wadsworth, 1970).

99. Substantial progress has been made by students of public administration in mastering behavioral technologies. Illustratively, see the integration of such materials in the popular text by Felix Nigro and Lloyd Nigro, *Modern Public Administration* (New York: Harper & Row, 1973).

100. Phillip O. Foss, "Policy Analysis and the Political Science Profession," *Policy Studies Journal* 2 (1973): 69.

101. Lowi, "What Political Scientists Don't Have to Ask About Policy Analysis," p. 62.

102. Quoted in Dye, "Policy Analysis and the Urban Crisis."

103. William Gorham hits this theme hard and also specifies the necessary conditions for "Getting Into the Action," *Policy Sciences* 1 (1970): 169-176.

104. Irving Louis Horowitz, "Social Science Mandarins: Policymaking as Political Formula," *Policy Sciences* 1 (1970): 340.

105. Ibid., p. 340.

Chapter 4

THE NEW PUBLIC ADMINISTRATION
Revolution by Rhetoric—Status Quo in
Skills and Technologies

Like many areas of inquiry and practice—including psychology,[1] sociology,[2] and (most proximately) political science[3]—public administration was shaken and affected by the turbulent or revolutionary 1960s. The purpose here is to take stock of some of the major reactions of public administrationists to those always significant and sometimes curious times. Even though definitiveness is beyond the grasp of this brief chapter, a review of the recent past can provide useful guidance for the future development of public administration; one convenient approach to such development will be described and illustrated in the companion to this volume.

Hopefully, a spirit of empathic criticism characterizes this chapter. In any case, that is my intent. For public administrationists, the 1960s were like a war. Although wars may be necessary, they imply levels of urgency and threat that contribute very unevenly to advances in knowledge and insight. Hence much picking and choosing—to some ears, perhaps, even yeahing and booing—is necessary to separate the useful from the understandable but ill advised emphases that were generated as each conceptual faction scrambled to keep on top of the mercurial developments of the 1960s. The strategy here is a hazardous one. For the new public administration has been characterized more by attack and defense. Hence, this chapter may get it from both sides, from proponent and opponent, as it seeks its own middle road.

Toward a Paradoxical Motivation

If the intended spirit of this chapter does not show through, it may be due to the paradoxical motivation of this chapter already signaled in the heading. That is, the new public administration must be counted a partial success, at best, and perhaps only a cruel reminder of the gap in the field between aspiration and performance. Moreover, that this has occurred is no fluke—the cards were stacked that way, most definitely. Still, this chapter sees much of value in the new public administration that deserves a better fate, which subsequent chapters will seek to provide in some measure.

Two Introductory Conclusions

Whatever else, the dual major conclusions of this chapter will not escape notice. First, the new public administration bravely and self-consciously sought to respond to multiple "revolutions"—whether in racial matters or involving the "generation gap" or as reflected in the growing mind set against science and technology or wherever.[4] But it is now clear, given some valuable years of perspective, that attractive aspirations and massive energies were not enough. Second, rhetoric of the new public administration neither reflected nor inspired the application and development of skills and technologies required to give life to words prescribing what should be a better world of public administration. Hence, the two themes in the chapter title: revolution or radicalism in words; and (at best) status quo in skills or technologies. These themes will be variously developed throughout this chapter.

Speculating About Inevitability
or Probability

There is no satisfactory explanation of this outcome for the new public administration, but three considerations imply that it was at least highly probable, if not foreordained. First, for whatever reasons, influential voices in public administration did not generate the kind of large-scale effort—for example, in medical schools and more recently in business schools—that was necessary to plan and implement the changes in curriculum, funding, and teaching resources and techniques that were implied by the new public administration and, indeed, that had been demanded with varying insistence by numerous observers over a long period of time. For example, Honey concluded that "the 'reform of the schools of public administration' cannot be accomplished in the same way that the medical schools were 'reformed' by the Flexner report and subsequent developments, or as the schools of business administration are being 'reformed' by the Gordon and Pierson studies."[5] Honey agreed that reform was necessary in public administration. But his opinion apparently was that this reform was dependent on major and prior reform in a range of broader institutions, such as "universities and the professions." Moreover, a dominant tone of Honey's major report was that there was nothing wrong with public administration that major new funding would not cure.

Honey clealry raises an issue of what is horse and what is cart, for which no resolution exists. The practical import of the Honey Report was significant, in any case. At the very least, it precluded the massive legitimation of "new times, new ways" that had been provided by the Flexner, Gordon, and Pierson reports.[6] Moreover, at least to some, the report signaled that "the establishment" was more intent on reinforcing old ties than changing them. In any case, the issue was more or less clearly joined. Thus Savage sees the 1967 Honey Report as fiddling with "venerable and eminently fatiguing issues," while neglecting the "perpetuation of social injustice and human misery."[7] In response to such massive charges, Honey assures that he is "aware of the dissidence which prevails among at least a minority, and the flabby talk which accompanies the dissidence—attacks on 'the establishment,' on 'materialism,' on 'our kind of of society.' "[8] And never the twain does meet.

Second, individual leadership in the new public administration was provided by Dwight Waldo, clearly a skilled user of traditional skills and technologies in public administration. Indeed, it may be that someone like a Waldo *had to* provide leadership, in that he so well represented where most public administrationists were, and are.

One can only speculate as to whether someone with less conventional skills and interests—a Herbert A. Simon or a James G. March, were they so inclined and/or so situated—could have given a different, or even any, direction to the new public administration. Sometimes the seas are so rough, as it were, that staying afloat is the maximum possible achievement of the most skillful and most fortunate captain of the ship. The seas were very rough in the late 1960s and early 1970s.

Third, the major reflections of the new public administration were all but devoid of emphasis on skills and technologies necessary to give concrete form to their intentions. Thus the two major books most closely associated with the new public administration do no more than allude to skills or technologies required for research or application, and then only in such abstract and very general terms as those calling for "confrontation" as a major mode of administrative behavior.[9] In contrast, for approximately the two preceding decades, other administratively relevant literatures had developed an associated approach to learning, had begun to differentiate designs appropriate for confrontation at various interpersonal and aggregate levels, including large organizations and even some aspects of nation-states, and also had begun accumulating data about the long-run effects of specific kinds of confrontations.[10]

Even this sketchy contrast leaves the new public administration limping badly. First of all, that literature is open to taunts of only thinking about reinventing the proverbial wheel when quite advanced models were already available. More significantly, the new public administration also generated some avoidable and cruel dilemmas. That is, expectations or desires are likely to soar highest when they are not tethered short by such mundane questions as the following:

- How can specific expectation or desires be achieved, if at all?

- Do we have the resources to do what is necessary to achieve those expectations or desires?

- If not, can those resources somehow be provided soon enough?

- Will developing those resources mean that traditional definitions of mission and role must change? And if so, in what more specific or less specific ways? And how probable is such a change?

There is both benefit and cost in giving free rein to expectations, of course. In the short run, for example, the previously unthinkable might not only be thought, but could actually gain support. In the longer run, however, the absence of skills and technologies for getting from here to there might only raise expectations so as to smash them more painfully.

There was no scot-free way out of the dilemmas thus energized by the new public administration. Consider only one ironic factor. Appropriate skills and technologies might have been provided by many others outside public administration, including even a few with some identification with public administration. But that would have helped meet one problem by exacerbating others. Such inputs could easily be stamped, "not invented here," and hence were subject to rejection or at least placement in a somehow different category.[11] Moreover, welcoming such contributions might in effect only underscore the already feared lack of viability of public administration. Relatedly, emphasis on advances outside public administration—which had rested on a decade or more of development in other literatures—might only alienate the broader audience of public administrationists, and at a time when all hands were desperately needed.

Why Disturb the Better Dead?

The argument, to this point, may read like a thumbnail brief for eliminating this chapter. The new public administration is associated with a variety of unpleasantnesses generated under stress. Hence, the choice of greater wisdom might be to simply allow its memory to further fade away.

But the considerations just discussed supply me with a heightened motivation to seek to build on the considerable value of the new public administration. That motivation has three components centering around the effort by Wald to assess the near-term future of public administration by a Delphi process. First, convincing evidence implies that the new public administration "will evaporate soon, if it has not already done so."[12] As Wald's informants see the future, more specifically, public administrationists will have to make up for a "chronic lag in methodology," which the new public administration exacerbated at a critical time by its neglect of skills and technologies. Moreover, Wald's futuristic guess is that conventional public administration is losing ground rapidly to a "supra framework of social technology."[13]

Second, Wald's evaluation is seen here as credible, understandable, and lamentable, in about equal measures. Specifically, the interest and enthusiasm generated by the new public administration could have provided major motivation for the development of appropriate skills and technologies, and might still be able to do so. Relatedly, the values emphasized in the new public administration seem like reasonable guides for the application of the "supra framework of social technology" that Wald foresees. Hence, the demise of the new public administration may be costly as well as understandable.

Third, major features of the new public administration can be approached by available skills and technologies in which public administrationists can perhaps develop early competence. The remainder of this book, in fact, attempts to highlight the general sense in which this linkage is both reasonable and useful. This book's companion volume gets more specific about this linkage. In this sense, the new public administration is a kind of convenient launching pad that would have to be invented if it did not already exist.

Features of the New Public Administration

The decision here is to evaluate critically the new public administration rather than to inter it, patent risks notwithstanding. It is easy enough, in any case, to pick a convenient place to begin. To wit: Nothing so clearly characterizes the new public administration as disagreement about even central issues, a general imprecision about even major features.[14] Consequently, developing categories to organize the new public administration experience is something like seeking a container for a universal solvent. One must become reconciled to substantial failure no matter how successful one is. The approach here is, for convenience only, to organize the treatment that follows in terms of three subsections: one dealing with what the new public administration seems basically against, another with what it is for, and a final section providing a brief summary. It is impossible to underestimate the matrix of events in which the new public administration was gestated. They truly are unprecedented in diversity and magnitude: U.S. involvement in Southeast Asia was so costly in terms of the human spirit here and abroad, in addition to being so profligate with material riches; a number of significant assassinations; the burning of American cities; diverse but equally insistent voices for more of whatever the Great Society had promised; and an awesome catalog besides.

A Trinity of Antigoals

Although emphasis will vary between commentators, three antigoals stand out in the new public administration. First, the literature is "antipositivist" in complex ways. Without doing justice to this complexity, being antipositivist in this case at least means:[15]

- Rejecting a definition of public administration as "value-free," which is generally seen as "a stance inherited from political theorists interacting with behaviorists a couple of decades ago"
- Rejecting a rationalist and perhaps determinist view of humankind, which view basically rested on a static image of "being" as contrasted with "becoming"
- Rejecting any definition of public administration that was "not properly involved in policy," as was the case with the naive politics/administration dichotomy and also with many varieties of Phase III described in Chapter 1.

Second, the new public administration is also caught up in part with the antitechnical chorus represented by this powerful theme: "I am human: do not fold, spindle, or mutilate." This chorus includes such voices as those of Mario Savio and Jacques Ellul, whose purposes and vocabularies may differ broadly. In general unison, however, they decry that the logic of emotive, creative mankind is being sacrificed to the logic of the machine and "the system." Up the human; down the system. That is their cry.

Third, the new public administration is more or less antibureaucratic and antihierarchical.[16] One theme is the clumsiness of large organizations, even at their best, and the inexorable way in which they ponderously create collective dross out of the contributions of potentially or actually creative organization members. For many observers, a catastrophic result is just around the corner unless major changes are made. Thus, Townsend urges that we "up the organization,"[17] which is not to be read as encouraging tender support. And Karl Marx earlier argued for an even more energetic approach to a far broader vision. Relatedly, even those willing to accept some repression or dilution of individual preferences for some greater common good, view large organizations as basically in the business of producing "surplus repression" far over and above that necessary to accomplish what requires doing.

Some Goals to be Approached

Often as reverse images, the preceding trio of antipathies implies what the new public administration stands for.

Five features provide a sense of the new public administration from a positive perspective.[18]

First, the new public administration implies a view of mankind as being substantially malleable and at least potentially perfectible. This view stands in marked contrast to that of humans as a more or less constant "factor of production." In the new public administration vision, people are at least in the act of "becoming" and, even more desirably, of "growing." This explains the attractions of humanist, existential, or phenomenological philosophies, in which persons are commonly seen as in some kind of growthful flux that continues except when institutions are massively punishing and repressive of the perfectible human spirit. This emphasis on "becoming" also explains the attraction of the several "growth psychologies" such as that represented by Maslow,[19] and as reflected in such technological innovations as sensitivity training.[20] To reverse and change one wise saying, the "bad" in human affairs is in our institutions, and not in ourselves.

Second, this view of the human forces the issue of "relevance." That is to say, if people are indeed in the act of becoming, what they could become *throughout their lives* is *the* central issue. The central tragedy is what persons are kept from becoming, however and whenever that occurs. In extreme cases, for example, "craziness" in this view might in part or whole be a reasonable reaction to corrupt and inhuman institutions, changes in which would buoy the human spirit.[21] More determinist views could finesse this issue by a central simplification: Humans will become only what they are or, as in the Freudian view, what they experienced prior to some quite early age. Such determinist views promise only a more or less successful adaptation to institutions, which are assumed to be relative constants. Only adaptation will preclude "craziness," in this view, with the onus for that adaptation being on the individual.

It is seldom possible to assess the impact of leading ideas, but the emphasis on becoming is clearly a potential powerhouse. If people are really becoming, for example, any limitation or inhibition or repression is tragically costly, for these deprive persons of some fraction of the ultimately human experience. Moreover, any opportunity, once gone, is lost forever.

The new public administrations's fixation not only on "relevance" but also on "style and tone," derives from a related core of ideas. For Willbern, for example, the new public administration is essentially characterized by "a more forthright and honest consideration of the relationship between the structures and processes of administrative efforts and their ends and goals, and a more conscious and deliberate selection of those goals on moral grounds."[22]

Because what we do personally and in organizations has such an impact on the becoming of both self and others, to spell out the point, the new public administration stresses the central role of personal and organizational values or ethics. How things are done become as significant as, perhaps even more significant than, what is done.

The moral emphasis in the new public administration has both personal and institutional components. The importance of personal morality or ethics is no new theme, of course. The emphasis on institutional morality is more uniquely characteristic of the new public administration, as, for example, in the crucial issue of what existing administrative arrangements do to mold the consciousness and character of their employees or clients. This is a new theme for public administration, and yet it is as old as Plato and Aristotle.

Third, it is essentially a reflection of the enormity of the challenge that the new public administration found only general ways to express its pervasive concern about the values appropriate for guiding human development. "Social equity"[23] became the most common vehicle for this task, as in Frederickson's verson. He argues that social equity, with specific reference to public administrators requires:[24]

- The recognition that administrative value-neutrality is improbable, perhaps impossible, and certainly not desirable

- A public service is a general public good that can be well or badly done

- However well or badly done, generally, public services vary in their impact on recipients depending on the recipient's social, economic, and political status

- Higher-quality services go to those with higher social, economic, and political status

- The public administrator is morally obligated to counter the tendency

- Equity in the delivery of services, so far as it is calculable, should be one of the standards by which the "goodness" of a public service is judged

- Variations from equity always should be in the direction of providing more and better services to those in lower social, economic, and political circumstances

- The isolation of administrators and public agencies from either political or administrative responsibility is not equity enhancing

Like other similar efforts, Frederickson's did not overcome a general obstacle. Specifically, one form of inequity was being resorted to in order to overcome a prior inequity that was reinforced by various social, economic, and political institutions. As attractive as the objectives were to many, they saw multiple dangers down this particular path. For example, would administrators know when to stop short of creating another system of inequities? Whatever the nuances, the difficulties were patent and so was the need. As Page notes: "Public administration as a professional discipline has no set of sound normative values, no prescriptive advice to offer student, practitioner, or citizen caught in the confusion of modern industrial or developing society."[25]

Fourth, the new public administration was determinedly relational, as contrasted with the emphasis on organizations and their internal processes characteristic of a Phase III concept of public administration.

This relational quality is manifest in a variety of ways. The new public administration urges a client-centered approach, with an emphasis not only on meeting client needs via goods or services, but also on providing them a major voice in how and when and what is to be provided. More broadly, Page emphasizes this new dimension: "The focus of public administration has been and remains public-administered organizations, but much greater emphasis and analysis should be devoted to the political and public context in which these organizations function."[26] The rationale is straightforward. Basically, the "organization context" is becoming increasingly central in influencing or determining the course of major events. Hence, the outcomes of administrative actions are more obviously critical than under a Phase II concept of public administration. Moreover, what happens *between* as well as within organizations becomes more central. The stress on this point distinguishes the new public administration from Phase III concepts. And given their growing importance, organizations must be made correspondingly more representative, as by an openness to a broad range of inputs from individuals and groups.

Ultimately, the relational thrust of the new public administration implies major reorientations of administrative study and practice. Traditionally, the focus has been on explaining why public bureaucrats behave as they do. In contrast, as Crenson explains, the new public administration urges attention to the "consequences of administrative action in terms of impact on the characters and attitudes of citizens."[27] This amounts to standing public administration on its head, in a central if not total sense. That is, Crenson implies that administration can shape politics in crucial ways, rather than the other way around. This feature at once illustrates and implies the crucial significance of relational emphases in public administration.

Fifth, for obvious reasons, the new public administration places a definite emphasis on innovation and change. They are the only ways out. Hence Bjur's note that the new public administration seeks to cope with the demands for change via a complex dialectic by "searching for philosophies applicable to theories about structures (or non-structures) in changing organizations."[28]

This strong thrust toward public administration as "applied" as well as "pure" has kaleidoscopic implications. For example, such a thrust clearly highlights the role of values, as in the central question: Change or innovation for what? Value issues could be made to seem less significant in a "knowledge for its own sake" concept of public administration, in the sense of "pure science." Of course, value-free science of the positivist variety is a central target for proponents of the new public administration. It could not be otherwise.

An Action Sketch of an Intended Balance

Given its mercurial qualities, the new public administration implies moving toward a new balance of emphases. To Frederickson, for example, it was "second generation behavioralism," which consciously sought to be:[29]

- More public and less generic
- More prescriptive and less descriptive
- More oriented toward changing reality—as in systematically changing policies and structures that inhibit social equity—and less oriented toward considering what exists to be an unalterable given
- More ready to influence policies that can improve the quality of working life, as well as more competent to implement such policies
- More oriented toward impact on client and less institution-oriented
- More normative and less neutral
- Less "sanguine about the applicability of the natural-science model to social phenomena"

The underlying hope is a lofty one. Only thus would a more relevant public administration evolve, one that, as Frederickson observes, will, "it is hoped, [be] no less scientific."[30]

A tragic quality represented in this intended balance also must be noted. That is, the new public administration is at once optimistic and buoyant that people and institutions are both malleable and perfectible. And yet such a view rests on the ashes of evidence that both people and institutions had messed up miserably, young and old, on a broad scale and on narrow issues, in America and worldwide.

History was unkind to the new public administration, to put the point directly, as a brief contrast with humanistic psychology can illustrate. Gestated in the buoyant 1950s and early 1960s, the several manifestations of humanistic, or third-force, or growth psychology had nearly two decades of grace to build confidence and to develop appropriate learning models and designs that gave some substance to their hopes that personally and organizationally more satisfying approaches to the good life could be found.[31] For a number of years, indeed, it appeared to many that glorious optimism about the human condition was appropriate. Hence, as late as 1964, Bennis announced that "democracy is inevitable" in organizations, given a goal-based technology usually called the "laboratory approach," whose best-known learning vehicle was the T-group or sensitivity training group. By 1970, society had so variously soured, and so quickly, that apocalyptic visions were severely readjusted. Bennis himself was led to observe in the title of an article in a professional journal that "A Funny Thing Happened on the Way to the Future."[32]

In contrast, the new public administration sought somehow to reconcile optimism about human perfectibility *and* massive immediate evidence of a pessimistic kind, without the period of benign grace available to humanist psychology during which its proponents could develop research strategies as well as skills and technologies for embodying their ideals in functioning human systems. Some dates are relevant. The famous Minnowbrook Conference, which perhaps best represents the aspirations of the new public administration, was held in September 1968. That date was tragically bracketed by the assassinations of the brothers Kennedy and Martin Luther King, the major urban disorders of 1967, the widepsread turmoil in many universities—the tragic litany could go on and on. To be optimistic about human perfectibility in 1968 was asking a lot of the new public administration, under awkward if not impossible conditions, and without a tradition for either research or application that was clearly appropriate for changing the world in ways that the new public administration envisioned. No wonder, then, that pessimism sometimes peaked through even exuberant visions of the new public administration.[33]

Does It Really Provide a Way Out?

So there it stands, at least in essential outline. And what about it? Does the new public administration provide a way out of the developmental difficulties facing public administration? What parts of it seem promising? And which woebegone?

An estimate of the viability of the new public administration here will depend on a three-step argument. First, the initial step will determine whether the new public administration reflects enough signs of newness or uniqueness to permit some enthusiasm that the approach might be a useful way out of the conceptual problems sketched in Chapters 1 through 3. Second, the focus will then shift to testing whether or not the new public administration simply falls victim to the dilemmas and difficulties so profusely apparent in the developmental history of public administration. Third, some guidance for a prognosis about the new public administration will be sought from comparative administration, which had a ten-year head-start over the new public administration in facing up to the difficulties in their often similar conceptual approaches.

Some Uniquenesses

Not a few observers argue that the new public administration possesses only a kind of difference by definition. Campbell, for example, argues that the "new" public administration differs from the "old" public administration "only in that it is responsive to a different set of societal problems from those of other periods."[34] Fewer argue that the new public administration is a kind of scholarly sheep-dip, one of those academic fads that have some impact only because they are periodically readministered to the largely unknowing and uncaring.

This chapter stands apart from such efforts to deny the unique birthright of the new public administration, despite the attractions for preserving needed links between past and future, and despite the sometimes alluring quality of gentle cynicism. The contrasting view here is that the new public administration is characterized by a number of uniquenesses that give hope of some light at the end of a long conceptual tunnel. Five will be emphasized here.

New Constituencies Available for Linking

In the present view, the new public administration at once reflects and gives life to some new and potentially powerful constituencies: teachers, students, and client groups. Given that major new sources of support are seen as necessary to meet the problems bedeviling public administration, it comes as no wonder to see proponents of the new public administration seeking to bring off a kind of grand union of new and variously separate constituencies. These constituencies do share in common the dislocations associated with our intervention in Vietnam, a number of major assassinations, and other dramatic forms of "bye, bye, Miss American pie."

Most of the story hardly needs telling, but one factor is too little noted. That is, common talk is full of notice about the post-Sputnik college crowds, as well as of the newly vocal constituencies of the poor or those on welfare or women or whomever. No wonder that a "new" anything would seek to provide a focal point for them. Little is heard of the newly large numbers of faculty in public administration, however, in the context of the critical fact that the field had not been "hot" for thirty years or thereabouts, with the exception of years immediately following World War II when a number sought to put to graduate-study use the three to five years they had served in various civilian or military administrative capacities. To simplify somewhat, public administration as a field was a child of the Great Depression, a field that quickly peaked and remained stable for several decades. As one consequence, relatively junior people—both scholars and practitioners—had early moved into senior positions and stayed there. By the late 1960s, major retirements were impending just as the demand for training in public administration and law enforcement escalated. This proved a heady combination and added impetus to the need to stake out new conceptual territory, and the earlier, the better. The need was exacerbated in many cases by another novel feature. The upwardly mobile were the first large generation of teachers who had been exposed to a range and intensity of training or at least to its professional advantages, beyond that of most of their mentors. This elemental fact may have heightened motivation and encouraged demands for a very specific kind of social equity.

There is no intent here to write off the new public administration as a mere case study in the sociology of occupations, but it was a factor.

New "Metaphysical Pathos"

Beyond such major constituencies that were newly available for the linking, the new public administration was characterized by a depth of concern, a sign of massive alienation, and sometimes a notable stridency of expression. All of the magnitudes in question were such as to promise that the feelings underlying the new public administration—whatever the fate of the specific approaches in which they became embodied—would long to be with us. In any case, moreover, those motivating feelings and concerns deserved caring notice and reaction even though the emphases were seldom novel *as content*. In this spirit, Friedland explains in one case that a need for a certain kind of analysis is "an important contribution to our understanding of the basic problem of public administration not because of its originality—for the need for such inquiry has long been noted—but because of the obvious intensity of [the author's] feeling about the need for it."[35] The medium is the important message, in short.

The point could easily get out of hand, but the uniqueness is essentially this. There were earlier critics of public administration, but their criticism was not embodied in such an unredemptive "metaphysical pathos" of associated ideas—of alienation, of (for want of better words) a lack of socialization or even an uncivility. Moreover, there were very many more critics and fewer places for them to go. That is, business schools were not hiring as frantically as in the 1950s, and they had eagerly and often generously provided refuge for a number of earlier expatriates from public administration.

In any case, these eruptions patently had to have deep and complex roots, even ominous roots. Gouldner draws attention to the significance of such deep-seated commonalities in these terms: "A commitment to a theory may be made because the theory is congruent with a mood or deep-lying sentiments of its adherents, rather than because it has been cerebrally inspected and found valid.... [Each theory] has its own silent appeal and its own metaphysical pathos."[36] Moreso than by the explicit language, many observers were concerned—even frightened—by the ominous metaphysical pathos reflected by many of the numerous, new generation who for good or ill would soon be the major carriers of public administration. That had never happened before in public administration either, and with many of the patriarchs of the field approaching retirement and with few back-ups of comparable status and attainments in the next several age brackets. In a few words, public administration was at once growing both younger and older in unprecedented ways. The combination was unsettling and volatile.

New Insistence on "Relevance"

Among the most pervasive themes in the new public administration was the demand for "relevance." This had numerous dimensions, only one of which was that the self-esteem of public administrationists was especially vulnerable to the fact that since (as Waldo explains) the 1948 publication of Simon's paper, their conceputal god had been dead and was not yet replaced.[37] La Porte's words graphically describe his reaction to the "shrieking demands" for relevance to which he had no ready reply. He noted that: "The young, the men on the job, and I suspect, we too seek a reaffirmation of worthiness—a sense of significance, and a promise that what we study and teach is worth the effort. . . ." The root difficulty is the poverty of empirical and normative guides in public administration, what La Porte calls "a state of antique or maladapted analytical models and normative aridity." The consequences are profound. Thus La Porte worries that there "is almost no basis for accepting or rejecting either substantive problems or analytical models save political-administrative crisis or academic fashion."[38]

In sum, public administration's ancestors at once stand indicted of trifling, as well as of failure to provide for their own posterity.

Some wicked conceptual dilemmas awaited those who sought early and comprehensive resolution of the need for some guiding gestalt for public administrationists, especially because much of the available huge literature was developed outside public administration. Witness the attendant dilemma of a La Porte. Concerning the numerous possible models for analysis he notes: "Clearly it is difficult to assess these models without some idea of the underlying directions implicit in them." And he completes the dilemma by noting that it is "equally difficult to complete the assessment if there is significant and unrecognized ambiguity in the assessor's values, that is, in the clarity of his own normative understanding of public organization."[39] La Porte saw how the student of public administration could be driven to desperation, if not despair.

Such dilemmas were not easily avoided, for the new public administration sought a lot, and fast. Witness the common desire for public administration to have both internal and relational emphases, which, as Campbell notes, involved public administrationists on many fronts. To illustrate:[40]

Internal thrusts	Relational thrusts
Attack or at least discipline hierarchy	Become more accountable to clients, provide better goods and services
Encourage broadening participation among clients as well as employees	Identify more with clients than with hierarchy
Provide meaningful and authentic interpersonal relationships at work	Encourage greater involvement of clients in agency operations

New Programmatic Missions for Public Administration

That La Porte and others saw public administration in a "state of antique or maladapted analytical models and normative aridity" did in no overt way tether expectations about what required doing. This may seem curious, or even self-defeating, but it is fact nonetheless. "Ends" were where it was at; "how to" was too distinctly a secondary concern. That is to say, a substantial family of programmatic "shoulds" characterized the new public administration. For convenience, we can rely on Elden's list. He emphasizes seven basic needs:[41]

- Discrimination by age and sex as well as race should be ended in government.
- Public administrators should be committed to "the public interest, social responsibility, and democratic principles."
- Participation in decision making should be increased for those "inside" a public agency as well as those "outside."
- Education in public administration should be reorganized so as to produce change agents rather than "status quo administrators."
- Professional organizations should be developed "to make public administration relevant and responsive to the times."
- Policymakers should have enhanced capacities to plan and administer social change.
- "Organizational communities within public agencies" should be created to increase the capacity for "heuristic decision, qualitative planning, and creative responsiveness."

Elden's view is not always shared in all particulars by all proponents of the new public administration, of course, but it is representative in two major senses. Elden does provide a programmatic profile for the new public administration that many of its proponents would generally support. Moreover, Elden is fascinated with what should be done rather than concerned with how or even whether it could be done.

New Role of Public Administrators

The new public administration also made it clear that the public administrators should change their concept of self and clients in ways consistent with a variety of the features detailed above. Table 4.1 presents one well-developed model of how the new public administrator required both a new role and a new associated self-concept.

TABLE 4.1   The Public Manager and Two Ideal Views of Self and of Recipients of Public Service[a]

Perceptions of public managers in relation to:	As Traditional Public Administrator	As New Public Administrator
Ideal View of Self		
Projects	An administrator of	A champion of
Policy	A policy implementer	A policymaker
Perception of political authority	Organizationally centered—vertically	Community centered— horizontally
Effectiveness criteria	Committed to economic and efficient government	Committed to social and economic justice
Change	An adaptor who copes	An advocate who influences
Ideal View of Recipients of Public Services		
Program design	Targets to impact	Consumers with choice
Political force field	Electors of representatives	Direct participators
Human needs	Categorical	Comprehensive
Resource allocation	Units or cases	Discrete individuals
Services	As a privilege	As a right

[a] Based on Ross Clayton and Ron Gilbert, "Perspectives of Public Managers: Their Implications for Public Service Delivery Systems," *Publc Management* 53 (November 1971): expecially 10.

Table 4.1 can stand on its own feet. Clearly, it implies a broad range of major changes on which a successful new public administration depends. Again, the "what" is quite clear. How the changes were to be brought off, or whether they could be, are far less clear.

The Same Old Tethers, Perhaps Worse

Convincing evidence implies, such uniquenesses notwithstanding, that the new public administration does not provide a viable way out of the field's developmental difficulties. Many of the old difficulties remain and are at least as potent as ever. Indeed, the brave words of the new public administration may make matters worse, as by increasing the gap between rapidly escalated aspirations and a stable level of achievement. The purpose here is to provide several major perspectives on this sad case of love's labors being variously lost.

The "One Best" Phantom

At least in retrospect, perhaps the major tether on the new public administration is the pervasive agreement about what may be called the "search for the singular." The limitations of this basic assumption can be sketched from two perspectives.

The search for the singular is most often reflected in the common view of the goal of disciplinary development—a yearning for a kind of conceptual Holy Grail that, once found, will provide uniform direction for public administrationists. The accompanying myth was that such a paradise had existed, and not so long ago, though it had been lost and not yet regained.[42] This is the sense of the influential Dwight Waldo's comment in a major retrospective piece. He observes: "For the twenty-year period [after 1948] begins with *the* problem posed and ends without *a* satisfactory answer, despite a wealth of 'contributions.' To understand this is to understand the essential quality of the period."[43] Nor is there for Waldo any apparent question as to what *the* problem and *a* satisfactory answer involve. In another place, he directs specific attention to the boundary issue as being the most central intellectual concern in public administration. Thus he sees "nothing more germane to contemporary public administration . . . than substantial research, exhibiting high scientific standards as these are measured in contemporary social science, devoted to the question, What distinguishes public administration, quantitatively and (or) qualitatively, from other administration."[44] It is instructive that, although most observers talk about such crucial research, little or no suitable work was (or is) being done. Kronenberg felt that an essential part of the answer to this apparent paradox lies in the general assumption about "*one* reality of public administration," which prevents meaningful response to Waldo's question. In contrast,

Kronenberg argues for "many realities." He explains: "Events do not cohere naturally and organize themselves. Theorists organize experience and search for patterns of meaning." Consequently, he warns, public administrationists "do little to advance the richness of description or the quality of explanation by clinging to monistic assumptions about reality and hoping for the big break-through."[45]

The search for the singular also appears in another form, with equally deleterious effects on real progress toward conceptual development within public administration. For example, Kaufman argues that there are in fact three major continuing yet shifting conflicts inherent in public administration's doctrine and practice. They are increased representativeness, better and politically neutral bureaucracies, and stronger chief executives. He explains: "At different points in time, enough people . . . will be persuaded by one or another of these discontents to support remedial action. . . . But emphasis on one remedy over a prolonged period merely accumulates the other discontents until new remedies gain enough support to be put into effect, and no totally stable solution has yet been devised." Hence, Kaufman concludes, a constant shifting in emphasis not only does occur and should occur but—even more to the present point—will occur as the effort to fixate on only one of the three major conflicting themes in public administration's practice and doctrine becomes more insistent.[46]

In these terms, the new public administration is merely a demand for increased representativeness, albeit a uniquely powerful demand. Rather than moving toward a "totally stable solution," then—which certainly would qualify as real developmental progress—reflections of the new public administration such as that shown in Table 4.1 are merely reactions to which many counter-reactions can be expected. The more "the singular" is emphasized, to paraphrase Kaufman's basic argument, the less probable the "stable solution" consistent with the notion of "*one* reality in public administration."

Some Well-lit Lamp Posts

The monistic assumption—reflected in the debatable hope that there should/ would be *a* comprehensive conceptual definition of public administration, as well as in the palpably false view that there had been such *a* definition that was more useful than troublesome—had a broad range of unfortunate conse-quences. Paramountly, it encouraged certain convenient but self-limiting approaches. The overall effect reminds one of the old joke about the person searching for a lost coin under a lamp post. Even though the coin was dropped on a dark section of the street, the person was searching under the lamp post because the light was better there.

Overemphasis on Maintenance Features. Primarily, the new public administration was akin to most effort directed at defining a concept for public administration in that it overemphasized maintenance features, as that term is defined in Chapter 2. Hence, the major concern with the "boundary question" about who is "inside" and who is "outside." Such concern is understandable in any "new" area, of course, where ownership claims are particularly important. But the paradoxical features remain, especially as they relate to spurning help from any quarter in elaborating the task aspects of public administration. Witness, for example, La Porte's apparent preference for maintenance over task in a curious particular: "Two men who have contributed very significantly to the general understanding of organizations," he notes, "have come to their present positions from initial studies in political science. I think it regrettably unfair, however, to include either Herbert A. Simon or James G. March in the company of public administration."[47] Some implications of this position do not reflect an attractive view of public administrationists. For example, the use of the term "regrettably unfair" in one view at least suggests that analogical inadviseability of matching Willie Pep and Joe Louis at their respective primes.

Such exclusivity is particularly curious in the context of the acknowledged need for help in grappling with the task features of public administration. Thus La Porte notes: "Normative bases for evaluating either organizational theory or action bring one squarely into the province of political philosophy." But that province is not very congenial. Political philosophy, he notes, "has left us trackless to venture largely unaided into a philosophically barren landscape."[48] La Porte no more gently evaluates the state of the empirical analysis of public organizations.

Neglect of Technologies and Skills. Relatedly, the new public administration gave short shrift to the development of specific technologies and skills that could have permitted some claim to special competence in research or application, and eventually might even provide some parts of an answer to Waldo's central question as to what (if anything) is unique about *public* administration. This conclusion is meant in four major senses, as they interact in complex ways. Together they imply that the new public administration gave awkward attention to task features, to describing managerial dynamics, and to prescribing how to achieve desirable conditions based on a knowledge of major empirical covariants.

First, the age in which the new public administration developed was more smitten with essence or policy than it was with specific technologies or skills. Revealingly, consider the two volumes most associated with the new public administration, Marini's *Toward a New Public Administration* and Waldo's *Public Administration in a Time of Turbulence.* Of the twenty-seven selections in the two volumes, only one reflects major concern with "how to" for either research or application, and that selection is largely tangential to the basic thrust of the new public administration. Other evidence supports the point. For example, I am aware of little subsequent research with a distinctly new public administration heritage. Similarly, suggestions about technologies and skills appropriate for the programmatic desires of the new public administration were, and remain, quite gentle and abstract.[49]

The reasons for this curious neglect are as patent as the costs. On the one hand, neglect of technologies and skills in effect (1) seeks to avoid scientism or narrow technician perspectives, (2) emphasizes that policy is where it's at, and (3) may endeavor to avoid overburdening by technical and practical considerations what Kenneth Boulding called "that heroic demand for social mutation which will not be stilled in the voices of our young radicals."[50] On the other hand, there clearly are limits on "social mutation," and especially on that variety supported more by wishes than by powerful technologies and skills. One electrical engineer is anxious to demonstrate by hyperbola that such limitations are very real. He observes: "In my own department ... there is not a single professor to expound the view that lightning is due to the anger of the gods; none of my colleagues in the physics department teaches out of Aristotle's well-known textbook; and the physiology department has no professor to teach that children are brought by the stork." He sardonically acknowledges the implied debilitating conformity and the obvious encroachment on academic freedom.[51]

Second, a monistic public administration demotivates an emphasis on technologies and skills, whether for study or application. Oversimply, perhaps, there are *so many* places from which the public administrationist might begin to seek for *the* guiding model—systems theory, decision-making approaches, small-group analysis, and so on and on.[52] To be sure, these approaches were basically developed outside public administration and hence have their own theoretical and normative features that might poorly suit the public context. Even so, the answer to the question about where to begin if one is at a mucking-around stage of inquiry is: Everywhere and immediately, so as to permit the earliest possible rejection of some alternative approaches. But the common view apparently was that public administration was not at such an early stage; what was seen as imminent, or at least what was assumed to be necessary and/or desirable, was *a* comprehensive guide for inquiry and action. Paradoxically, this stacked the deck against any major developmental work, given the assumption that all but one starting point will not provide *the* monistic approach that could inspire the whole of public administration. Hence the search for *a* comprehensive model can encourage nonsearch among *alternative* models.

Third, relatedly, the focus of the new public administration is almost exclusively on prescriptive "shoulds" rather than on ways and means of attaining them. White's treatment is exceptional only in that he devotes far more attention to implementation than do most writers associated with the new public administration. For example, he details these three major new public administration "shoulds":

- Communication of the whole truth should be straightforward and voluntary. Underlying this premise is the empirical assumption that people *can be* completely honest with each other or, indeed, that the most effective type of relationship is one characterized by the absence of defensiveness.

- All parties to the relationship should be placed in equal positions in the sense that power and authority is allocated *functionally* in the manner described earlier.

- Interactions should continually take place within an explicit framework of principles based on a specification of what men and women are and what their purposes are. The concepts of decision by compromise, reasonableness, tolerance, or balance of interest would become irrelevant for a much wider range of issues than at present.[53]

In a twenty-four-page article, he then devotes about three pages to a very broad sketch of a supporting "technology of administrative politics," including less than a page on "the problem of transition," where he notes basically that the transition is far from certain. And no small wonder, given this slim aid promised by White: "One can only hope that by developing appropriate techniques for changing conditions we can effectively make a transition which will avoid a societal state in which suppression is widely used."[54]

Fourth, the new public administration thus basically fixates on desired *outcomes,* as opposed to the scientific *processes* by which knowledge can be accumulated as well as in contrast to the applied *dynamics* by which desired states can be attained, based on knowledge about the empirical world. This is certainly a convenient approach. It permits free rein to the imaginative faculties; and it is clear that taking a stand about what is desirable ranks very high among human priorities.

A number of significant difficulties derive from this pervasive bias toward outcomes, however. Primarily, what is missing in the new public administration is a consistent distinction between "empirical theory" and "goal-based, empirical theories." Empirical theory seeks to describe the network of relationships in the empirical world, what is related to what under which conditions. Goal-based, empirical theories, in contrast, attempt to prescribe how specific ends can be achieved, given a knowledge of the relationships in nature. If you want to achieve end *x,* goes the general form of such theories, do *x, y,* and *z* under conditions *a* and *b.*[55]

The general failure to respect this basic distinction between types of theories is associated with substantial mischief. At an extreme, enthusiasm about outcomes often gets confused with other, broader objectives in ways that come close to postulating that only intrasubjective processes exist for testing the truth value of statements about the empirical world. This injects a know-nothing quality into a movement whose primary emphasis is that so much needs doing so very badly, and hence so much needs knowing.

It is instructive to describe how a much needed emphasis sometimes got transmuted into a position that set observers from other empirical sciences to shaking their heads in disbelief. Basically, the goal of the new public administration is to make a solid place for values in analyses for action where its proponents saw only value-free positivism run riot. It is in this sense that La Porte argues for an "integrated theory of public organizations" that (as Friedlander observes) "cannot be built on a purely behavioral basis, but instead must be founded upon a conception of 'the valuable.' . . ."[56] La Porte thus sees the need for goal-based, empirical theories built around values congenial to the new public administration. And such theories, in turn, rest upon the development of increasingly comprehensive fragments of empirical theory. So far, so good. Excellent, in fact.

However, the tide of the times was running strong, and overkill was common. The progression from reasonable need to conclusion *in extremis* can be sketched briefly. There is a major problem with getting enough of the right values into scientific work; however, the problem was oversimplified as one involving "science" rather than the unavailability of appropriate goal-based, empirical theories; and some even went so far as to argue that no processes exist that can lay reasonable claim to being guides for isolating and testing truth.

The irony need only be expressed. The deep need for appropriate goal-based, empirical theories sometimes was expressed in ways that inhibited the scientific development of empirical theory on which those applied theories depend. This reflects that there can be too much even of the very best things.

Blankenship nicely sketches the ironical situation in an essay aptly titled "Public Administration and the Challenge to Reason." He notes that scientific and technical advancement has been associated with pollution, overpopulation, alienation, and a plethora of other social ills. And "science" is also seen as a servant of power in a consumption-oriented economy, serving to discipline or manipulate people into accepting war, keeping up with the Joneses, and generally acting on a set of contrived needs in place of really human priorities. And the negative catalog drones on. Blankenship also sketches a broad range of reactions to the "failing of science." Some experts call for a rethinking of priorities, with reallocations of resources from elite problems to mass issues, from "pure" to "applied" science, from technological to human problems. Others argue that enough is now known to start effectively changing things that desperately need changing. From this perspective, eschewing implementation for more study is a crass cop-out. Blankenship goes on to describe a more extreme reaction, a denial of the very possibility of approaching some transpersonal objectivity or rationality, a suspension if not a denial of the basic premises of the scientific enterprise in the name of action and commitment to social or political causes. Blankenship reacts in this way:

> If objectivity is impossible (or immoral—the two get confused), the argument goes, and theories and research in the past have had negative costs including maintenance of an illegitimate status quo, then let us give up our pretensions to science and refuse to accept the legitimacy of any knowledge it produces, especially that which conflicts with our own subjective experiences of a situation. Let us do only what will change a status quo which we find, on the basis of that subjective experience, intolerable. This is clearly a major "challenge to reason."[57]

If I Say It, It Is. The neglect of processes for research and skills or models for application was profoundly beside the point for some proponents of the new public administration. They were consciously about the business of "creating a new public administration."[58] Hence, while they were at it, why not create the kind of field that pleased them most? Their orientation is well illustrated by Kariel, who urges that scholars not sweat about defying existing paradigms or expectations involving "political science" or the "free world" or "private property" or whatever. He jauntily recommends creating a new political reality whose paradigms or expectation *would not* have to be defied. He explains: "We would thus indicate that these marvels are 'so-called,' that we have made them all up and that—given wit and passion, courage and luck—we might yet remake them to suit ourselves."[59]

There is much that is attractive in Kariel's advice. Up to a substantial point, we are our own ideas about ourselves, and there seems precious little sense in saddling ourselves with awkward notions. So change merely requires that we shuck inhibiting ideas, and we are home free. One does not have to be a therapist to observe how people's ideas or attitudes are often self-imposed prisons, for example. Making parks out of conceptual prisons has much to recommend it, as a general policy. And what is true for individuals must be even more applicable to social groups or to societies, where the impact of an awkward idea is felt by so many.

There is also liberal humbug in Kariel's advice, however. The essential humbug inheres in the qualifier "up to a substantial point" used in the preceding paragraph. In at least six senses, the new public administration's emphasis on creating appropriate verbal constructs goes too far, too fast, and zips well beyond that "substantial point." Altogether these six senses may reflect only that it is difficult or impossible to fine tune a revolution or even to steer it some. But the effects remain nonetheless.

First, patently, there are large classes of phenomena that retain certain characteristics whatever we may think or believe or feel about them. Indeed, some of these characteristics are neglected only at one's peril. At some point,

in some way, that is, one must distinguish attitudes or values or preferences—
which may be changed, sometimes even at will—from statements about aspects
of reality that change slowly or not at all. The issue is clearest in the case of
physical laws or regularities, which ostensibly stay much the same under more
or less constant conditions whatever our attitudes or values or preferences
related to them. Stepping out of a fourth-story window will have one class of
highly predictable consequences, whether we get good or bad "vibes" thinking
about it, or whatever the value we place on our own life or on those of unwary
and unlucky passersby.

Similarly, creating realities to correspond to ideational constructs also may
be variously and severely limited by lack of physical, economic, or social
resources. For example, prevailing concepts of what constitutes a "good day's
work," or what degrees of bribery and corruption are tolerable, or what level
of taxation is acceptable, are clearly not as inexorable as the reality of gravita-
tion. They are not iron laws, to use terminology from another but similar
American time. In the short run, however, such understandings can as effectively
block efforts to achieve some desired states as the "law of gravity" can frustrate
my desire to soar like an eagle.

Second, far more subtly, some observers seem to have become vague about
the difference between reality-as-perceived and reality-as-it-is, which is at least
careless about a central distinction and at worst implies that no intersubjective
knowledge is possible. For some cases, there is no difference between reality-as-
perceived and reality-as-it-is, and no dearth of skills or will to do something
desirable with that reality. This is presumptively the case in complex physical
and psychological senses for the rare basketball player who converts 90 percent
or more of his foul-shot attempts. Moreover, all perceptions of reality are
variously filtered through complex subjective processes, which can color it in
significant ways. Thus if I read hostility into a benign greeting, hostility is what
I am likely to give and receive. Acknowledging such complexities, however,
hardly constitutes a proof that there are no processes appropriate for sifting
some kinds of truth from some kinds of error.

Third, much of the talk about creating an appropriate reality is simply not
very specific. Even given absolute malleability of all humans and all natural and
institutional resources, it is not at all clear what many proponents of the new
public administration wish to create even if they could. As Meade observes in the
case of one popular prescription:

> The current dissatisfaction with the performance of public bureauc-
> racies has spawned a rhetoric of reform and change which takes
> participative administration as one of its central themes. But one
> of the problems in responding to the demand lies in the generality
> with which participation is often advanced as a solution to the
> administrative ills of the day. That is, what, precisely, is meant by

the term "participation" is not usually specified, and there is not necessarily agreement among all proponents of the concept as to its meaning. To put it briefly, advocacy does not always make clear the referents: *who* is to participate in *what way*? These are, after all, critical issues.[60]

Fourth, most proponents of the new public administration give too little attention to the elemental fact that there is a monumental difference between articulating a value or preference and being able to act on it. Suppose, for example, that I firmly resolve to be more loving. If I lack the skills required, I may be worse off for my new resolve. Here, patently, the new public administration's inattention to technologies and skills is especially striking, and perhaps even tragic. Moreover, various conditions may curb my success at being more loving. For example, if others persist in seeing me as manipulative, no matter how objectively wrong they may be, even ostensibly skillful efforts by me at being loving are likely to go for naught.

Fifth, relatedly, proponents of the new public administration dwell very little on a central concern. Given that the "politics of love" is preferable and perhaps necessary, and given that "participation" is desirable, how do we approach those ends? And what can be done if the world, or powerful segments of it, do not wholeheartedly accept the end states? Or even if acceptance exists, what if many are puzzled as to how to go about the "politics of love" or vague as to how to bring off "participation." Here, the new public administration has been mute, and essentially remains so.

Sixth, most charitably, proponents of the new public administration view public administration far too much as creation and far too little as creature. Although he joins in the general enthusiasm to create an appropriate discipline, for example, Savage confronts the sobering possibility "that part of our trouble lies beyond our control." He explains that "public administration does *reflect* rather than create a political culture, that it behaves very much the way society *expects* it to behave, and that what is missing from public administration is not just representation and participation but the impetus of political and social will flowing from the public realm."[61]

This obviously escalates the challenge facing the new public administration, and it implies a cruel taunt as well. Either the new public administration prescribes techniques for inducing "the impetus of political and social will," or it must remain a kind of prophetical scold.

A Central Conundrum

The above catalog of particulars could be extended, but mostly in the sense of merely adding variations on a theme. A central conundrum—perhaps *the* central conundrum—should be manifestly clear. The central question about why the new public administration went too far, perhaps too soon, certainly with too little emphasis on the technologies and skills appropriate for achieving the new administrative state, can be framed by the following epigram:

> One need not be a weatherman to know which way the wind is blowing; but meteorological technology and training are very handy indeed when tornadoes are to be predicted; and they are patently vital for creating or aborting a tornado, disregarding some cosmic-scale dumb luck.

This analogical point certainly could not long have escaped public administrationists. And yet they sought their brave new world with, at best, passing attention to the technologies and skills that would be required if they were to be able to build and maintain what they so enthusiastically conceived. How is that apparent paradox to be explained?

Attention here will be on a single, cruel feature of the new public administration that helps explain the curious lack of attention to the obvious. In an important particular, the new public administration was engulfed by the very wave of public mood on which it had ridden. Even though technology and skills are patently necessary, the mood of the times was in pervasive senses oriented toward spontaneity rather than development of skills. Savage sensitively isolates the ironic double bind in these terms:[62]

- Any technological advances will constitute a greater temptation for elites to use that capacity for their own purposes of social control, as well as to increase their capacity to achieve broad social ends.

- The logic of various technologies can exclude significant social and political options, especially those in the moral realm, even as those technologies might facilitate more effective approaches to desired ends.

- Technological development can induce a diminution of personal responsibility for wrongdoing, even as it increases the potential for creative pursuit of desirable social, political, and economic goals.

It may be oversimple to see the new public administration as basically hoisted on its own petard in a crucial particular, but no doubt part of its difficulties inhere in the central double bind just illustrated.

Comparative Administration as Prototype

Further perspective on the probable fate of the new public administration can be gained from a brief survey of comparative administration, the other major star in the public administration skies following World War II. The motivation is direct—comparative administration and the new public administration share major similarities, and there has been a decade or so of additional experience with the comparative administration approach. Hence, this effort seeks to go to school on the experience of comparative administration and to derive from such schooling insights about the developmental future of the new public administration.

A Thumbnail Characterization

Comparative administration can be briefly characterized in terms of three themes, without pretending to do any but summary justice to a burgeoning and balkanized literature. These themes are (1) significance of focal concerns, (2) magnitude of resulting effort, and (3) motivation for the approach.

First, the significance of the focal concerns of comparative administration is easy to establish. Waldo saw comparative administration as intimately associated with major developmental issues faced in American public administration, which to him "clearly posed questions that only serious attention to comparative study could answer. Is public administration culture-bound, but a manifestation of parochial interests? Are truly general principles of administration possible? Or: what kinds of general principles are possible?"[63]

Second, massive effort was devoted to addressing such issues, beginning with the early 1950s.[64] A large number of summary evaluations of that effort exist in various places,[65] and present purposes can in any case be satisfied with Waldo's description. He concludes: ". . . these efforts, these foci of interest have in the past decade become extremely important: they have developed a large literature, they are carried on in special organizations set up for the purpose of concentrated attention, many of us find them the center of our professional-intellectual lives."[66]

Third, the effort in comparative administration derives from solid and substantial motivation. Comparative administration was rooted in the huge American involvement in "technical assistance," which made available the full spectrum of specialized aid to countries in all parts of the world. Hence, the magnitude of the comparative administration effort was stimulated both by the promise of substantial resources, and by an ideological commitment to share with others the benefits of our several modern technologies, disciplines, and arts.

An interesting advantage also motivated work in comparative administration. That is, specialists in "American-culture public administration" were involved in tussles of variable intensity with those who emphasized generic, as opposed to *public*, administration. There was no such conflict about turf in comparative administration, at least overtly and early on.[67] Students of comparative administration were largely "comparative politics" specialists, who could claim considerable knowledge about the various countries or cultures that comparative administration defines as its context.

Some Impressive Contributions

Like the new public administration, comparative administration emphasizes a number of useful perspectives or challenges relevant to both a pure and an applied science of public administration. Indeed, major comparative administration contributions are similar to, or even identical with, new public administration emphases that were to come later. Four of these contributions may be highlighted. Comparative administration, in brief, emphasizes this related family of conclusions:

- That, for many purposes, organizations must be viewed as imbedded in specific cultures and political settings[68]

- That, more broadly, the "principles of public administration" are seriously inadequate

- That both the study and practice of administration are pervasively value-loaded

- That any proper discipline must have complementary pure and applied aspects, even if these aspects are difficult to keep in reasonable balance

The Present Condition

The present status of comparative administration may be instructive for the new public administration. Overall, three summary conclusions describe that status. First, much of the external push for comparative administration disappeared behind the smoke of Watts and was scaled down by the new prominence of various cankers on the domestic social and political body. Second, however, the development of comparative administration while it was a hot area was such that it is vulnerable in diverse ways. Third, comparative administration is now experiencing its own identity crisis.

The major developmental inadequacies of comparative administration may be suggested in terms of only one of its significant features. That is, especially following Riggs, comparative administration essentially adopted the approach via grand theory on the model of system sociology.[69] To illustrate, Riggs's approach emphasizes the development of elaborate models—adorned with exotic verbalisms such as "prismatic society"—that "might *eventually* help us understand more about administrative behavior."[70] As ingenious as such constructs often are, they have a basic fault. Essentially, "eventually" is likely to be a very long time indeed. That is, followers of Riggs seem to believe that there is simply no other way (following Heaphey) "of coming into contact with administrative reality except through our theory."[71] Apparently, also the guiding assumption is that the more elaborate and comprehensive that "theory," the better.

Heaphey isolates the essential weakness of the Riggs's approach to comparative administration. He explains: "The hitch in this vision is the undefined 'administrative reality.' If there are theoretical definitions on one hand, and an undefined reality on the other, how does one know when he has learned someting about the undefined reality?"[72] That central question, seldom isolated so starkly, bedevils Riggs's dominant approach to comparative analysis. Basically, Riggs took an awkward approach to a complex reality, which is understandable enough. But the consequences thereof are no less real because of that fact.

Two such consequences stand out most prominently. Thus, comparative administration is inadequately developed as a social science, and only fitfully applies its methodology. Moreover, comparative administration's lack of development as an applied science for facilitating administrative change or development is even more notable.

This dual conclusion about comparative administration will be developed in two ways. First, the point is not only that comparative administration's development is lacking in terms of empirical theory. In addition, comparative administration efforts are often ascientific, if not antiscientific. In 1960—somewhat more exuberantly than sensitively—I noted at a national meeting two concerns about the dominant comparative administration approach. I pointed out that the various papers for discussion created an image in my mind of kind of an intellectual baptismal ceremony, with exotic new names being given wholesale to recognized subjects. Moreover, I emphasized a curious quality of those papers. The special quality of scientific theorizing is that it proceeds from what we are relatively certain about, and makes imaginative leaps via hypotheses or extrapolations toward what we do not know, which leaps ideally are in testable form. In contrast, the papers impressed me as beginning with models or verbalisms that implied what we did not know, and probably never could test in any way. And such models or verbalisms then were shown to be related to what we already knew. Like Riggs's uses of theory somehow to approach an undefined "administrative reality," the approach seemed to me to start the wrong way around. More awkwardly still, even if one's theory somehow got "there," the analyst would never be in a position to know it.

I have not changed my mind, although I would today change my expression.

Henderson nicely expresses my now preferred style for articulating the failure of comparative administration to test empirical theory fragments in a systematic way, its general inability to frame theory in testable terms. He notes that would-be researchers were frustrated by inadequate "statistics, problems of access, language barriers, expenses which foundations seemed reluctant to share, hostile or indifferent governments and study subjects, and other obstacles. . . ." Henderson adds that even when such "obstacles were partially overcome, the results were sometimes disastrous nonetheless." A major part of the difficulty apparently was the inadequate methodological base in comparative administration, its lack of experience and traditions for empirical research, which limited students who (in Henderson's words) "could not operate from a firmer base than comparative public administration." Henderson concludes that empirical field research ran a very distant second to the development of "grand theoretical models in the tradition of Weber and Parsons."[73]

Second, comparative administration did not develop a viable applied aspect. That is, it did not develop a family of what were earlier called goal-based, empirical theories. Generally, to be sure, the need for practical application was central in comparative administration's early formative period.[74] But Henderson tells us, the need soon became "a very weak urge."[75] More specifically, the grand theory common in comparative administration did not prove very useful to practitioners, who basically needed to be informed about what they did not know rather than to have illustrated what they did know. Relatedly, the lack of a viable applied aspect encouraged some (at least) incipient splits in comparative administration, as in the case of development administration. Comparative administration is seen as "academic analysis" and as more beholden to the "knowledge for its own sake" bias of university settings.[76] In contrast, development administration was generally related to an "action-oriented goal-oriented administrative system,"[77] as well as to "major societal transformation, a change in system states," especially in the developing countries of the world.[78]

Five Lessons for New Public
Administration

It seems useful for the new public administration to go to school on the comparative administration experience. Five lessons seem most prominent, and they seem applicable whether one comes out relatively optimistic[79] or pessimistic[80] about comparative administration's accomplishments or about its future prognosis.

First, the experience of comparative administration demonstrates what should have been obvious from the start. That which lasts, both analytically and practically, rests on the *logic and processes* of the approach. The locus of the focal problem is a very minor concern; and the same is true, sad to say, whether the problem is a "relevant" one or not, whether the intervenor really intends to do good, or whether few or many people will profit from what the intervenor does.

The "old" comparative administration never got this message. Even sympathetic observers now note that comparative administration was clearly motivated by lofty intent, but failed to develop (indeed, usually failed even to recognize the need for) a methodology for empirical analysis. Savage makes this point, saying that he speaks for most of those associated with comparative administration, as he was. Comparative administration has not, he concludes, "isolated and identified a manageable and distinct piece of the terrain of human political behavior, posed an agenda of compelling questions and problems within the terrain, and established an appropriate logic of inquiry."[81] When all is said and done, that is the central tragedy of comparative administration, a tragedy made more poignant by the undoubted concern of comparative administration with "human needs and human liberation."[82]

Matters seem no better as Waldo describes the "new" comparative administration, which he sees as required by the recent shift of attention to domestic concerns. He notes: "There is no escape, no alternative: if we are to rise to our responsibilities and opportunities, if we are to remain (I use it again) *relevant* and not become obsolete, we must become 'urbanists,' 'metropolitanists,' or whatever the proper term may prove to be."[83] Waldo's boosterism is encouraging for obvious reasons, but it is also frightening in that it still implies a definition of comparative administration in terms of a kind of problem for the week rather than in terms of processes of inquiry that are broadly applicable to a range of problems. Learning from history does not seem to have occurred, in short.

Second, public administration should take full notice of the fact that comparative administration's failure rests substantially on a self-imposed failure experience. It set an unattainable goal, that is, in its early and persisting choice to seek a comprehensive theory or model in terms of which to define itself. Savage nicely encapsulates this fixation. Comparative administration, he notes, "has produced much one could, with some generosity, label theory; particularly grand theory."[84]

Comparative administration's experience implies that the search for a grand vision is premature and even dangerous, probably in direct proportion to the initial intensity of that search. Untethered by a useful set of logic and processes for empirical inquiry, particularly, and fueled by the obvious needs of the moment, many aficionados of comparative administration took fanciful flight. Hence, the prominence of formulations such as the following—complete with geometric figures—in the writing of many of the most prominent in comparative administration: ". . . assuming that we can determine the degree of structural differentiation and the level of performance of any system, we can then determine the degree to which it is diffracted or prismatic utilizing the Pythagorean formula for the length of the hypotenuse of a right-angled triangle."[85]

Third, any viable approach to public administration must provide explicit places for both empirical and normative concerns, as well as relatively specific interfaces between them. The prime need is for a substantial balance between the two.

In this sense, comparative administration was far more faith than it was good works. Specifically, La Palombara had all but unanimous support for his statement of comparative administration's normative posture, which appears in what Savage calls "one of the signal works of the decade"[86] of comparative administration's hegemony. La Palombara prescribes: "There should be more open and conscious effort to export not merely American technical know-how, but our political ideology and reasonable facsimilies of our political institutions and practices as well."[87] The tragic rub, of course, derived from two points. Comparative administration did not have available an empirical theory for bringing such "shoulds" into being by suitable manipulations of relationships that were known to exist or could be cultivated via known empirical regularities. Moreover, comparative administration did not rest on processes of empirical inquiry suitable for even beginning the development of such knowledge.

Even more insidiously, comparative administration also reflected an unsatisfactory confusion of empirical and normative concerns in a crucial particular. When push came to shove, comparative administration typically did not deal with normative differences. On technical issues, for example, it generally accepted one set of value-loaded prescriptions for organizing work, those patterned after Max Weber's legal-rational bureaucracy.[88] This choice for homogeneity of values was not made easily, so the choice must be significant, and especially so because alternative models for organizing work were available that implied sets of values very different from Weber's.[89] Siffin formulated the rationale for a choice other than Weber's model: "The inadequacies of this view were obvious to a lot of people: It largely ignored the human side of administration and the real problem of incentives. It afforded no foundation for the study of policy making and administrative politics. And it simply did not fit the realities of most of the developing countries of the world."[90]

Value homogenity also was the general order of the day, more broadly. "The thematic value," Siffin notes, "was the idea of administration as *instrumental.* From this derived supportive values: *efficiency, rationality, responsibility,* and (sometimes) *effectiveness.* Along with these there was the burgeoning value of *professionalism.*"[91] Such notions were comfortably nestled in American experience, beginning especially in the late nineteenth century. Development suitable for the American goose, to risk an awful usage, was assumed to be good enough for the underdeveloped gander. If spoils politics were "bad" for America, why not just skip to "responsible political parties" in Southeast Asia, for example? Such developmental jumps were doubly dangerous. Thus, they assumed that development $_1$ = development $_2$, despite huge difference in culture and historical experiences. Moreover, such jumps often were incautious. For example, spoils politics no doubt was useful in helping develop political parties, American style, and perhaps may have been similarly useful elsewhere.

Discordant voices were heard about this convenient way of simplifying the melding of empirical and normative concerns in comparative administration, of course. Witness the troubling question: Development for what?[92] But these were not early mainstream voices.

Fourth, any viable approach to public administration must provide explicit places for both pure and applied knowledge. Again, the prime need is for a substantial balance between the two. That message is also crystal clear in comparative administration's experience.

Sometimes comparative administration seemed right-on in its appreciation of the need to produce both basic and applied knowledge, but matters typically came unglued. Basically, the task was overpoweringly formidable, and that practically guaranteed very limited success at best. Other factors—the lack of a solid basis for empirical inquiry, the lusting after grand theory, the gross imbalance between the goals of comparative administration and the technologies and skills to achieve them—did not permit a fair shot at even this very limited success.

Fifth, the experience of comparative administration implies another hard lesson: Useful theory and technology are infinitely preferable to loyalty and shared allegiances when it comes to problem solving, and when the choice is technology *or* loyalty. Of course, technology *and* loyalty are everyone's dream. One of the contributions that Savage attributes to comparative administration, for example, is that it "stood as a domain for fertile interaction between public administrationists and political scientists involved in a compelling movement." With a suggestion of considerable pride, Savage concludes:

> With ample evidence of shared literature, it is also probable that comparative administration may well have served to maintain the links between . . . political science and . . . public administration during a time when the original and historic bonds were under strain *and* elements of . . . public administration were breaking away to find homes under organizational arrangements other than the traditional one in departments of political science.[93]

Pride may be appropriate, of course. But it is at least possible that those persisting links also had something to do with comparative administrations's limited success in responding to its problems via processes of inquiry that were comfortably nestled within political science. Although such processes were accepted by many political scientists, they were not particularly useful for the task at hand.

Notes and References

1. Here the pot has been bubbling longest, as in the development of "third force" and "humanistic psychology." The roots go back to various complex sources, as these are reflected by such works as Abraham E. Maslow,

The Farther Reaches of Human Nature (New York: Viking Press, 1971); and Arthur Koestler's *The Ghost in the Machine* (New York: Macmillan, 1967).

2. Most prominently, see Alvin Gouldner, *The Coming Crisis of Western Sociology* (New York: Basic Books, 1970).

3. For example, consult George J. Graham, Jr., and George W. Carey, eds., *The Post-Behavioral Era: Perspectives on Political Science* (New York: David McKay, 1972).

4. The spirit of the times is both reflected and created in Dwight Waldo, "Public Administration in a Time of Revolution," *Public Administration Review* 28 (July 1968): 362-368.

5. John C. Honey, "A Report: Higher Education for Public Service," *Public Administration Review* 27 (November 1967): 302.

6. See Robert A. Gordon and James E. Howell, *Higher Education for Business* (New York: Columbia University Press, 1959); and Frank Pierson et al., *The Education of American Businessmen* (University-College Programs in Business Administration, 1959).

7. Peter Savage, "What Am I Bid for Public Administration?" *Public Administration Review* 28 (July 1968): especially 391.

8. John C. Honey, "Honey Responds," *Public Administration Review* 28 (September 1968): 483.

9. The reference is to Ira Sharkansky, "Constraints on Innovation in Policy Making," in *Toward a New Public Administration,* ed. Frank Marini (Scranton, Pa.: Chandler, 1971), pp. 261-284. The other major book referred to is Dwight Waldo, ed., *Public Administration in a Time of Turbulence* (Scranton, Pa.: Chandler), 1971. For examples of the abstract and general treatments referred to here, see especially Orion White, "Social Change and Administrative Adaptation," in Marini, *Toward a New Public Administration,* pp. 59-80.

10. For a summary treatment, see Robert T. Golembiewski, *Renewing Organizations* (Itasca, Ill.: F. E. Peacock, 1972), especially pp. 19-202. For details of design and longitudinal studies of the effects of one level of organizational confrontation, see Michael Blansfield, Robert R. Blake, and Jane S. Mouton, "The Merger Laboratory," *Training Directors Journal* 18 (May 1964): 2-10; Robert R. Blake, Jane S. Mouton, and Richard L. Sloma, "The Union-Management Laboratory," *Journal of Applied Behavioral Science* 1 (January 1965): 25-57; Richard Beckhard, "The Confrontation Meeting," *Harvard Business Review* 45 (March 1967): 149-155; Robert T. Golembiewski and Arthur Blumberg, "Confrontation as a Training Design in Complex Organizations," *Journal of Applied Behavioral Science* 3 (December 1967): 525-547; and Robert T. Golembiewski and Arthur Blumberg, "Persistence of Attitudinal Changes Induced by a Confrontation Design," *Academy of Management Journal* 21 (September 1969): 309-318.

11. For example, see the determined boundary-defining effort of Todd La Porte, "The Recovery of Relevance in the Study of Public Orgnaization," in Marini, *Toward a New Public Administration*, p. 24n.

12. Emmanuel Wald, "Toward a Paradigm of Future Public Administration," *Public Administration Review* 33 (July 1973): 372.

13. Ibid., pp. 366-372.

14. For summary treatments, see Marini, *Toward a New Public Administration*, especially pp. 346-364.

15. Wesley E. Bjur, "Communication," *Public Administration Review* 30 (March-April 1970): 202.

16. The most extreme statement in the public administration literature is in Frederick C. Thayer, *An End to Hierarchy!* (New York: New Viewpoints, 1973).

17. Robert Townsend, *Up the Organization: How to Stop the Corporation from Stifling People and Strangling Profits* (New York: Knopf, 1970).

18. See Marini, *Toward a New Public Administration*, especially pp. 349-350; and Waldo, *Public Administration in a Time of Turbulence*, especially pp. 192-197.

19. Abraham Maslow, "Self-Actualization and Beyond," in *Challenges of Humanistic Psychology*, ed. James F. T. Bugental (New York: McGraw-Hill, 1967), pp. 279-286.

20. Robert T. Golembiewski and Arthur Blumberg, eds., *Sensitivity Training and the Laboratory Approach* (Itasca, Ill.: F. E. Peacock, 3rd ed., 1977).

21. This theme is one of the emphases in R. D. Laing, *The Politics of Experience* (New York: Pantheon Books, 1967).

22. York Willbern, "Is the New Public Administration Still With Us?" *Public Administration Review* 33 (July 1973): 376.

23. The seminal treatment—much interpreted and misinterpreted—is usually considered to be that of John Rawls, *A Theory of Justice* (Cambridge, Mass.: Belknap Press, 1971).

24. H. George Frederickson, "Creating Tomorrow's Public Administration," *Public Management* 53 (November 1971): 3.

25. Richard S. Page, "A New Public Administration?" *Public Administration Review* 29 (May 1969): 304.

26. Ibid., p. 304.

27. Matthew A. Crenson, "Comment: Contract, Love, and Character Building," in Marini, *Toward a New Public Administration*, p. 88.

28. Bjur, "Communication," p. 202.

29. H. George Frederickson, "Toward a New Public Administration," in Marini, *Toward a New Public Administration*, p. 315.

30. Ibid., p. 316.

31. For a summary introduction, see Golembiewski and Blumberg, *Sensitivity Training and the Laboratory Approach.*

32. Philip E. Slater and Warren G. Bennis, "Democracy Is Inevitable," *Harvard Business Review* 42 (March 1964): 51-59; and Warren G. Bennis, "A Funny Thing Happened on the Way to the Future," *American Psychologist* 25 (July 1970): especially 597-603.

33. As in White, "Social Change and Administrative Adaptation," in Marini, *Toward a New Public Administration,* pp. 82-83.

34. Alan K. Campbell, "Old and New Public Administration in the 1970's," *Public Administration Review* 32 (August 1972): 343.

35. Edward Friedland, "Comment: The Pursuit of Relevance," in Marini, *Toward a New Public Administration,* p. 49.

36. Alvin Gouldner, "Metaphysical Pathos and the Theory of Bureaucracy," *American Political Science Review* 44 (December 1955): 496.

37. Dwight Waldo, "Public Administration," *Journal of Politics* 30 (May 1968): 447.

38. La Porte, "The Recovery of Relevance in the Study of Public Organization," in Marini, *Toward a New Public Administration,* p. 21.

39. Ibid., p. 31.

40. Campbell, "Old and New Public Administration in the 1970s," p. 343. See also Frederick Thayer, "Presidential Policy Processes and 'New Administration,'" *Public Administration Review* 31 (September-October 1971): 552.

41. James M. Elden, "Radical Politics and the Future of Public Administration in the Postindustrial Era," in Waldo, *Public Administration in a Time of Turbulence,* pp. 36-37.

42. The myth is that, more or less until Herbert Simon published his attack on the "principles of public administration," they were essentially unchallenged, at least by major figures. As a simplification, this may be tolerable. But the careful reader should consult such revisionary sources as Francis W. Coker, "Dogmas of Administrative Reform," *American Political Science Review* 16 (August 1922): 399-411; Charles S. Hyneman, "Administrative Reorganization: An Adventure into Science and Theology," *Journal of Politics* 1 (February 1939): 62-74; Earl H. Latham, "Hierarchy and Hieratics," *Employment Forum* 2 (April 1947): 1-6; and Herbert A. Simon, "Proverbs of Administration," *Public Administration Review* 6 (Winter 1946): 53-67.

43. Waldo, "Public Administration," p. 447.

44. Dwight Waldo, "The Administrative State Revisited," *Public Administration Review* 25 (March 1965): 26.

45. Philip S. Kronenberg, "The Scientific and Moral Authority of Empirical Theory of Public Administration," in Marini, *Toward a New Public Administration,* pp. 194-195.

46. Herbert Kaufman, "Administrative Decentralization and Political Power," *Public Administration Review* 29 (January 1969), p. 4.

47. La Porte, "The Recovery of Relevance in the Study of Public Organization," in Marini, *Toward a New Public Administration*, p. 24n.

48. Ibid., p. 33.

49. For example, Marini highlights the lack of concern among Minnowbrook participants with research technology. See Marini, *Toward a New Public Administration*, p. 5. See also pp. 58-89 and 224-225, among other locations in the Marini volume.

50. Kenneth E. Boulding, "Economics as a Moral Science," *American Economic Review* 59 (March 1969): 11.

51. Peter Bechman, letter to the editor, *Wall Street Journal*, December 23, 1967, p. 11.

52. La Porte emphasizes the point in "The Recovery of Relevance in the Study of Public Organization," in Marini, *Toward a New Public Administration*, p. 29.

53. White, "Social Change and Administrative Adaptation," in Marini, *Toward a New Public Administration*, p. 79.

54. Ibid., p. 83.

55. Consult Robert T. Golembiewski, *Behavior and Organization* (Chicago: Rand McNally, 1962), especially pp. 47-61, for details about the distinctions between types of theory.

56. Friedland, "Comment: The Pursuit of Relevance," in Marini, *Toward a New Public Administration*, p. 52.

57. L. Vaughn Blankenship, "Public Administration and the Challenge to Reason," in Waldo, *Public Administration in a Time of Turbulence*, pp. 190-191.

58. The emphasis was pervasive. For example, see Frederickson, "Creating Tomorrow's Public Administration."

59. Henry S. Kariel, "Creating Political Reality," *American Political Science Review* 64 (December 1970): 1098.

60. Marvin Meade, " 'Participative' Administration: Emerging Reality or Wishful Thinking?" in Waldo, *Public Administration in a Time of Turbulence*, p. 169.

61. Peter Savage, "Contemporary Public Administration," in Waldo, *Public Administration in a Time of Turbulence*, p. 51.

62. Ibid., pp. 51-52.

63. Waldo, "Public Administration," p. 470.

64. Generally, see Keith M. Henderson, "Comparative Public Administration," in Marini, *Toward a New Public Administration*, pp. 234-243.

65. For an extensive critical bibliography, consult Henderson, "Comparative Public Administration," in Marini, *Toward a New Public Administration,* p. 235. More specifically, evaluations of comparative public administration or development administration cover a broad range, mostly from bad to worse. Thus some observers see that experience as a costly one, due to the basic mistake of expecting developmental outcomes from concepts and tools that are more suitable for system maintenance. See William J. Siffin, "Two Decades of Public Administration in Developing Countries," *Public Administration Review* 36 (January 1976): 61-71. Others are more critical, with development administration being seen as great in aspiration but more or less puny in outcome due to asking far too much, too soon. See Garth N. Jones, "Frontiersmen in Search for the 'Lost Horizon': The State of Development Administration in the 1960s," *Public Administration Review* 36 (January 1976): 99-110.

66. Waldo, "The Administrative State Revisited," p. 23.

67. Today, some latent conflict over turf seems to exist. See D. Woods Thomas et al., eds., *Institution Building* (Cambridge, Mass.: Schenkman, 1972).

68. Fred W. Riggs, "Relearning an Old Lesson: The Political Context of Development Administration," *Public Administration Review* 35 (March 1965): 70.

69. Fred W. Riggs, *Administration in Developing Countries* (Boston: Houghton Mifflin, 1964).

70. Ibid., p. 401.

71. James Heaphey, "Comparative Public Administration: Comments on Current Characteristics," *Public Administration Review* 28 (May 1968): 243.

72. Ibid., p. 243.

73. Henderson, "Comparative Public Administration," in Marini, *Toward a New Public Administration,* p. 239.

74. Ferrel Heady and Cybil L. Stokes, eds., *Papers in Comparative Public Administration* (Ann Arbor, Mich.: Institute of Public Administration, 1962), especially p. 3.

75. Henderson, "Comparative Public Administration," in Marini, *Toward a New Public Administration,* p. 239.

76. Heaphey, "Comparative Public Administration," p. 246.

77. Edward W. Weidner, "Development Administration: A New Focus for Research," in Heady and Stokes, *Papers in Comparative Public Administration,* p. 98.

78. Milton J. Esman, "The Politics of Development Administration," in *Approaches to Development: Politics, Administration, and Change,* ed. John D. Montgomery and William J. Siffin (New York: McGraw-Hill, 1966).

79. Jamil L. Jreisat, "Synthesis and Relevance in Comparative Public Administration," *Public Administration Review* 35 (November 1975): 663-671.

80. Jones, "Frontiersmen in Search for the 'Lost Horizon,' " pp. 99-110.

81. Peter Savage, "Optimism and Pessimism in Comparative Administration," *Public Administration Review* 36 (July 1976), p. 417.

82. Ibid., p. 422.

83. Waldo, "The Administrative State Revisited," p. 20.

84. Savage, "Optimism and Pessimism in Comparative Administration," p. 416.

85. Fred W. Riggs, "Administrative Development," in Montgomery and Siffin, *Approaches to Development,* p. 240.

86. Savage, "Optimism and Pessimism in Comparative Administration," p. 416.

87. Joseph La Palombara, ed., *Bureaucracy and Political Development* (Princeton, N.J.: Princeton University Press, 1963), p. 60.

88. William J. Siffin, "Two Decades of Public Administration in Developing Countries," *Public Administration Review* 36 (January 1976): especially 62-63.

89. The most popular expression of the contrasting sets of values underlying the organization of work in the theory X versus theory Y formulation of Douglas McGregor, *The Human Side of Enterprise* (New York: McGraw-Hill, 1960), especially pp. 33-57.

90. Siffin, "Two Decades of Public Administration in Developing Countries," p. 90.

91. Ibid., p. 63.

92. Denis Goulet, "Development for What?" *Comparative Political Studies* 1 (July 1968).

93. Savage, "Optimism and Pessimism in Comparative Administration," p. 420.

"DEMOCRATIC ADMINISTRATION" AS THE PARADIGM*
A New Synthesis and Some Old, Tough Problems

Public administration often must be sheltered from its friends as well as saved from its enemies. So it is with Vincent Ostrom's "democratic administration," which is the focus of this chapter. He is clearly a long-time friend of public administration, and a major contributor to its development. Despite his welcome effort to define a mission and role for public administration, however, the view here is that Ostrom's work is not particularly helpful, and may even be seriously counterproductive. Hence this effort to shelter public administration from one of its friends.

Three Contrasts of Promise and Performance

This chapter intends to show in three central particulars how Ostrom's analytical performance is short of his promises. First, Ostrom promises to go beyond the procrustean distinctions of Phase II politics/administration and especially seeks to improve upon its incautious and inadequate treatment of values. However, the core ideas on which Ostrom rests his work are themselves based on a very

*This chapter is one reflection of a substantial history of an exchange of ideas and papers that I have had with a colleague, Dr. Keith Baker. I warmly acknowledge that interchange. Other reflections appear in Baker's works: "Public Choice Theory: Some Important Assumptions and Public Policy Implications," in *Public Administration*, ed. Robert T. Golembiewski, Frank Gibson, and Geoffrey Y. Cornog (Chicago: Rand McNally, 1976); and "The Search for A New Paradigm in Public Administration" (Paper delivered at the Annual Meeting of the Southern Political Science Association, New Orleans, La., November 1974).

A version of this chapter will appear in the *American Political Science Review*.

restrictive treatment of values. In this critical sense, democratic administration is not up to the job either of specifying the central phenomena in public administration, or of providing guidance for how they should be studied. Even if public administration were in need of *a* paradigm, that is to say, democratic administration would be seriously lacking.

Second, Ostrom proposes to outline and illustrate a methodology that would provide the empirical complement to the consideration of values that Ostrom so rightly emphasizes as necessary. Unfortunately, Ostrom's empirically relevant methodology does not appear to be useful. His methodological guides no doubt will hinder empirical analysis and, indeed, may even preclude it. Patently, these are unattractive probabilities.

Third, Ostrom promises to provide guidance for the applied aspects of public administration, as well as for its analytical or descriptive aspects. Here Ostrom correctly senses a major challenge to be overcome by any viable guidelines for public administration. Those guidelines must variously specify *linkages for action.* That is, they must prescribe how the goals of the just state can be approached, via knowledge of the empirical world and through the skillful application of technological ways and means that permit inducing desired conditions. Ostrom's performance falls short of his perceptive vision, however. His approach is not particularly helpful; indeed, probably, that approach may even positively hinder the development of public administration as effective and sensitive application.

In sum, Ostrom promises to deal with three old and tough problems related to the mission and role of public administration. That promise is attractive and urges serious attention to Ostrom's work.

In overall effect, however, Ostrom's new synthesis will be shown to be incapable of coping with those three problems. In critical particulars, indeed, Ostrom's hopeful synthesis may only make those old problems even tougher and more intractable. Hence, this effort to shelter public administration from one of its friends.

Some Good News before the Bad

In the ongoing ferment about leading ideas to guide public administration, most attention has centered on Ostrom's effort to make democratic administration *the* paradigm of the 1970s.[1] This chapter acknowledges that centrality, while it also seeks to provide some of the critical treatment that Ostrom's ideas require. This critique necessarily includes the broad ideational infrastructure of public-choice theory on which Ostrom relies, as it seeks to deal with his democratic administration.

Given the critical tone of much of what follows, it is important to note where this chapter stands with Ostrom. There are five important points of agreement:

- There is no disagreement with Ostrom about the inadequacy of sharply separating politics and administration: "The structure of public administration cannot be organized apart from processes of political choice," as Ostrom observes.[2]

- There is no disagreement with Ostrom for his joining the long-standing criticism of monocratic bureaucracy.

- There is no disagreement with Ostrom in arguing for a broader role for individuals in influencing public policy and its administration, as both members and clients of public agencies.

- There is no disagreement with Ostrom in urging greater administrative responsiveness to clients' perceptions of needs or in emphasizing the critical need for improved productivity in providing public services.

- There is no disagreement that economic modes of thought and analysis can be powerful aids to enlightened choice making.

More generally, the present view is often one of agreement with Ostrom's conclusions, but an agreement burdened with concern that his argumentation is not adequate. In any case, the bulk of this chapter will emphasize areas of Ostrom's position that are unacceptable as presented. Because the argument will be long and sometimes complex, its major thrusts may be introduced usefully at this point. Four emphases do the job. Two early sections introduce Ostrom's view of the major contenders for providing the dominant paradigm to guide the study and practice of public administration, with special attention to how these paradigms apply to such central questions as determining the scale of public delivery systems. A long and multisectioned argument then provides a detailed analysis of the ideation supporting Ostrom's democratic administration, with that ideation being seen as basically inadequate from five central perspectives. A brief concluding section seeks to encourage a contingency approach to the issues Ostrom addresses, as opposed to the more unidirectional prescriptive approach he actually takes.

Two Contenders for the Reigning Paradigm

More or less, Ostrom has two goals. First, he seeks to approach the "intellectual crisis" of public administration in terms of two broad and contrasting paradigms. In this sense, "paradigm" means roughly the set of guiding ideas that express the sense of which problems are significant, how these problems are to be analyzed, and in what priority they are to be dealt with. Thus posed, the crisis is shown to be conveniently resolvable. Second, Ostrom argues simply that it is high time that one of those models be supplanted, root and branch, by the other.

A Familiar and Long-lived Gestalt

The first set of guiding ideas, or the Traditional Paradigm—usually identified by Ostrom as derivative from Woodrow Wilson,[3] but also clearly recognizable as close kin to the monocratic bureaucracy of Mex Weber—has a "top, down" bias, as Table 5.1 demonstrates. And it also has had a long-lived influence. Chapter 2 contains a discussion of this Traditional Paradigm, along with its associated organizational arrangements. For this reason brief analysis suffices here.

The overall image of the Traditional Paradigm in Ostrom's telling is that of an overflowing font of sovereignty, authority being concentrated at high levels but allowed to trickle variously down the hierarchy of the state enterprise.

TABLE 5.1   Basic Propositions of the Traditional Paradigm[a]

---

1. There will always be a single dominant center of power in any system of government; and the government of a society will be controlled by that single center of power.

2. The more power is divided the more irresponsible it becomes; or, alternatively, the more power is unified and directed from a single center the more responsible it will become.

3. The structure of a constitution defines and determines the composition of that center of power and establishes the political structure relative to the enactment of law and the control of administration. Every system of democratic government will exalt the people's representative to a position of absolute sovereignty.

4. The field of politics sets the task for administration, but the field of administration lies outside the proper sphere of politics.

5. All modern governments will have a strong structural similarity so far as administrative functions are concerned.

6. Perfection in the hierarchical ordering of a professionally trained public service provides the structural conditions necessary for "good" administration.

7. Perfection in hierarchical organization will maximize efficiency as measured by least cost expended in money and effort.

8. Perfection of "good" administration as here defined is a necessary condition for modernity in human civilization and for the advancement of human welfare.

---

[a]From Vincent Ostrom, *The Intellectual Crisis in American Public Administration* (University, Ala.: University of Alabama Press, 1973), pp. 28-29.

Table 5.2 Basic Propositions of Democratic Administration[a]

1. Individuals who exercise the prerogatives of government are no more or no less corruptible than their fellow men [and women].

2. The exercise of political authority—a necessary power to do good—will be usurped by those who perceive an opportunity to exploit such power to their own advantage and to the detriment of others unless authority is divided and different authorities are so organized as to limit and control one another.

3. The structure of a constitution allocates decision-making capabilities among a community of persons; and a democratic constitution defines the authority inherent in both the prerogatives of persons and in the prerogative of different governmental offices so that the capabilities of each are limited by the capabilities of others. The task of establishing and altering organizational arrangements in a democratic society is to be conceived as a problem in constitutional decision making.

4. The provision of public goods and services depends upon decisions taken by diverse sets of decision makers, and the political feasibility of each collective enterprise depends upon a favorable course of decisions in all essential decision structures over time. Public administration lies within the domain of politics.

5. A variety of different organizational arrangements can be used to provide different public goods and services. Such organizations can be coordinated through various multiorganizational arrangements, including trading and contracting to mutual advantage, competitive rivalry, adjudication, as well as the power of command in limited hierarchies.

6. Perfection in the hierarchical ordering of a profesionally trained public service accountable to a *single* center of power will reduce the capability of a large administrative system to respond to diverse preferences among citizens for many different public goods and services and cope with diverse environmental conditions.

7. Perfection in hierarchical organization accountable to a *single* center of power will *not* maximize efficiency as measured by least-cost expended in time, effort, and resources.

8. Fragmentation of authority among diverse decision centers with multiple veto capabilities within any one jurisdiction and the development of multiple, overlapping jurisdictions of widely different scales are necessary conditions for maintaining a stable political order which can advance human welfare under rapidly changing conditions.

[a]From Vincent Ostrom, *The Intellectual Crisis in American Public Administration* (University, Ala.: University of Alabama Press, 1973), pp. 111-112.

Hence the centralized character of its associated organization structure, as Chapter 2 shows. In brief, the Traditional Paradigm postulates that there will be a single dominant center of power in any system of government. Consequently, all modern governments face the same challenge in organizing their administrative activities: To perfect their hierarchical organization into a unitary structure under a single executive, leading a corps of trained and politically neutral professionals, so as to maximize efficiency as measured by least money and effort expended, as well as to advance human welfare.

These notions, which are patently consistent with the naïve separation of politics and administration detailed in Chapter 2, long influenced the organizing of work and men, Ostrom advises. That they did, essentially although not without growing opposition, for a half-century or more.

Democratic Administration as the Alternative Paradigm

Ostrom offers a contrasting, alternative, and (to him) more useful paradigm, democratic administration. That alternative has a "bottom, up" emphasis, as Table 5.2 clearly reflects, and its overall quality suggests a kind of sociopolitical Brownian movement far more than it implies the ordered symmetry of a hierarchy. The contrasts between the two paradigms are numerous. For example, Ostrom tells us that the "overlapping jurisdictions and fragmentation of authority" prescribed by democratic administration "can facilitate the production of a heterogeneous mix of public goods and services in a public service economy." A contrary presumption is built into the Traditional Paradigm, which (Ostrom notes) sees "overlapping jurisdictions and fragmentation of authority [as] the principal source of institutional failure in American government."[4]

The Two Paradigmatic Contenders and Determining the Scale of Public Delivery Systems

Although they are no more than barely illustrative, the descriptions in Tables 5.1 and 5.2 clearly imply that democratic administration must deal with major problems that are superficially finessed by the Traditional Paradigm. These problems will only be sampled here in terms of two questions that Ostrom's alternative must face. What should be the scale of public-service delivery systems? And how should they be differentiated and coordinated?

Such questions seem easy to solve within the framework of the Traditional Paradigm, which implies a dominant bias toward centralization consistent with its ideal of an increasingly integral authority structure. Both the implied theoretical and practical urgencies of the Traditional Paradigm, that is simply require

TABLE 5.3   Criteria for Determining the Scale of Public Delivery Systems[a]

1.   *Control.* Requires that the broad "boundary conditions" of a political jurisdiction be so defined as to "include the relevant sets of events to be controlled." Because relevant events are not uniformly distributed in space or time, these boundaries can be defined only "with more or less precision." But these events—whether they involve a watershed basin or patterns of human interaction—can be described and bounded in determining the scale of a public agency. Too narrow boundaries will result in a public agency that "is disabled in regulating a set of events in order to realize some preferred state of affairs," and the "likely result" will be a transfer of that agency's function to a governmental unit "scaled to meet the criterion of control more adequately."

2.   *Efficiency.* "The most efficient solution would require the modification of boundary conditions so as to assure a producer of public goods the most favorable economy of scale, as well as effective control."

3.   *Political Representation.* This criterion requires "the inclusion of the appropriate political interests within its decision-making arrangements."
       The issues are complex, but the ideal solution—assuming "criteria of responsibility and accountability consonant with democratic theory"— would require that "three boundaries be coterminous." These boundaries are: (1) the *scale of formal organization,* or the size of the government unit providing some public good; (2) the *public,* consisting of those affected by the provision of that good; and (3) the *political community,* or those "who are actually taken into account in deciding whether and how to provide" that public good.

4.   *Local Self-determination.* The application of the three preceding criteria to local governments in the United States is usually to be "subordinated to considerations of self determination," that is, application is usually to "be controlled by the decisions of the citizenry in the local community."
       The basic assumption is that public goods can be appropriately "packaged" or "internalized," so that those outside the boundaries of a local unit of government can be excluded from the public goods produced by that unit. Looked at from another perspective, the assumption is that the "purely 'municipal' affairs of a local jurisdiction, presumably, do not create problems for other political communities."
       Relatedly, also, this fourth criterion implies that the local citizenry be both capable of, and motivated toward, holding public officials accountable, in ways that do not create major problems for other political communities.

[a]From Vincent Ostrom, Charles M. Tiebout, and Robert Warren, "The Organization of Government in Metropolitan Areas," *American Political Science Review* (December 1961): especially 835-837.

reducing any extant autonomy of component government units so as to increase the reality of *a* "chain of command." Hence, in answer to the issue of how big a public-service delivery system should be, proponents of the Traditional Paradigm would state that such a system should be as big as necessary to create a unitary organization under a single executive. The prescription is for a monolithic giantism, clearly. This may be difficult to achieve in practice, and even counter-productive, but the prescription is directly and simply derived from the Traditional Paradigm.

Beyond this central point of agreement, opinions of those supporting the Traditional Paradigm tend to fall into two camps. One camp maintains that "effective centralization must precede effective decentralization."[5] Its pro-ponents presume that acting on the urgencies above is only a necessary prelude to dealing with the issues of fine tuning the system, of determining the scale of component units as well as defining a rationalized system of differentiated or integrated subsystems. In some more extreme versions, the achievement of the totally rationalized system is seen as *the* goal,[6] rather than a prelude to some newly reachable goals.

Democratic administration cannot take such a superficially convenient route, if only because of its emphasis on "different organizational arrangements" and its rejection of "*a* single center of power." The obvious next questions are numerous and momentous. If not *a* center of power, then how many? And of what size?

To respond to such next questions, Ostrom offers a set of four criteria for dealing with problems of scale in governmental units. He deals with these central and complex problems in an uncomplicated way. Basically, his goal is suitably to define a "package" for the boundaries of a unit of government that would exclude those outside the boundaries from the use of the public goods produced or provided by that unit. The criteria are sketched in Table 5.3, which will be discussed at several points below.

A Critical Analysis of the Ideation
Underlying Democratic Administration

The criteria for determining the scale of governmental units have received little critical analysis,[7] despite the burgeoning attention devoted to the "public choice" context of which the criteria are both creator and creature. To be sure, Ostrom does note that the criteria are "sometimes in conflict." And Ostrom does allow that when the criteria are not applied adequately in local govern-ments, for example, the "package" for the production and provision of public goods by the governmental units whose boundaries are being drawn will be faulty. This will result in "externalities [that] spill over into neighboring communities."[8]

The critical analysis here is more ambitious than Ostrom's brief qualifications and seeks to go beyond the admission that the criteria are sometimes in conflict. The subsequent argument seeks to establish a broader indictment, which includes these five central points relating to Ostrom's argument generally, to his criteria for determining the scale of government units more specifically, and also to their underlying ideation:

- The methodology underlying democratic administration is awkward.
- Major assumptions in Ostrom's argument are at least improbable descriptors and may be seriously incongruent with reality.
- Critical content or meaning is lacking in major concepts underlying democratic administration.
- Opposite and simultaneous courses of action are implied by central aspects of Ostrom's system of thought.
- Democratic administration can lead to unexpected practical consequences that are sometimes the polar opposites of those intended.

Methodological Concerns

The central concerns with Ostrom's position are methodological and constitute slippery targets because his usages (and the usages of those on whom Ostrom explicitly relies) are so alluring as to invite incautious acceptance. This section will list and briefly discuss several of these methodological concerns, while subsequent sections will add substance to the spare argument that immediately follows. Note that attention is directed both at Ostrom and at the core ideational infrastructure on which Ostrom relies so much, the theory of public choice.

Basically, the public-choice position rests upon a methodology that emphasizes a closed-system circularity, and at the same time permits incautious building upon assumptions that are often suspect. The circularity is often explicit in the key questions for inquiry. For example: "When will a society composed of free and rational utility-maximizing individuals choose to undertake action collectively rather than privately?" It comes as no surprise to learn that collective action will occur when (enough?) individuals realize that they can increase their utility in a cost-efficient manner by so organizing.[9] The line of argumentation is tendentious because "free and rational utility-maximizing individuals" could hardly have done it any other way. Worse still, rather than identifying or describing or predicting, this approach permits only a posteriori classification, as in: "Aha! There is a collective action; ergo, someone's utility has been maximized." The lack of caution in argument can be conveniently established here by merely noting the strong attention De Gregori draws to it in the literature on property rights, because the tendency will be illustrated at several points in the following discussion. De Gregori concludes that "one finds a tendency for authors to begin with assumptions, or borrow other theorists' models with their assumptions, which are in conflict with reality. One author assumes zero transaction costs, another zero information costs. By the time the conclusions are reached, somehow these assumptions are forgotten."[10] Patently, these methodological propensities toward circularity and incaution are very awkward and raise serious concerns about the argument built on such foundations.

Four points provide further perspective on the character of the method- ology common to Ostrom and many of the public-choice theorists on whom he relies. First, consider how several prominent public-choice theorists seek to have the best of all analytical worlds in casually shifting the base of their argument. The point could be illustrated in many ways. The sole focus here is the central notion of methodological individualism, on which the public-choice argument is typically predicated and which Ostrom tells us he accepts.[11] Methodological individualism seeks to explain collective decision making as a simple summation of the individual decisions made by separate and distinct persons. The core concept is deliberately contrasted with "normative individualism," which Buchanan and Tullock stress is rooted in the "explicit acceptance of certain value criteria."[12] Perhaps the intent is to represent the public-choice argument as one of science rather than of personal bias. Whatever the intent, Buchanan and Tullock are not sufficiently restrained by their own tethers. For example, they also announce early on that they "are not directly interested in what *the* State or *a* State actually is, but propose to define quite specifically, yet quite briefly, what we *think* a State ought to be."[13] De Gregori arches an analytic eye- brow: "Methodological or normative?" he asks rhetorically of this elastic aspect of the Buchanan and Tullock system of thought.[14]

Second, related major concerns about Ostrom's argument inhere in the assumptive and derivative nature of the core ideational infrastructure of the theory of public choice. Numerous evidences and consequences of this assump- tive and derivative character will be developed shortly in some detail. Here note only one elementary fact: The character of the assumptions is vital, because such assumptions predetermine the range of derivations, given nimble minds and consistent logic. This cruciality of its assumptions does not get sufficient respect in the ideational infrastructure on which Ostrom relies. This neglect is puzzling, for some of those assumptions are at least controversial, and others are in fact increasingly denied by some of those involved in the technical development of public-choice theory.[15] So flexible is the underlying methodology, indeed, that such controversiality or denial is taken in full stride, without apparent concep- tual pause. When pushed on the issue of the "real-world inapplicability" of one of his assumptions, or about a conflict between them, for example, Ostrom only allows that "it might be necessary" to make another assumption as to the "prevailing condition."[16]

Such flexibility might be useful, of course, but only if great care were taken to emphasize what was being done and when, and when appropriate efforts were made to test assumptions that relate to the empirical world. Such care and efforts do not appear probable, given Ostrom's broad system of thought, for reasons which should become increasingly clear. Hence, Long goes for what he sees as the jugular of this kind of reliance on those types of assumptions. They may not mirror reality, and both practically and methodologically, reliance on them is counterproductive and derivations from them are highly suspect. Referring to two well-known public-choice theorists, for example, Long concludes that they "can argue with elegant and impeccable logic about unicorns. The cogency of their logic, however, does not demonstrate the existence of unicorns."[17]

Third, Ostrom's argument also induces concern because of what is here conveniently labeled the "direction" of its methodology, as well as that of its ideational infrastructure. This directionality adds force to conclusions like that of Long just sketched above.

Ostrom's basic thrust is from assumptions about reality to prescriptions about how the real world should be. This directionality makes the public-choice theorist more central than the testing of reality, and provides no defense at all against the human bias to see in reality what we are predisposed to see. Hence, the centrality of testing reality, of raising the probability that intersubjective judgments will reflect more of reality than the specific life experiences or preferences of single observers. Building complex ideational systems on assumptions about reality is hazardous, especially in the absence of major motivation to test those assumptions early in the game. In the main, this motivation characterizes neither Ostrom nor the public-choice literature. Indeed, one careful observer regards "the virtual absence of empirical concern as a major weakness in the collective choice literature."[18] Moreover, as Baker notes: "It is difficult to determine unequivocally the extent to which assumptions proceeding from or incorporated with the theory stem from ideological concerns, from what public-choice analysts believe or value as persons."[19]

In sum, it is unclear whether and to what extent public-choice theory reflects the world or ideological concerns; it is moot regarding the degree to which its theoretic agreements mirror reality or the life experiences, beliefs, or preferences of the theorists. The only certainty is that Ostrom takes no great pains to safeguard his theory against being an analytical Rorschach, a structure reflecting individual needs or beliefs but that purports to deal with the phenomenal world.

Of course, one may build a theory based on any assumptions that one fancies—for example, the practice of an architecture may be grounded on the assumption that the only building materials are spaghetti and gum drops. Even such bizarre assumptions can sometimes prove useful. Whether that occurs, however, depends not so much on the assumptions as on how the derivative theory is used. One could regard such theory as hypotheses to be tested, as some theorists of public choice are careful to do.[20] Such testing can do multiple duty: It might provide evidence as to whether the assumptions underlying the theory are more or less correct; it might suggest that the original assumptions are so simplistic as to generate theory that ill suits reality; and so on. Alternatively, one could treat such derivative theory as the basis for making action plans for intervening in reality or (worse still) for describing how things should be. This is a very dangerous business indeed. Far more rather than less, Ostrom's methodological approach encourages the latter treatment as theory as an end of the road rather than as hypotheses to be tested.

Fourth, neither Ostrom nor public-choice theory provides an acceptable place for values. Indeed, in concepts critical to the ideational structure, the value judgment is made that almost all value judgments cannot be made or should not be made. The purpose is to avoid making subjective, nonempirical judgments; but the approach also seeks to legitimate that avoidance via subjective nonempirical judgments. That does not wash.

The present point has a paradoxical character. That is, Ostrom's democratic administration is value-loaded in critical senses, a fact concerning which both writer and readers could hardly be unaware. And critics like De Gregori and Baker are quick to emphasize the metavalues of the public-choice system—a "conservatism," a clear preference for those exercising economic power as contrasted with electoral or political power, a bias toward serving some extant preferences rather than encouraging the development of other preferences, a commitment to the status quo rather than to change, and so on.[21]

When theoretical push comes to shove, however, the public-choice approach variously makes a value judgment that excludes almost all other value judgments. Consider the Pareto criterion or optimum, which proposes that a change is desirable if it makes at least one person better off in that person's own judgment, while at the same time it leaves not even a single person worse off in their own judgment. Proponents of the criterion argue that it has two basic attractions: (1) It is ethically appropriate; and (2) the decisions made consistent with it are potentially verifiable by empirical analysis alone.[22] To develop the point, the underlying position is that of logical positivism, which considers as scientifically meaningful only those statements whose truth or falsity can be demonstrated by empirical test, at least in principle. Superficially, the Pareto criterion nicely fits this requirement. As Merewitz and Sosnick explain: "If one adopts the Pareto criterion and then states that a change is desirable, the statement becomes equivalent to two other statements" which, at least in principle, can be empirically verified or rejected—"first, the change would move some persons to more preferred positions and no one to a less preferred position; second, the person making the statement approves the change."[23]

This line of argument may seem attractive, but it has the liability of walking away from most or all issues that are morally or ethically troublesome, as well as away from those issues that are likely to be encountered in practice.

Morally or ethically, the Pareto criterion in effect (and one supposes, by design) seeks to limit attention to these three values: (1) It is desirable to let people have what they want; (2) it is undesirable to impose on people anything that they do not want; and (3) it is legitimate to neglect all else save that which people want or do not want.[24] Most of the interesting issues in choice, and many of the significant ones, are thereby discarded. Hence, what may seem an unexceptionable criterion may have profound consequences, not all of them desirable for those unwilling to make the value judgment that almost all value judgments cannot or should not be made. Merewitz and Sosnick effectively state the case for the unwilling:

> Giving people what they want, or not imposing on them what they do not want, may have doubtful merit. This is clearly so if the people involved are ill-informed (as with hazardous products or complicated medical care), if the people are incompetent (as with youngsters, oldsters, and morons), or if they have lost self-control (as with addicts, drunks, and the bereaved). Moreover, what the affected persons want may not be everything that matters to the person passing judgment. He may be concerned about national interests, about accurate reporting, about due process of law, about making prison unpleasant, and so on. Even a humanitarian, then, and certainly a dictator, may find the Pareto criterion unacceptable at times.[25]

Practically, the Pareto criterion gains internal consistency only at the cost of defining out of its domain many issues of practical moment, if not all of them. For example, it does not deal with the class of situations in which some individuals would be better off and some worse off if an action were taken. The putative reason for the exclusion is that such situations require an interpersonal comparison of gains and losses that in turn rests on some evaluation of the relative work or value of what specifics are gained or lost by specific individuals. This evaluation, of course, is not in principle possible on empirical grounds, and hence is eschewed. This exclusion of a massive class of situations is apparently motivated by the attractions of the approach underlying the Pareto criterion, which requires only gross resultant judgments by individuals as to whether they are better off or not, no matter what they are better off about. This convenience finesses value issues, except for the three detailed above. In addition, the domain of the Pareto criterion is even further narrowed by the requirement that the affected persons and their reactions are known with certainty. The narrowing is especially severe in those cases in which persons not yet born will be affected, or when the effects are probabilistic tendencies whose actual impact is dependent upon complex conditions that are themselves uncertain.[26] Patently, this means that the Pareto criterion will apply to very few issues of public policy. It conceptually avoids value judgments by practically avoiding most classes of significant choice.

Not all public-choice theorists accept the full conceptual baggage of the Pareto criterion,[27] but few avoid the extreme simplification of values that is so clearly a part of its theoretical development. Indeed, the Pareto criterion is broadly attractive, definitely a "now" notion with its dominant undercurrent of "do your own thing." Moreover, both the idea and its associated metaphysical pathos convey a strong commonsensicalness that can lull even the wary, a let's-get-right-to-the-heart-of-it quality that promises to order nicely what would otherwise be complex imponderables.

Ostrom is not one of those who succeeds in resisting the allures of the extreme simplification of the central issues of values. There is a central irony here. For Ostrom in some places, as in Tables 5.2 and 5.3, rejects the notion of any separation of politics from administration and urges that the latter be disciplined by the former. But he otherwise accepts an ideational network that in effect removes from politics so much of its essence, that tumultuous clash of values that inheres in the effort to define the role of the good citizen in the just state.

In Ostrom, to develop the point, the clearest evidence of the simplification of values is the insistent emphasis on consumer preference or utility as sovereign, as in the concept of methodological individualism or "individualistic choice." De Gregori apparently either does not appreciate fully how "preference" or "utility" have become value surrogates in public-choice theory, by way of such conceptual inventions as the Pareto criterion, or he strongly rejects that surrogate status. Hence he hammers hard at the fact that "Ostrom and the public-choice theorists have a strange concept of freedom"; and he stresses how they in effect consider one set of tastes or preferences as clearly superior to another, for which judgment he sees no theoretical justification in public-choice theory. De Gregori complains:

> It does not matter [to public-choice theorists] that the electorate may have opted for collective action; only market decisions are acceptable data. Again, there is an a-historical element. Tastes are always taken as "given." "Given" by whom? God? Human nature? Or are our tastes and preferences a product of past behavior and conditioning? ...[28]

We have the further question of freedom from what? Or freedom for what? In effect, Ostrom and the public-choice theorists—by their insistence

that only market decisions provide acceptable data and appropriate "freedom"—
consider one set of tastes or preferences as clearly superior to others, for example, to those reflected in elections. De Gregori sees no theoretical justification
for that superiority and, moreover, is troubled by the lack of associated
specificity. He asks: "Freedom from what? Or freedom for what?"

De Gregori insists on seeing the full array of values that provide specific
content for generic terms like "tastes," "preferences," "freedom," and other
similar concepts, so that priorities may be determined when tastes are in conflict. De Gregori is at once profoundly correct in this insistence and yet
irrelevant for public-choice theorists. For the methodology and derivative theory
of public-choice theory define what De Gregori insists upon as of no consequence, as nonexistent at least for purposes of analysis and—given some
incaution—as nonexistent, period. Recall that a central feature of the public-
choice argument is that almost all value judgments cannot or should not be
made. The three value judgments that can or should be made from the public-
choice position are:

- That it is desirable to let people have what they want.

- That it is undesirable to impose on people anything they do not want.

- That it is legitimate to neglect all else save that which people want or do
  not want.

Probably Improbable Assumptions

Concern about Ostrom's ideational structure is especially appropriate because
some of his central assumptions are at least probably improbable, a fact that
his methodology will fail to highlight. At the broadest level, consider an
elemental concern about the probability that market or decentralized strucures
can solve our public problems, their alleged absence being Ostrom's basic
diagnosis of what ails us and their reinvigoration being his prime prescription
for remedial therapy. If they worked so well, to paraphrase De Gregori, one
wonders how we generated our present problems that need solving. Of course,
some may argue that our present problems derive from our relatively recent
abandonment of good political-economic sense. Again, one wonders why it was
abandoned in the first place by rational, utility-maximizing individuals who are
at the very center of public-choice theory.

But let such one-liners pass. The probable improbability of Ostrom's
assumptions will be demonstrated in detail. Let us conveniently return to
Ostrom's central commitment to "methodological individualism." Essentially,
Ostrom proposes a model of man that seeks to explain public policies in terms of
the rational decisions of individuals which act as an unseen hand of market
forces that determine the supply of public goods as well as the demand for them.

This basic commitment, in turn, requires a host of definitions and assumptions about how people behave. Thus decisions are considered rational so long as they contribute to the attainment of specific goals or objectives, which are taken to be mutually consistent as well as transitive, so that if a person prefers decision A to B and B to C he also will prefer A to C. In sum, the assumptions and definitions are that the decision maker also will act consistent with:[29]

- Self-interest

- Rationality

- The quality of information available

- Law and order

- The choice of a maximizing strategy, a least-cost way of achieving preferences

It is tempting to be picky with such necessary underpinnings of methodological individualism. For example, what if the actual expressions of self-interest conflict with the assumption of law and order? In the "absence of any law and order assumption," Ostrom can only advise, "it might be necessary" to make another assumption as to "the prevailing human condition."[30]

The mind boggles because, to score a debater's point, it might on the same grounds also be necessary to abandon many of the other assumptions and definitions just listed. Rather than being so congenial as to easily acknowledge that different assumptions might be necessary, that is, the prudent course is to make as certain as possible that different assumptions are *not* necessary because the ones used are adequate expressions of our existing knowledge of the world around us. The prudent course is not taken, however. Consequently, the admission that it "might be necessary" to make other assumptions is far too mild a formulation. For example, the public-choice theorist's insistence on transitivity in individual decision making required for least-cost decisions is troublesome. Transitivity would exist in the case of voting, for example, if a voter who prefers alternative 1 to 2 and alternative 2 to 3, also prefers alternative 1 to 3.

The public-choice theorists' insistence on transitivity seems a prime example of how the assumed need to preserve ideational integrity can be multiply mischievous. To wit: Serious reasons urge believing that transitivity is not common in individual choice, that our social and political institutions are such that they present few transitive choice situations, that even Ostrom denies the voter the volume and quality of information on which transitivity must rest, and that in any case insistence on transitivity in important choices like voting would lead to very curious consequences except under quite limited conditions. Consequently, transitivity seems too restrictive a central condition to build into a theory of choice.

The case for each of the three counterpoints to the insistence on transitivity can be outlined. First, psychologists have not been able to establish that transitivity is characteristic of human behavior. Indeed, Weinstein concludes flatly that "most empirical tests of choice behavior appear to reflect intransitive preference patterns."[31] Second, the complex concurrent and multiple majorities characteristic of American politics and political parties do not encourage the posing of policy choices in ways that facilitate or even permit transitive choice.[32] Third, insistence on transitivity in voting typically would lead to consequences diametrically opposed to the values that public choice theorists publicly espouse, including the freedom of the individual decision maker.[33] We cannot here present the straightforward but lengthy argument that establlishes this irony, but we can conveniently quote Dahl on the central point. Dahl notes: "Arrow shows that if there are more than two alternatives, any method for making social decisions that insures transitivity in the decisions must necessarily be either dictated by one person or imposed against the preferences of every individual." Dahl concludes: "This brilliantly developed and quite startling argument has, unfortunately, so far been totally ignored by political scientists."[34] Dahl wrote these words in 1956. The last two decades have seen an extensive literature develop around the voting paradox but, despite subtle qualifications and issues in doubt, Dahl's conclusion still appears more appropriate than not.[35]

The prudent implication is caution about accepting any derivations from such public-choice assumptions, thus used, an impression that is reinforced by considering one central aspect of methodological individualism. Is the intent to deny the independent existence of supraindividual collectivities like "groups"? Generally speaking, the answer is yes, for such a view is consistent with the emphasis on methodological individualism in public-choice theory. But some public-choice theorists seem to want to have it both ways, as do Buchanan and Tullock. They note:

> Our conception of democratic process has much in concert with that accepted by the school of political science which follows Arthur Bentley in trying to explain collective decision-making in terms of the interplay of group interest. Throughout our analysis the word "group" could be substituted for the word "individual" without significantly affecting the results.[36]

This denial of the need for multilevel analysis is clearly convenient, but it almost certainly means a major reduction in the explanatory power of any derivative theory. Whether the answer is a straightforward denial of supraindividual collectivities, or pained efforts to suggest some kind of equivalence between "individual" and "group," reality is too recalcitrant to fit such economizing fomulations. To be sure, only individuals can perceive and make decisions. But what of the common experience that the same individuals typically behave in radically different ways, following deliberate manipulations of the "climate" of the successive groups of which they are members?[37] Such effects clearly require a supraindividual level of description and explanation. Or better still, what of groups in which all or many members come to decisions that they personally do not prefer, or even abhor, on profoundly serious[38] as well as trivial[39] matters? The alternative to denying multiple levels of social organization is to presume the irrationality of mankind, or to postulate their "herd" or "crowd" quality, which names or villifies but does not explain.

What does this catalog imply? Clearly, public-choice theorists do not seem sensitive to such critical dilemmas in their ideation. Pretty clearly, also, Ostrom would like to increase the role of the individual decision maker in public-policy choices. All well and good, and many of us applaud that intent. And there is no doubt that assumptions like methodological individualism provide conceptual support for such an intent. But it appears that too much is made of a convenient thing. Not only does Ostrom articulate a "should," which is proper enough, but he accepts a theoretical infrastructure that conveniently recognizes only separate individuals. He thus empirically flies in the face of what is common and long-standing experience. As noted, Ostrom's flexibile methodology encourages such practices. But so much the worse for the methodology. As De Gregori concludes, if any theorists assume "that large numbers of people do not consider themselves members of economic and social classes [and consequently that they do not] act politically in these terms (that is, collectively) [the theorists] have a sizable body of data to refute."[40] Methodological sleight of hand does not change that stubborn fact. The neglect also may imply tragic misdirection if, as many argue, the individual needs to define self largely in social interaction, and if freedom is possible only in a special kind of society. Consequently, emphasis on the separate individual will in such cases result in not asking many of the appropriate questions.

Critical Gaps in Content and Meaning

Beyond relying on improbable assumptions, Ostrom's position and its underlying public-choice theory also lack critical content or meaning. Indeed, this puts the point mildly, as will be shown in two central particulars. The focus, in turn, is on the unsatisfactory (indeed, peculiar) treatment of self-interest and efficiency in Ostrom's formulation specifically, and then in public choice theory more broadly.

Whose Self-Interest about What?

Public-choice theory waffles badly on the issues of self-interest and consequently finds itself between the analytical rock and a hard place. In an assumed attempt to be comprehensive, it ends up saying little clearly or consistently. De Gregori's conclusion is harsher still. Referring to two central figures in public-choice theory, he concludes that their writings about "self-interest contain neither a concept of self nor a concept of interests, and we are left with a logical or mechanical construct without content."[41]

The basic point is easy enough to document, whatever the harshness of the overall evaluation. One of the patent things that should be true of methodological individuals is that they operate in terms of their self-interest narrowly defined. This preserves the sense of the "separate individual" as well as other associated ideation of public-choice theory. However, some public-choice theorists apparently recognize that the narrow definition of self-interest is inadequate for describing reality. In any case, some significant public-choice theorists take care to emphasize that their methodological individuals have a broad-banded self-interest. Their motivation is not only "narrowly hedonistic," but it can also be (and often is) "egoistic or altruistic."[42]

Ostrom accepts the broad-banded notion of self-interest,[43] and, however motivated, that acceptance creates far greater theoretical problems than it solves. Indeed, the irony may be that there is no solution, only a dilemma. Perhaps De Gregori is correct in concluding that self-interest as a postulate is either false in its narrow form, or trivial as a broad-band notion.[44]

Both falsity and triviality can be established by considering three kinds of problems for public-choice theory implied by broad-band self-interest. First, the "what" of self-interest is no longer clear, and the predictive power of public-choice theory thereby suffers. De Gregori nicely makes the point by observing that if individuals are assumed to be profit maximizers, it is then reasonable to talk "about a form of behavior in which individuals seek to maximize an empirically definable function that is called economic gain." But this advantage vanishes in broad-band self-interest. De Gregori makes the contrast vividly: "Call the motivating principle 'utility' or 'ego' or whatever, and one has a principle that can be defined [only] in terms of the ensuing action.... It does not explain or predict the action, it merely names it...."[45]

The same point, indeed, was apparently clear to Buchanan and Tullock in one of the early and seminal books on public choice. Broad-banded self-interest, they recognize, permits an economic assumption of only the "barest essentials." As they note: "The economic assumption is simply that the representative or the average individual, when confronted with real choice in exchange, will choose 'more' rather than 'less.' "[46] This is neither a powerful assumption nor a comforting one, what with the authors' single quotation marks around what are fundamental concepts in their system of thought. Note also that "more of what" is not specified. Descriptively, then, the assumption permits only such a gentle a posteriori statements as: When I observe an economic choice, I know it was motivated by the chooser's judgment that the choice provides more of something, but more of what and how what is measured I cannot now say, and may never be able to say. Such a statement can never be tested and hence cannot be shown to be false. Consequently, it provides a questionable foundation for theoretical development.

Second, broad-band self-interest obscures a second issue that is crystal clear in narrow concepts. *Whose* self-interest becomes a major unknown rather than a given. To explain, it is the separate individual's self-interest that is patently at the center of narrow concepts. In allowing altruism (or whatever) as a motive, in contrast, the issue of whose self-interest is involved takes on complex proportions. The conceptual door is thereby opened to various social or collective processes, including group formation as one way that individuals can act in terms of the best interests of others as well as of themselves. Some public-choice theorists follow Sen in this regard. He explains that:

> The society in which a person lives, the class to which he belongs, the relation that he has with the social and economic structure of the community, are relevant to a person's choice not merely because they affect the nature of his personal interests but also because they influence his value system including his notion of "due" concern for other members of society. The insular economic man pursuing his self-interest to the exclusion of all other considerations may represent an assumption that pervades much of traditional economics, but it is not a particularly useful model for understanding problems of social choice.[47]

Other public-choice theorists—including Ostrom—avoid such an admission, presumably because it undercuts the "methodological individualism" so central in public-choice theory. Perhaps that is why Buchanan and Tullock go as far as— but no further than—noting that the word "group" can be used interchangeably with the word "individual" in their analysis without significantly affecting their results. But this requires walking an analytical tightrope. As De Gregori observes of Buchanan and Tullock's admission of broad-band self-interest:

> [They] are talking about persons acting in terms of the best interest of others, clearly a social, judgmental process. Proceeding along this train of thought, one is not far from allowing individuals to conceive of themselves as members of a group and to make decisions and act upon them as members of groups.[48]

Third, these problems with what and whose self-interest unfortunately do not disturb the flow of the public-choice argument. De Gregori attributes this major oversight to the illusion of understanding the phenomena that are only named by the broad-band concept of self-interest. He explains:

> Economists prefer models with determined behavior patterns. Buchanan and Tullock are no exception. With legerdemain, they

forget their original disclaimer, and the methodological individual of their model is acting like the plain old garden variety, the economic man of their disciplinary colleagues.[49]

Efficiency for What?

The gaps in meaning or content in Ostrom's approach also are especially prominent in the second criterion in Table 5.3 for determining the scale of public organizations consistent with democratic administration. The deficiences are conveniently expressed in the context of the critical question with which Ostrom does not deal: Efficiency for what? Note that much the same analysis applies to such similar questions as: Effective for what?

In contrast to Ostrom's generic usage, "efficiency" can be approached only from at least five distinguishable if sometimes related perspectives. To illustrate an "efficient" organization may be one that (1) makes timely response to market or clientele demands, (2) is innovative in developing new missions and roles, (3) is sized appropriately for its dominant technology, (4) is big enough to take advantage of economics of scale but not so big as to generate offsetting diseconomies, or (5) provides a variety of conveniences, including short-run control over markets, customers, suppliers, or unions.

It is not altogether certain what meaning Ostrom wishes to attach to the term "efficiency." At one point, for example, he notes that consumer preferences are central in providing the required content; perhaps they even exclusively provide that necessary meaning. This is the sense of this proposition, which Ostrom italicizes in the original: "Producer efficiency in the absence of consumer utility is without economic meaning."[50] This effort is not analytically satisfying, however. Clearly, it runs afoul of the several considerations raised earlier in connection with self-interest. Ostrom's dictum about economic meaning itself has no tolerably precise meaning, then, to put it bluntly.

Ostrom's failure to deal effectively with the goals defining efficiency also impacts significantly on his broader argument, as can be shown by illustrating the lack of content or meaning in his criteria sketched in Table 5.3. Recall that Ostrom prescribed in part that: "The most efficient solution would require the modification of boundary conditions so as to assure a producer of public goods the most favorable economy of scale, as well as effective control."[51]

The prescription has no tolerably specific meaning, in the absence of an unambiguous answer to the question of efficiency for what purposes. During World War II, for example, it was the common experience that the most monopolistic industries were "most efficient" in a number of then relevant senses. Thus, it was easier for government officials to deal with Alcoa than with the multitudinous producers of feeds and grains, for more or less obvious reasons. Of course, Alcoa also was in a position to be more troublesome if it so chose, but wartime conditions were well suited by central control and planning

over the production of aluminum, given acceptable combinations of patriotism
and whatever. Because short-run control was facilitated, the answer to how big
Alcoa should be was: the bigger the better, and the greater share of the market
the better. In the immediate postwar period, different considerations became
prominent in public policy, and different answers consequently were appropriate. Both before and during the war, however, the central question was the
same—efficiency for what purpose?

The emptiness of the phrase "the most favorable economy of scale" also
can be demonstrated in less obvious ways. Consider Ostrom's contrast of two
ways of viewing efficiency: "One way views efficiency as being expressed
through principles of hierarchical organization," by which he refers to concepts
such as "unity of command, span of control, chain of command, depart-
mentation by major functions, and direction by single heads of authority in
subordinate units."[52] Ostrom notes that these principles are alleged to be
universally applicable and that this first way of viewing efficiency is direct and
uncomplicated. "The greater the degree of specialization, professionalization,
and linear organization in a unitary chain of command, the greater the
efficiency." The bigger the unitary organization, in short, the better. Ostrom
adds by way of contrast: "The other way views efficiency in terms of a cost
calculus," which Ostrom asserts will permit the "accomplishment of a
specifiable objective at least cost; or a higher level of performance at a given
cost."[53]

Several observations are relevant to this significant contrast. First, there
is no available cost calculus of the kind required. Even the traditional tools
and approaches for financial analysis imply serious issues and deficiencies.[54]
Worse still are the problems of taking into account a broader range of considerations that are typically neglected in managerial accounting and financial
reports, factors such as the motivation or morale of the work force, the long-run
versus the short-run consequences of managerial actions, and so forth. Perhaps
the most that can be said here is that such work is only a little way down the
track.[55] Most chronic by far are the problems with "social accounting," which
seeks to relate organizational costs to broad goals or ends.[56]

It is not clear why Ostrom chose to introduce cost calculus reorganization
scale, but he does so at the cost of some violence to central notions of public-
choice theory, as well as at the substantial loss of creditibility of his own
argument. Let us avoid the morass of intent and focus on consequences. Consistent with Ostrom's emphasis on markets, methodological individualism, and
so on, it would have been seemly to argue that the scale of public organizations
on the supply side would be, or should be, a function of the same invisible-hand
market forces that public-choice theorists seek to energize and legitimate on the
demand side. In contrast, he introduces the cost calculus, which implies a cadre
of experts, with data far beyond that available to his individual choice makers

and ostensibly with some power or authority to influence the scale of public organizations. Suddenly, Ostrom finds himself squarely facing the kind of problem that PPBS enthusiasts had promised to solve, those very centralizing, rationalist, elitist proponents from whom Ostrom otherwise seeks to distance his argument.[57] Ostrom is not successful at transcending their failure. Indeed, he basically promises a "cost calculus" without actually providing one. On this issue, Ostrom is in the same boat as the conceptual enemy. The conclusions applying to PPBS efforts thus apply to Ostrom in this regard. Consider their hope to justify appropriations or expenditures for public programs. Merewitz and Sosnick quash that hope by recalling the harsh and unavoidable realities. "To *justify* an appropriation," they observe, "it is necessary to show that the benefits to be obtained outweigh the benefits that could be obtained by spending the same amount of money for other purposes or by cutting taxes. *And this cannot be shown.*" They conclude: "No procedure is available that will show whether expenditures are or are not justified. The answer is a matter of subjective judgment."[58]

Second, as the reference to social accounting implies, and as the excerpt from Merewitz and Sosnick explicitly notes, there *can be no* cost calculus for determining the appropriate scale of any organization until an answer to a key question is reasonably in hand. That key question: Efficiency for what? The point should be momentously obvious, a fact that stands in curious contrast to its neglect by Ostrom and others.

Third, Ostrom's juxtaposition of hierarchical perfection and the cost calculus constitutes a straw man. That is to say, for nearly the preceding half-century, the "principles of organization" have been attacked with great gusto and even with some effect.[59] Although "contingency theorists" will argue that the principles describe the appropriate form of organization under certain technological and product-line conditions,[60] the definite drift of research and commentary argues the appropriateness of guidelines for organizing that differ significantly from the "principles." These guidelines were long ago sketched in the public administration literature,[61] and also have received fulsome attention in the literature on both generic[62] and business[63] administration. The most common citations in Ostrom predate this work by a decade and usually far longer, with most attention going to the central *Papers on the Science of Administration* (1937) by Gulick and Urwick, and to Simon's powerful but early (1946) critique of the "principles" literature.

There is no point here in detailing these emerging guidelines for organizing work, for that has been done much earlier in detail elsewhere. Moreover, a brief primer to these guidelines appears in Chapter 2, which the reader might consult with profit. Here note that those emerging guidelines constitute an alternative to the cost calculus that Ostrom proposes will decide the scale of organizations but on which no one can deliver.

Simultaneously Opposed Courses of Action

Still more troublesome, Ostrom's prescriptions have the common unhappy feature of recommending two or more courses of action that are at least potentially antithetical. Consider Table 5.3, in which the scale of public organizations is to be determined, *inter alia,* by the criterion of control and the "democratic ideal of local self-determination." There are two basic difficulties. First, Ostrom provides little or no guidance as to appropriate decisions when choices between the criteria must be made. As Baker asks:

> ... how does one account for the scale of a public enterprise which, in the process of "internalizing" the consequences of producing or providing a public good or service under the criterion of control, exceeds the boundary conditions necessary to achieve optimal economies of scale requisite under the criterion of efficiency? The boundary conditions required for regulation purposes may not coincide with the boundary conditions necessary for obtaining optimal economies of scale. Or in attempting to meet the requisites of the criterion of political representation, how does one *make* coterminous the scale of formal public organization, the public affected, and the political community?[64]

Because these choices always must be made, and because they are often fiendishly complex ones in the bargain, it is not useful to prescribe a decision rule that is moot in this central particular.

Second, it is not clear how a kind of runaway-train effect is to be avoided, or stopped once it starts. To rely on Baker again: "There appears to be virtually no upper limit to the scale of American public enterprise if the control criterion were to take precedence over the other criteria"[65] in Table 5.3. The problem is especially compounded by the fact that a critical issue in the scale of a public enterprise is the number of levels of organization. Assume, for example, that it is possible to define some optimum size for a federal land-reclamation project in Arizona, using cost calculus or whatever. Still open are questions of the size of the regional suborganization of which that project may be a part, of the size of the federal cabinet-level organization of which that region may be a part, and so on. What is clearly local to one of these levels of aggregation may be cosmopolitan to some and yet impossibly provincial to still others. In such a case, moreover, control may take on more compelling qualities than local self-determination. This will especially be the case if one of the economies of scale is the ability to compete successfully for funds at the congressional level where, all things considered, being bigger may be very useful whatever the scale of enterprise consistent with local self-determination. In addition, pressures for adding overhead levels are often generated by lower hierarchical levels as well. Thus hierarchies have many uses in addition to monitoring or even coercing lower cadres. They include broader perspective, taking the heat attendant to a decision that should be made but that local officials fear making because it violates some powerful interests or figures,[66] and so on through a very long list.

Some Awkward Probable Answers to Four Central Questions

Worse still, both Ostrom's approach and that of the public-choice theorists can have major consequences opposite to those intended. The broader family of unanticipated consequences can be viewed in connection with four main questions:

- Is decentralized government better, more democratic, and more moral?
- Are smaller public organizations more effective and more responsive?
- Is nonintervention clearly more appropriate when resources are growing scarcer?
- Do "cycles of governance" make a difference?

The examples of unexpected and unintended consequences imply that the ideational infrastructure of public choice is not yet ready to provide a framework for public policy. By implication, the consequences imply the need for a contingency theory rather than the unidirectional theory of public choice espoused by students such as Ostrom.

Is Decentralization Better, More Democratic, and More Moral?

One nativist thrust of the public-choice position is that decentralization is preferable to a unitary hierarchy responsible to one man. The logic underlying this basic bias of public-choice theory seems clear enough. Individuals possess only what March and Simon call "bounded rationality," which means that no one decision maker can pretend to a broad knowledge of utility preferences needed to achieve maximum efficiency. Thus, public-choice theorists prefer decentralized price or market systems, because they make fewer demands on the decision maker by reducing the scale of the system of choices to be coped with.

There is no particular objection to this emphasis in public-choice theory, if it is not pushed too far. But public-choice theorists are not restrained in this regard, perhaps because they are coerced by their own fixation on individualistic choice and the representative individual. Indeed, ample reasons suggest the validity of this broad equivalency between public-choice theory and Ostrom's political theory. Taste or preference is the basic value surrogate in public-choice theory; and decentralization of government plays much the same role in Ostrom's thought. Thus public-choice theory avoids this question: Whose preferences about what? And Ostrom usually neglects a similar question: What degree of decentralization, when, for which purposes? Both approaches commonly simplify the issue of values. In both cases, also, cautionary comments are required because of their similarly inadequate approach. To be fair, there are points where Ostrom argues (as in Table 5.2) that a "variety of different organizational arrangements can be used to provide different public goods and services." To be equally fair, however, Ostrom is on balance not very interested in that "variety."

Decentralization is far from simple, but some brief and meaningful things may be said about it here. Primarily, public choice theorists see centralization and decentralization as opposite extremes of a continuum. More useful is a tripartite notion, such as that shown in Figure 5.1. Public-choice theorists generally, and Ostrom specifically, neglect this distinction. And one major consequence is that their strong preference for decentralization may result in chaotic localism, which, in turn, may only make more likely the very centralization that public choice theorists say they abhor.

The underlying argument can be sketched. In sharply contraposing centralization and decentralization, public-choice theorists in effect might support chaotic localism, a situation in which effective powers are lodged in small units of government wherein local minorities may be poorly treated, policies can vary enormously between local constituencies, and so on. This is a possible, perhaps even probable, consequence of championing decentralization without reference to the values to be served thereby. Such a consequence occurred, for example, when race relations were considered a local matter. There are two probable outcomes in such cases: (1) The need deprivation will persist over long periods of time; or (2) superordinate units of government are likely to

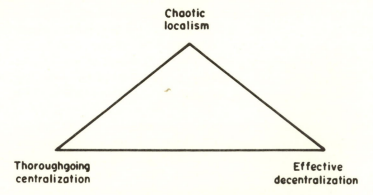

Fig. 5.1   Tripartite notion of decentralization/centralization.

centralize decision making in the particular issue area in question, all the more decisively the longer the status quo persists. Presumably neither outcome is the one desired by public-choice theorists.

It seems reasonable to surmise, however, that neither Ostrom's nor the public-choice logic permits any other way out. To illustrate, the distinction between the two brands of decentralization—that is, chaotic localism and effective decentralization—clearly rests on value judgments. However, public-choice theory overtly seeks to avoid most value judgments. Hence, by hypothesis, the failure to distinguish between varieties of decentralization may rest on the failure to specify values. This may also explain the public-choice theorist's typical failure to stress that centralization also might serve important values. It is more or less obvious, in contrast, that decentralization is congenial to individualistic choice. Decentralization it is, then, in the absence of the specification of values that will permit judgments as to which mixes of centralization or decentralization or whatever are appropriate for specified purposes or goals at specific times.

This elemental sketch illustrates the conceptual difficulties about which careful observers like Fesler sought to warn those zealously committed to decentralization as a doctrinal *summum bonum,* a "greatest good."[67] Their warning stresses three points. First, the preference for centralization or decentralization cannot be a matter of either/or, but should be a dynamic, evolving, and oscillating process of fine tuning institutions to current problems. Failure to recognize the point implies only trouble, if not an Alice-in-Wonderland state where even benign intentions yield unwanted effects. As Friedrich notes: "This continual change is a matter of fact; but unless it is clearly recognized and institutionally provided for, all decentralization of power [is] apt to become [a] source of tension and conflict. . . ."[68]

Second, it is specious to link democracy, freedom, and decentralization, as Ostrom does,[69] in common with much of the public-choice literature. This easy marriage neglects a reality that often has been painfully obvious. As Hart notes: "Democratic processes do not necessarily result from nor are democratic ideals necessarily maximized by decentralization. In fact, the opposite has often occurred, and independent local political structures have worked against democratic ideals."[70] Moreover, the linkage of decentralization with democracy and freedom equates values with means, and also creates major analytical and practical difficulties. We cannot improve on Fesler's formulation: "In extreme principle [such a conceptual linkage] can mean anarchy; and in muddled practice it can be so closely associated with islands of group or community self-determination that subordination of the individual to a local autocracy may be lost from view, as can the potentially liberating infuence of a national leadership committed to development of social and economic opportunities for individual achievement of personal goals."[71]

Third, the doctrinal approach to decentralization neglects the critical role of the central government in facilitating movement toward those goals that decentralization is intended to achieve. Briefly, decentralization implies a viable definition of the parameters within which local governments can act without becoming so balkanized that the necessary context of unity about fundamentals is destroyed, that a chaotic localism comes to be and persists. Without such a viable definition of value parameters, to illustrate, decentralization could equally serve reactionary as well as ameliorative politics, with the worst-case potential for such polarization as that which led to the Civil War. In the absence of specified values, that is, decentralization is like an unguided missile. In Fesler's more restrained and detailed language:

> National legislation, overriding local objections and implemented by national administrative action, is often required to democratize the selection of local officials, to establish viable units of local govern-ment with the size, resources, and diversity of interests that are preconditions of effective local self-government, to recruit and train skilled staff for local administration, to minimize corruption and regularize fiscal practices, to provide grants from national revenue to help finance the more impoverished communities. . . .[72]

Patently, these interventions by the central government are not consistent with a doctrinal vision of the decentralized polity, even if their motivation (as Fesler notes) is "often to save local self-government from itself."[73]

Are Smaller Public Organizations More Effective and More Responsive?

Perhaps the most dominant emphasis in Ostrom's thought is that "smaller government" will bring more effective and responsive provision of services, and Ostrom thereby sets himself a substantial challenge. To be sure, every age seems to have a retrospective vision of an uncomplicated and pleasing "prior condi-tion," a kind of nice sociopolitical predecessor of extant nastinesses and nuisances. Early on, there were the Garden of Eden and Marx's vision of pre-industrial society; more recently, the vision of a nation of "family farms" substained many; and there is an important theme of "back to fundamental nature" in some of today's communal experimentation.

Such nativist traditions notwithstanding, the vask bulk of the literature gives small-scale government no clear edge in being better,[74] more democratic,[75] or more moral,[76] given a gentle fuzziness about what "small scale" really means. Quite the opposite, in fact.

Let us begin with a debater's point or two. For one thing, Ostrom is never clear on what "small" is. Nor does it do for him to praise "smaller" more than "larger," thereby seeming to avoid the issue. For once any organization gets larger than one in which cozy face-to-face interaction is both possible and convenient, major differences in communication and influence patterns quickly develop.[77] This is the profound wisdom in Rousseau's observation in *du social contrat* that people can be free only where the I = They, that is, the condition under which the individual ego is the only monitor of its own behavior. Hence also, Rousseau's judgment that social man is "born free" but will "everywhere be in chains," for I = They only under very special and rare circumstances.

The profundity of such issues grossly outweighs the attention Ostrom gives them. And severe problems relate to even his very general and far from obvious position that the appropriate scale will vary "with the boundary condition of different fields of effects inherent in the provision of different public goods and services."[78] Even given maximum generosity, the word "inherent" still rankles. Only complex mixtures of empirical conditions and value positions will define what is an optimal scale. There is no more an inherent optimal scale for a public agency than there is an inherent optimal family size, independent of complex empirical conditions and especially value preferences. It all depends, within very wide limits.

But let us put aside such initial if basic concerns, in the spirit of seeking help wherever it is offered. What is Ostrom's argument for small (or smaller) public units? The preference in public-choice theory and Ostrom for smaller units is offered almost as a matter of fact, a given beyond any serious question or qualification. Or if that is too strong, the arguments of public-choice theorists like Ostrom are far from convincing. In the main, Ostrom refers to three basic public-service areas—education, police, and fire—and provides some data about the last two in seeking to establish that smaller is better. Briefly reviewing his evidence will be instructive.

Big-city education is in turmoil, Ostrom notes, turmoil that he attributes mostly to large and centralized school systems that are unresponsive to citizen preferences or tastes.[79] This attribution is buttressed only by minimal documentation and is characterized by an unseemly neglect of factors such as race, dislocated families, decaying center cities, plummeting tax bases, escalating public services, and so on. Not mentioned, also, is the fact that a common rationale for larger school systems rests on the perceived failure of smaller systems to do the required job.

Ostrom's contention that smaller is better in big-city education is coupled with a straightforward remedy, but not a convincing or even an entirely consistent one. As for the remedy, Bish and Ostrom note that the "big-city school systems are too large, and they should be broken up into smaller systems serving children in more homogeneous neighborhoods. . . ." Decentralized school districts, they conclude, "would give city residents control over their own schools such as that presently enjoyed by suburban residents."[80] The remedy has some troublesome features, however. Thus the overall record suggests that at least electoral participation varies directly with the size of jurisdiction;[81] hence, smaller scale may generate effects counter to those Ostrom hopes for and expects. This contrary consequence is no doubt due to many factors, including the media's regional and national focus. Decentralization of schools does not clearly dominate such factors, which need more direct confronting by those presenting decentralization as a more or less unqualified good. Moreover, Ostrom's remedy is basically inconsistent with the massive Coleman report, which—despite its own internal limitations—convincingly and persistently traces educational outcomes to the quality of the home and of the immediate environment of students.[82] Finally, Ostrom does not follow his own advice in some particulars, at the cost of possible inconsistency. "Accompanying decentralization would be expanded area-wide or state-wide financing," Bish and Ostrom note, "so that poorer districts would be able to provide a greater level of support for education. Wealthier districts would be free to tax at higher rates and provide more educational inputs above that general level."[83] Bish and Ostrom do not deal with the several possible inconsistencies, as between area-wide or state-wide financing and greater local control over schools.

Ostrom's case against police service is similar,[84] but is presented with more supporting data. Three empirical studies are referred to. More or less, services of larger police departments are said to cost more per capita,[85] and residents of small, independent communities are represented as more satisfied with the service their police departments provide.[86] These empirical efforts are to be applauded and encouraged, but they do not yield unequivocal interpretation. The central problem is that the underlying cost-benefit analysis is quite incomplete. For example, larger police departments studied did cost more per capita in two of the three cases, but no one knows whether or not they yielded commensurate benefits. It does seem that residents of larger jurisdictions have less favorable attitudes toward their police, but, as important as this trend may be, it clearly falls far short of a complete measure of benefits. Calculating these benefits would be very difficult, but that alone can permit specific comparisons of the kind required. Moreover, of course, it is anybody's guess as to how stable such attitudes are, how deeply they are rooted in experience or reliable information, and to what degree individual judgments of efficiency and effectiveness are made within a matrix of values or goals that meaningfully relate to the full range of police work. Such differences should be important in political debate and dialog.

The evidence about fire services is limited to one study, and it curiously supports a conclusion opposite to the one advertised: Smaller is not clearly better. To explain, Bish and Ostrom cite Ahlbrandt's study[87] of fire protection in Scottsdale, Arizona. Ahlbrandt provides important evidence supporting the efficacy of unorthodox arrangements, for Scottsdale's fire services are provided by a business firm, which seems to do an innovative and economic job, compared to reasonable estimates of what the costs would be if the service were provided by a traditional fire department. Ostrom proposes that this is due to the fact that the firm can be unbuckled by Scottsdale if it does poorly, a pressure for performance not felt so directly by a traditional fire department. This is perhaps true, although one could imagine alternative scenarios in other similar cases. Sweetheart arrangements between a firm and local politicans are possible, for example. Such possibilities aside, moreover, note that at least part of the firm's advantage comes from the fact that it serves not only Scottsdale, but "several other cities and unincorporated areas in Arizona."[88] Smaller is not necessarily better, that is to say, and it is incautious to compare the firm's costs with those of a traditional fire department restricted to Scottsdale.

Indeed, when all is said and done, large scale is not the only (or perhaps even the central) issue for Ostrom. Thus, in big-city education he himself identifies three causes of problems: "professionalization, large scale, and uniformity."[89] At other points, he observes that the "combination of professionalization and unionization has [made] organized teachers . . . relatively invulnerable to the directives of elected officials."[90]

There is a wicked probable paradox in all this: The emphasis on smaller scale may not only fail to achieve Ostrom's goals, but it may in fact be counterproductive in his own terms. The point is meant in several senses. Let us grant—though it is neither obvious nor necessarily true—that the development of narrow professionalization, unionization, and uniformity are causally related to size of school systems. Even then, it is doubtful whether those conditions would disappear if public units could somehow now be scaled down in size. Assume that Ostrom is successful in reducing the size of (let us say) school systems. Will the scale or policies of professional associations or unions, especially at state or national levels, be very much affected by such reductions? Not likely. The more probable consequence, in fact, is a substantial increase of the power of professional associations, unions, and government bureaucracies vis-à-vis the elected or appointed heads of the now-smaller school systems. This is precisely opposite to Ostrom's stated intentions, of course, and does nothing to reduce his concern about monopolistic powers of public unions and professional associations. Similarly, it is not clear that smaller scale implies less "uniformity," especially if by that term Ostrom excludes nonuniformity of the chaotic localism variety. Indeed, some evidence suggests that a substantial minimum size is required for many diversified educational programs,[91] such as those for exceptional children, for "organization development" in schools, for various forms of experimentation with curricula, forms of governance, and so on. Finally, uniformity need not always be an evil to be avoided—for example, there is nothing wrong with uniform agreement about the pursuit of high-quality educational outcomes.

To be fair, the rigorous comparison of larger versus smaller governmental units is extremely difficult, so it is understandable that Ostrom provides no convincing comparisons. But it is inadequate to argue, as does Ostrom basically, that smaller is preferable to larger in governmental units because, among other things, the latter lack a market with its accompanying "competitive force" and thus are less likely than businesses to be aware of diseconomies of scale; hence large units will simply grow larger rather than wisely or well.[92] That may be so. But it would have been useful to do more than proclaim the point, as in explaining why an organization like AT&T—which lacks a market in Ostrom's sense—is not only mammoth but effective as well as innovative. Much might be learned from such obvious cases. Or perhaps Ostrom could have explained the substantial differences in the effectiveness of similar-sized units within federal agencies like the Social Security Administration, because neither those units nor SSA possess markets. Such analyses would be critical in developing a full-fledged theory of the covariants of the effectiveness of public organizations. And, finally, Ostrom does not begin to test a fundamental assumption: Under which conditions is a "business" with a market in fact more effective than "government," size being held relatively constant.

In contrast to recommending such complex and demanding questions for analysis, Ostrom basically presumes what is at best a very complicated proof. And he is content with such general statements as "opportunities for improvements in efficiency through increased size will have been exhausted *for many services* in communities that reach a size of 50,000-150,000 population."[93] Among the signs he reads as portents of institutional failure of massive proportions, and which he attributes to large size, Ostrom notes that streets "can no longer be kept clean in many areas" of New York City;[94] and Los Angeles school administrators "can no longer cope with cockroaches."[95]

Is Non-Interventionism Clearly More Appropriate When Resources Are Growing Scarcer?

Perhaps the most subtle snare in the public-choice argument inheres in its assumption of relative resource affluence and in the related prescription for governmental noninterventionism. To preview, the public-choice argument has a variety of conceptual attractions. In overall probable impact, however, that argument seems well designed to generate awkward unintended consequences, even opposite those desired, by its basic prescription of a pattern of decision making by individuals and government that is more appropriate to an extractive or exploitative phase of economic development, with great or even apparently limitless resources there for the taking.

The proof of this broad contention requires some stage setting. Consider the methodological individual intent on individualistic choice. As Ostrom explains:

Individualistic choice occurs whenever each person is free to decide for himself in the pursuit of his own interest. Individualistic choice is characteristic of the market and occurs whenever the only requirement is the willing consent of those individuals who freely agree or contract with one another to exchange some good or undertake some action.[96]

This multiple higgling and piggling is crucial, for it is a fundamental postulate of public-choice analysis that Pareto optimality can be achieved only through market dynamics. A Pareto optimum is defined to exist after some transaction if, and only if, in their own judgements, at least one party to the transaction is better off and not even a single party is worse off as a consequence. The essential argument is not complex. A Pareto optimum is the ideal outcome; hence a market is indispensable; and thus also is the minimum of government intervention the preferred strategy.

The summary does not do full justice to this central position of the public-choice argument, but it does suffice to illustrate several of its related weaknesses. Four of these weaknesses will be introduced here, by way of brief illustration of the far broader family.

First, Pareto optimality seems increasingly unapproachable in the world as we are coming to know it. Witness the potentially chronic energy deficits, compounded by OPEC (Organization of Petroleum Exporting Countries) policy; apparently shrinking reserves of some commonly used raw materials; the "revolution of rising expectations" of so many more than ever expecting so much more than before in terms of wages, goods, and public programs; and the demands of some efforts (for example, at pollution abatement) being at cross-purposes with historic expectations about reasonable prices or costs, return on investment, levels of employment, uses of energy, and so forth. That is to say, a Pareto optimum implies a sufficiency of resources, if not an overabundance. Otherwise, a Pareto optimum would be unlikely or impossible, and individuals pursuing it might succeed only in impoverishing one another. For if resources are scarce—and especially if they are growing scarcer and/or more expensive quickly—logrolling or market dynamics will typically result in many or even all parties to a transaction being worse off than before.

The significance of the point deserves underscoring. Shepsle notes that the only cases in which the Pareto rule applies are "free of conflict," which hardly constitutes "a very political situation."[97] Relatedly, van Dalen concludes that the rule is a "fair weather friend" that applies only "when times are good, *very* good."[98]

Even these brief comments suggest a wicked trap. Individualistic choice seems most applicable when available public resources are able to satisfy effective demand with some slack; but that is also the condition under which increases in central influence and programs often will meet least resistance.

For example, it is unlikely that we would have slipped so quietly into our vast expenditures for that gold-plated but ill-fated adventure in Vietnam except for the fact that tax receipts were running so far ahead of historic expenditures that concern was registered in important circles about what was to be done with anticipated budget surpluses of very large size. Much the same historic accident no doubt motivated massive increases in health, education, and welfare spending. There seemed, albeit for a short time only, more than enough to go around. We could have butter and guns, and the "Great Society" in the bargain. Similarly, when demand comes to exceed available resources, individualistic choice may only compound the problem, as by inducing inflation, labor/management conflict, civil strife, and so on. The choice then is whether to increase available resources, as by changes in the tax structure or in the pace of economic development, and/or to determine which demands are to be scaled down or deprived by how much and by whose action. Some sort of central influence on programs is most appropriate, but it is also the case that relevant proposals are likely to meet greatest resistance during such periods. Political life, as Charlie Brown might say, is a paradox wrapped in a conundrum.

The point can be approached from another angle. The politics of bargaining and incrementalism require a definite "morality of restraint," with restraint being defined in terms of the delicate balance between expectations that are realistic or even modest in terms of existing resources. As Gawthrop notes, "Self-control, moderation, and circumspection are the cardinal virtues of prudential politics,"[99] and these qualities cannot be limited only to professionals. Broadly, the required condition is that bargaining/incrementalist "expressions would be—indeed, must be—made within the given limits of the rules of the game."[100] Present conditions—more individuals and groups than ever before making greater and more insistent demands for resources that are not being increased rapidly enough, and may even be becoming depleted—are precisely those that encourage testing, or breaking, those "given limits" of self-control, moderation, and circumspection. Individualistic choice adds probable fuel to what is already a roaring blaze of newly heightened expectations, and thus qualifies as an idea for which the times may be very inauspicious.

In fact, Ostrom recognizes as a special case one variety of the condition at issue here, and he graphically sketches the probable consequences of an unrelieved emphasis on individualistic choice. His special case is a "common-property resource with a renewable yield or supply," such as a water supply.[101] Individualistic choice, Ostrom informs the reader, "has great advantages in reducing the costs of entrepreneurship so long as supply exceeds demands." The "so long as" is crucial. When demand exceeds supply, and as each individual pursues narrow self-interest, so will the supply diminish and so also will increase the social costs of the community of users. Should voluntary actions to limit demand be agreed to by some, this would only encourage others to pursue a holdout strategy and thus to profit disproportionately from the limited usage by others. Bad can easily lead to worst, Ostrom advises. Not only will the community of users suffer a loss, but other more tragic consequences may be expected. "Individuals in weak economic positions will be forced out," Ostrom notes. "The neighborhood effects which are generated may include poverty, deprivations, threats, and even violence."[102] Shades of Watts, Hough, and other sites of urban unrest.

Second, patently, the strong preference in public-choice theory for decentralization also is ill suited to growing—and even less to chronic—resource scarcity. Distributive resource allocations of relatively plentiful resources among people with moderate, even if growing, expectations as to what they have a legitimate claim on constitute a tame class of problems, and it is to this class that public-choice theory applies more directly. In contrast, really scarce resources will, as Baker notes, "require more direct policy responses to the questions of who gets what,"[103] which implies critical value issues and the differential weighting of contending tastes and preferences that exist, that might come to exist, or whose development should be encouraged.

Third, a pursuit of Pareto optimality implies a very restricted range of reactions to problem situations. Consider the case of the polluter, as developed by De Gregori. He explains that a Pareto optimum could be achieved only if the victims of the pollution "voluntarily assessed themselves and bribed the polluter not to pollute or to pollute less." De Gregori explains:

> All actions would have been voluntary, and consequently everyone would have acted so as to make their condition better, not worse. Any solution that required the polluter to pollute less would not fit Pareto because the polluter would be worse off, because he would have either had to absorb the cost directly or, in passing the increased costs on, lower the quantity demand of his product and therefore lower his profit.[104]

There are paradoxes in such "solutions." For example, this approach to alleviating pollution would be likely to aggravate it. For if you bribe a polluter to pollute less or not at all, it may encourage him initially to pollute a great deal in order to increase the bribe. Indeed, the improbability of such voluntary action implies what is the probable action in such cases—none, at least until matters get very bad.

Fourth, the theme of government nonintervention is not meant lightly in public-choice theory. In the special case of Ostrom's excerpted near footnote 101, for example, he notes that individualistic choice "will lead inexorably to tragedies," unless one of two things is done. He notes: "The common property can be partitioned into separable private properties or decision-making arrangements can be modified to enable persons to act jointly in relation to a common property."[105] Government intervention would seem a reasonable alternative in such cases, perhaps even a preferred one in the case in question. Failure to note this option may have been inadvertant, but there is no doubting the pervasive bias of public choice theory. As Baker concludes:

> Public choice theory prescribes a basically noninterventionist approach to the making of public policy. It is based upon the perspective of the representative individual in combination with a stated preference for decentralized markets as the best means of producing and providing public goods and services. The theory would replace controlled markets with the unfettered forces of a laissez faire market for the purpose of determining the substance, scope and direction of public policy.[106]

Some public-choice zealots push noninterventionism even further, much further. Consider government interventions intended to get manufacturers to produce safe products and to accept liability for unsafe ones. Some advocates of public choice argue that even such interventionism is ill advised, because, as McKean notes, the "only thing that would happen" to the consumer's position would be "loss of an opportunity to take a risk." The underlying logic is instructive. McKean explains that "some consumers, especially . . . the poor," would prefer the risk rather than the greater cost of a safer product. Any shift toward safer products, he concludes, would then work "to the detriment of the poor."[107]

De Gregori sees two assumptions in the bias of public-choice theory toward noninterventionism. He concludes: "The assumptions of this theory lead to one public policy conclusion: do virtually nothing. More fundamental is the hidden assumption that honoring tastes expressed in the marketplace is freedom; honoring those expressed in the voting booth is repression."[108]

Perhaps more moderately, it is at least clear that public-choice theory has an ahistorial bias toward preserving the status quo, toward serving the existing preferences of favored consumers and the power relations underlying their having come to be favored. Apparently bypassed thereby are major questions historically at the heart of the debate over what constitutes the just state. Among many such questions are:

- Are all "preferences" or "tastes" to be evaluated equally?

- Does the state direct early attention to the consequences for others when some act on their own preferences?

- What is to be done when one segment of the citizenry comes to feel that its preferences conflict in serious ways with the preferences of others?

An extended comparison will help illustrate the sense of the present point, as well as the implication that the issues just listed are bypassed because of the basic simplification of values at the center of the public-choice argument. As with pluralism, the ideal of public choice is defined in terms of a process. In public choice, a kind of "unseen hand" is said to be generated by individual choices that determine what public goods and services are provided; and in pluralism, the bargains are essentially struck by large interests or groups. The difference is that government intervention, by definition, is minimal in public-choice theory.[109] For pluralists, government is another set of interests to be represented in the bargaining and exchange process. The difference can be consequential.

What to do in public-choice theory when some historical policy consequences have developed in unattractive or undesirable ways, as in racism or sexism or thalidomide or whatever? Baker worries that public-choice theory would be impotent in doing anything much about such issues, as a matter of principle, perhaps not even able to recognize them. More broadly still, Baker concludes that public-choice theory "allows, if not encourages, racial, sexual and other forms of discrimination. That is, to what extent do discriminatory policies result from the preference patterns of the representative individual? Should he be a racist or sexist, he no doubt would not be sympathetic toward distinctions made between his preference for a particular brand of soap, say, as compared with his preference for 'his own kind of people.' "[110] It may be that such consequences are not intended by public-choice theorists, but they do seem probable.

Do "Cycles of Governance" Make a Difference?

Another major source of probable but unintended consequences for public-choice theory inheres in its broad assumption that there is a single best approach to governance, which in turn presumes a kind of standard set of governmental issues or challenges.

Granting the convenience of this assumption, it appears to be seriously inadequate. In Kaufman's terms, for example, it is necessary at a minimum to distinguish three major emphases in our public administrative history: representativeness; politically neutral competence; and executive leadership.[111] These three values appear in complicated mixtures, but with definite central tendencies over time. "None of these values was ever totally neglected in any of our past modifications of governmental design," Kaufman notes, "but each enjoyed greater emphasis than the others in different periods." The dynamics of change are uncomplicated. As Kaufman explains: "At different points in time, enough people (not necessarily a numerical majority) will be persuaded by one or another of these discontents to support remedial action—increased representativeness, better and politically neutral bureaucracies, or stronger chief executives, as the case may be." The condition is far from static. Indeed, an emphasis on one of the classes of discontent in effect accumulates the other classes of discontent and, sooner rather than later, this motivates a change in emphasis. As Kaufman concludes ". . . no totally stable solution has yet been devised. So the constant shift in emphasis goes on."[112]

These shifts in the cycle of governance are responses to broadly felt changes in central clusters of problems. Approaches and structures sensitive to one cluster of problems are likely to be unresponsive to the second or third clusters, if indeed they are not seriously counterproductive in dealing with them. Adaptive slippage is likely to increase under two conditions: (1) when the tasks of governance are seen as homogeneous and constant over time; and (2) when zealous allegiance is given to approaches and structures appropriate for only one of the central values of governance.

To translate a bit, Ostrom's prescriptions seem intended to emphasize representativeness as a central value. But those prescriptions are in various ways potentially out of kilter with the goal of a competent public service, and they are seriously at odds with the central value of executive leadership.

Zealous commitment to public-choice theory, that is to say, may prove too much of a good thing as conditions change, which they almost certainly shall. It is well and good, consequently, for public-choice theorists to propose for argument and debate that the American public economy was intended to avoid concentrations of power, that it has prospered because of that basic structural bias, and that this bias should continue where it exists, should be reinstituted where backsliding has occurred, and should be inaugurated wherever it has not existed. But it is awkward to advocate the bias without conditions, as awkward as it is to argue that reliance on markets or decentralization is always utopian and unrealistic. The awkwardness has three sources. First, the public-choice propositions for argument and debate are at least questionable. Second, necessary and sensitive adjustment to changing conditions may be complicated, if not precluded, by the emphasis on *a* structuring bias. Third, participants may become so intense about either/or arguments that the goals of attack or defend get more attention than truth seeking and problem solving. Waldo nicely captures the essence of these awkward consequences. He notes:

> As I view it, the situation presented is akin to classical tragedy, wherein all the protagonists are "right," but tragedy ensures. One task of the public administrator will be to try to avert, from the conflict of two legitimate principles, a denouement that could be tragic for all.[113]

Toward a Contingency Model

The preceding analysis should suffice to support three major points. First, there are sufficient methodological inelegancies to encourage great caution in accepting Ostrom's democratic administration and the ideational infrastructure on which it rests.

Second, there is consequently sufficient reason to look critically at any prescriptions for action derived from public-choice theory. A number of its major assumptions are either questionable or clearly inadequate as empirical descriptions of existing conditions. Moreover, it seems that public-choice theory is likely to generate major unanticipated consequences, some of them directly contrary to intended consequences.

Third, the critical survey of Ostrom's views suggests the greater usefulness of a contingency analysis, rather than the either/or contraposition that he has attempted. Indeed, Ostrom himself at times comes close to advocating a contingency approach. Thus he observes: "It is the exigencies of national defense that peculiarly require a system of one-man rule inherent in the prerogatives of the commander in chief—not the exigencies of community assistance programs, rural development, poverty, or the public security of neighborhood streets."[114] But Ostrom does not go on to detail the classes of exigencies to which various contingent approaches and structures could be shown to be variously appropriate by a range of empirical tests. His argument is more monolithic—to replace "one-man rule" across the full range of conditions encountered in governance.

The virtues of contingency analysis are multiple. Basically, it directs attention away from polarizing and polemical formulations and puts the emphasis on the attempt to describe the sets of more or less specific conditions under which one approach or another to providing public goods and services is variously applicable, and with more or less specific consequences. That is to say, contingency analysis puts the emphasis where it belongs.

Notes and References

1. The central source is Vincent Ostrom, *The Intellectual Crisis in American Public Administration* (University, Ala.: University of Alabams Press, 1973).

2. Ibid., p. 66.

3. Ibid., pp. 23-29.

4. Ibid, p. 74.

5. This proposition is not obviously valid, of course. For contrary evidence, see Robert H. Guest, *Organizational Change: The Effect of Successful Leadership* (Homewood, Ill.: Dorsey Press, 1962). Indeed, Guest's argument is more nearly that ineffective centralization helped provide the foundation for effective decentralization.

6. This premise has been shared by zealots for any number of management systems, including PPBS and Scientific Management. Some exotic forms of the premise have a Catch-22 flavor, as in the case of arguments that Scientific Management (or PPBS, or whatever) cannot really exist anywhere until it exists everywhere.

7. For exceptions to the lack of critical attention, see Thomas R. De Gregori, "CAVEAT EMPTOR: A Critique of the Emerging Paradigm of Public Choice," *Administration and Society* 6 (August 1974): 205-228; and Keith Baker, "Public Choice Theory: Some Important Assumptions and Public Policy Implications," in *Public Administration,* ed. Robert T. Golembiewski, Frank Gibson, and Geoffrey Y. Cornog (Chicago: Rand McNally, 1976), pp. 42-60.

8. Vincent Ostrom, Charles M. Tiebout, and Robert Warren, "The Organization of Government in Metropolitan Areas," *American Political Science Review* 55 (December 1961): 835.

9. James M. Buchanan and Gordon Tullock, *The Calculus of Consent* (Ann Arbor: University of Michigan Press, 1962), especially pp. 43-48.

10. De Gregori, "CAVEAT EMPTOR," p. 217.

11. Ostrom, *The Intellectual Crisis in American Public Administration,* pp. 50-51.

12. Buchanan and Tullock, *The Calculus of Consent,* p. vii.

13. Ibid., p. 3.

14. De Gregori, "CAVEAT EMPTOR," p. 208.

15. William A. Niskanen, Jr., *Bureaucracy and Representative Government* (Chicago: Aldine-Atherton, 1971), especially p. 218.

16. Ostrom, *The Intellectual Crisis in American Public Administration,* p. 52.

17. Norton Long in a book review, *Journal of Politics* 36 (August 1974): 804.

18. Kenneth A. Shepsle, "Theories of Collective Choice," in *Political Science Annual,* ed. Cornelius P. Cotter (Indianapolis: Bobbs-Merrill, 1974), 4.

19. Baker, "Public Choice Theory," p. 43.

20. As in, for example, Niskanen, *Bureaucracy and Representative Government,* especially p. 8.

21. De Gregori, "CAVEAT EMPTOR," especially pp. 207, 217-219; and Baker, "Public Choice Theory."

22. Leonard Merewitz and Steven H. Sosnick, *The Budget's New Clothes* (Chicago: Markham Publishing, 1971), p. 79.

23. Ibid., p. 80.

24. Ibid., p. 79 n.

25. Ibid., p. 79 n.

26. Ibid., p. 80 n.

27. Illustratively, the Kaldor-Hicks and Little criteria have been developed to loosen the conceptual limits of the Pareto criterion. See J. R. Hicks, "The Rehabilitation of Consumer Surplus," *Review of Economic Studies* 8 (1940-1941): 106-116.

28. De Gregory, "CAVEAT EMPTOR," p. 219.

29. Ostrom, *The Intellectual Crisis in American Public Administration*, pp. 50-51.

30. Ibid., p. 52.

31. Arnold A. Weinstein, "Individual Preference Intrasitivity," *Southern Economic Journal* 34 (January 1968): 335.

32. Robert A. Dahl, *A Preface to Democratic Theory* (Chicago: University of Chicago Press, 1956), especially pp. 34-50.

33. Kenneth Arrow, *Social Choice and Individual Values* (New York: Wiley, 1951), pp. 51-59, 75-80.

34. Dahl, *A Preface to Democratic Theory*, pp. 42 n, 43 n.

35. Shepsle, "Theories of Collective Choice," especially pp. 31-42.

36. Buchanan and Tullock, *The Calculus of Consent*, p. 9.

37. This was the case, for example, in the famous 1930 studies of group atmospheres or climates. See especially Robert Lippitt, "Field Theory and Experiment in Social Psychology: Autocratic and Democratic Group Atmospheres," *American Journal of Sociology* 45 (July 1939): 26-49.

38. Irving Janis, *Victims of Groupthink* (Boston: Houghton Mifflin, 1972), deals with a number of major political and military decisions that fit this characterization.

39. The classic experimental demonstration is that of Solomon E. Asch, "Effects of Group Pressure upon the Modification and Distortion of Judgments," in *Groups, Leadership, and Men,* ed. Harold Guetzkow (Pittsburgh, Pa.: Carnegie Press, 1951), pp. 177-190.

40. De Gregori, "CAVEAT EMPTOR," p. 210.

41. Ibid., p. 209.

42. Buchanan and Tullock, *The Calculus of Consent*, pp. 3, 17.

43. Robert L. Bish and Vincent Ostrom, *Understanding Urban Government* (Washington, D.C.: American Enterprise Institute for Public Policy Research, 1973), p. 18.

44. De Gregori, "CAVEAT EMPTOR," p. 209.

45. Ibid., p. 209.

46. Buchanan and Tullock, *The Calculus of Consent*, p. 18.

47. Amartya Sen, *Collective Choice and Social Welfare* (San Francisco: Holden Day, 1971), p. 6.

48. De Gregori, "CAVEAT EMPTOR," p. 209.

49. Ibid.

50. Ostrom, *The Intellectual Crisis in American Public Administration,* p. 62.

51. Ostrom, Tiebout, and Warren, "The Organization of Government in Metropolitan Areas," pp. 835-837.

52. Ibid., p. 35.

53. Ibid., p. 48.

54. Abraham J. Briloff, *Unaccountable Accounting* (New York: Harper & Row, 1972).

55. Consult William J. Bruns, Jr., and Don T. De Coster, eds., *Accounting and Its Behavioral Implications* (New York: McGraw-Hill, 1969); and Thomas Burns, ed., *Proceedings of the Symposium on Accountancy* (Columbus: College of Administrative Sciences, Ohio State University, 1972).

56. Bertram M. Gross, *The Managing of Organizations,* vol. II (New York: Free Press of Glencoe, 1964), especially pp. 467-501; and Meinoff Dierkes and Raymond A. Bauer, eds., *Corporate Social Accounting* (New York: Praeger, 1973).

57. Ostrom, *The Intellectual Crisis in American Public Administration,* especially 49-50.

58. Merewitz and Sosnick, *The Budget's New Clothes,* p. 63.

59. Francis W. Coker, "Dogmas of Administrative Reform," *American Political Science Review* 16 (August 1922): 399-411; Charles S. Hyneman, "Administrative Reorganization: An Adventure into Science and Theology," *Journal of Politics* 1 (February 1939: 62-74; Earl H. Latham, "Hierarchy and Hieratics," *Employment Forum* 2 (April 1947): 1-6; and Herbert A. Simon, "Proverbs of Administration," *Public Administration Review* 6 (Winter 1946): pp. 53-67.

60. Charles Perrow, *Organizational Analysis* (Belmont, Calif.: Wadsworth, 1970), especially pp. 75-91.

61. Robert T. Golembiewski, "Civil Service and Managing Work," *American Political Science Review* 56 (December 1962): 961-973.

62. Robert T. Golembiewski, *Men, Management, and Morality* (New York: McGraw-Hill, 1955), among many others.

63. Alfred D. Chandler, Jr., *Strategy and Structure* (Cambridge, Mass.: The MIT Press, 1962); and E. Raymond Corey and Steven H. Starr, *Organization Strategy: A Marketing Approach* (Boston, Mass.: Graduate School of Business Administration, Harvard University, 1971).

64. Baker, "Public Choice Theory," pp. 51-52.

65. Ibid., p. 51.

66. The welcome opportunity for lower-level officials to kick upstairs decisions that are locally too hot to handle is graphically illustrated in Paul B. Crooks, Harold Lakin, and Frederick J. Pratt, "Three Cases in Field

Administration," Inter-University Case Program, No. 16 (1953), especially pp. 5-13.

67. James W. Fesler, "Approaches to the Understanding of Decentralization," *Journal of Politics* 27 (August 1965): especially 548-549. See also the useful treatment by David O. Porter and Eugene E. Olsen, "Some Critical Issues in Government Centralization and Decentralization," *Public Administration Review* 36 (January 1976): 72-84. They see decisions about decentralization and centralization as involving a complex simultaneous juggling of three classes of variables: values, tasks, and structure.

68. Carl J. Friedrich, *Man and His Government* (New York: McGraw-Hill, 1963), p. 667.

69. Ostrom, *The Intellectual Crisis in American Public Administration,* especially pp. 75-81.

70. David K. Hart, "Theories of Government Related to Decentralization and Citizen Participation," *Public Administration Review* 32 (October 1972): 606.

71. Fesler, "Approaches to the Understanding of Decentralization," p. 549.

72. Ibid., p. 549.

73. Ibid., p. 549.

74. Herbert Kaufman, *The Limits of Organizational Change* (University, Ala.: University of Alabama Press, 1971), pp. 101ff.

75. Fesler, "Approaches to the Understanding of Decentralization," especially pp. 539-546.

76. George Graham, *Morality in American Politics* (New York: Random House, 1952), especially, pp. 42-53.

77. Arnold S. Tanenbaum et al., *Hierarchy in Organizations* (San Francisco: Jossey-Bass, 1974).

78. Ostrom, *The Intellectual Crisis in American Public Administration,* p. 118.

79. Bish and Ostrom, *Understanding Urban Government,* pp. 36-37.

80. Ibid., p. 38.

81. James A. Reidel, "Citizen Participation: Myths and Reality," *Public Administration Review* 32 (May 1972): 211-220.

82. James S. Coleman et al., *Equality of Educational Opportunity* (Washington, D.C.: Office of Educational Opportunity, 1966).

83. Bish and Ostrom, *Understanding Urban Government,* p. 38.

84. Ibid., pp. 41-46.

85. Elinor Ostrom et al., *Community Organization and the Provision of Police Services* (Beverly Hills, Calif.: Sage Publications, 1973); and Elinor Ostrom and Gordon Whitaker, "Black Citizens and the Police" (Paper delivered at the Annual Meeting of the American Political Science Association, Chicago, Ill., 1971).

86.   S. T. IsHak, "Consumers' Perception of Police Performance: Consolidation vs. Deconcentration" (Ph.D. diss., Indiana University, 1972); Ostrom et al, *Community Organization and the Provision of Police Services*; and Ostrom and Whitaker, "Black Citizen's and the Police."

87.   Roger S. Ahlbrandt, Jr., *Municipal Fire Protection Services* (Beverly Hills, Calif.: Sage Publications, 1973).

88.   Bish and Ostrom, *Understanding Urban Government,* p. 47.

89.   Ibid., pp. 40-41.

90.   Ibid., p. 36.

91.   It is also correct that larger urban schools do pose more challenging targets for change, in part because of the organizing concepts prevalent in them, as Ostrom argues. See Richard A. Schmuck and Matthew B. Miles, eds., *Organization Development in Schools* (Palo Alto, Calif.: National Press Books, 1971), especially pp. 236-237.

92.   Ostrom, *The Intellectual Crisis in American Public Administration,* p. 59.

93.   Ibid., p. 119.

94.   Ibid., p. 121.

95.   Ibid., p. 121.

96.   Ibid., p. 56.

97.   Shepsle, "Theories of Collective Choice," p. 30.

98.   Hendrik van Dalen, "Some Theoretical Perspectives on Government's Role in Consumer Protection" (Paper delivered at Southwestern Public Administration Meetings, Phoenix, Ariz., November 12, 1975), p. 12.

99.   Louis C. Gawthrop, *The Administrative Process and Democratic Theory* (Boston: Houghton Mifflin, 1970), p. 439.

100. Ibid., pp. 439-440.

101. Ostrom, *The Intellectual Crisis in American Public Administration,* pp. 56-58.

102. Ibid., p. 57.

103. Baker, "Public Choice Theory," p. 59.

104. De Gregori, "CAVEAT EMPTOR," p. 210.

105. Ostrom, *The Intellectual Crisis in American Public Administration,* p. 57.

106. Baker, "Public Choice Theory," p. 54.

107. Roland McKean, "Product Liability," *Quarterly Journal of Economics,* 84 (November 1970): 623.

108. De Gregori, "CAVEAT EMPTOR," p. 219.

109. Witness the extreme position of McKean concerning product safety, for example. Most public-choice theorists incline to somewhat more government intervention, as in providing information about product safety. See W. Y. Oi, "The Economics of Product Safety," *Bell Journal of Economics and Management Science,* Spring 1973, p. 26.

110.   Baker, "Public Choice Theory," p. 55.

111.   Herbert Kaufman, "Administrative Decentralization and Political Power," *Public Administration Review* 29 (January 1969): 3.

112.   Ibid., p. 4.

113.   Dwight Waldo, ed., *Public Administration In a Time of Turbulence* (Scranton, Pa.: Chandler Publishing, 1971), pp. 259-260.

114.   Ostrom, *The Intellectual Crisis in American Public Administration,* p. 125.

SECTION 3

WHERE PUBLIC ADMINISTRATION MAY GO
Toward Miniparadigms in the Future

Chapter 6

THE CASE FOR MINIPARADIGMS
IN PUBLIC ADMINISTRATION
Some Guidelines Implicit in Historical Development

There is no doubt that public administrationists of the early 1970s were both paradigm aware and paradigm fixated. The signs are unmistakable. For example, at the 1974 annual meeting of the American Political Science Association, a panel that focused on the theme "paradigms in public administration" not only lasted a full day—which is unusual in itself, perhaps even unprecedented—but also attracted the second largest attendance of any panel. The 1974 meetings of the Southern Political Science Association also gave attention to public administration paradigms, as did the 1975 annual meeting of the American Society for Public Administration. Several books also have addressed themselves to the loss of an old paradigm. Moreover, the crying need for a new comprehensive paradigm is often noted, and several candidates therefor have been offered.

In sum, concern about paradigms has been in vogue, despite a definite ennui in the later 1970s. This concern has consumed major amounts of energy, and it has raised academic blood pressures on any number of occasions.

The earlier paradigmatic preoccupation is unfortunate, and the present ennui is even worse. In sum, this chapter argues that the energy, concern, or annoyance associated with the scholarly warfare about paradigms is not particularly helpful, as understandable and even desirable as it is compared to withdrawal or resignation. This conclusion is not lightly made. Nor does it intend to demean the substantial energies that have been lavished on paradigms by many proponents and a few opponents. But there is no virtue in being coy about a basic conviction.

This chapter seeks to be constructive about its basic conviction in two ways. First, today's public administrationists generally have accepted the need for a comprehensive paradigm as part of a revolutionary process of scientific progress. Reliance is placed on the formulation of Thomas S. Kuhn.[1] Even though he himself has severely qualified his early notions, paradoxically, those qualifications have little influenced the debate in public administration. The uncritical acceptance of Kuhn's early formulation will be shown to be a bad bargain, overall, for it diverts attention from an approach to "science" that seems to be more promising than the wholesale replacement of one comprehensive paradigm by another. Second, an alternative approach to seeking comprehensive paradigms will be sketched as a way out of the difficulties in which public administration presently finds itself.

This chapter should stand on its own analytical feet, like any chapter. But its more basic purpose is to provide a set of guides or benchmarks to be approached and illustrated by the second volume of this work, to sketch the developmental directions in which the public administration of the immediate future might usefully go. That is to say, the present "intellectual crisis" is here seen as simply the result of scholars having made a few wrong turns, analytically speaking. These understandable errors in judgment are now correctable in substantial part, given the benefit of hindsight and of major progress in various areas of inquiry, neither of which was available to the scholarly pioneers.

So this chapter proposes a kind of constructive hindsight. It seeks to point out some useful developmental directions which the chapters of the second volume will seek to respect as they go about illustrating what should and can be done to improve the present condition in public administration. Directly, this chapter provides the generic introduction to the companion volume, which seeks to detail various aspects of one scientific approach that follows the directions specified in this chapter as to where public administration might usefully go.

Primer about Paradigms in Public Administration

This section will sketch how public administrationists got matters wrong-way-around, as far as the character and role of paradigms is concerned. Three immediate steps will serve as a foundation for a following section, which will present guidelines for the future development of public administration as a field. These three steps involve (1) a sketch of the concept "paradigm" common among public administrationists; (2) an outline of the major senses in which the usual understanding is not adequate to describe the development of science, let alone to prescribe how that development should occur; and (3) a proposal to set the common search for a paradigm on its head, as it were, as an alternative approach to facilitating the development of public administration.

Paradigms as Comprehensive and Revolutionary

Vincent Ostrom well represents the usual usage of the term "paradigm" in public administration, and his treatment will be used here to represent related uses of the notion. Two major emphases characterize his interpretation of Kuhn's development of revolutionary paradigms, and they can be briefly outlined without compromising Ostrom's argument.

Public Administration's Crisis of Identity

Ostrom first draws attention to the widely remarked ferment in public administration. That ferment has many faces, one of which is that Herbert A. Simon effectively demolished the "principles" of public administration,[2] but neither Simon nor anyone else has been able to replace that long-time tethering point for many public administrationists. Ostrom notes that by late 1967, influential opinion perceived the patent crisis in confidence among public administrationists as a crisis of identity. Thus he quotes Waldo to this effect:

> Both the nature and the boundaries of the subject matter and the methods of studying and teaching this subject matter become problematical. Now, two decades after the critical attacks, the crisis of identity has not been resolved satisfactorily. Most of the important theoretical problems of public administration relate to this continuing crisis, to ways in which it can be resolved and to the implications and results of possible resolutions.[3]

Ostrom sees the crisis of identity as having two major aspects—"this failure to know what we are (subject matter) or how we should proceed (methods.)."[4]

Revolution as Rx for Identity Crisis

Ostrom proceeds to diagnose the identity crisis of public administrationists as generic rather than particularistic, as an example of a common enough feature of scientific development. Interpreting Kuhn, Ostrom explains that the identity crisis derives from the lack in public administration of the prerequisite for "normal science," specifically, a "basic theoretical paradigm or framework in which a community of scholars shares common theoretical assumptions, and a common language defining essential terms and relationships."[5] This framework directs the scholars' attention, and also gives them something to identify with as well as a convenient image for describing self. In terms of the vocabulary introduced earlier, an adequate paradigm thus serves both task and maintenance needs.

To put the point briefly but with essential accuracy, Ostrom sees today's public administration as "extraordinary science" rather than normal science. Extraordinary science, in effect, has learned that its paradigmatic god is dead. And rather than proceeding step-by-step and cumulatively, as in normal science, a conceptual great leap forward is needed. More specifically, Ostrom's views can be listed as follows:

- The old paradigm in public administration has been shown lacking by its failure to explain satisfactorily a growing number of "anomalies."

- "A proliferation of competing articulations of the prevailing paradigm will occur,"[6] and the failure of these articulations to resolve anomalies will result in broadening frustration and discontent.

- The processes of normal science having failed, "a radically different [paradigm] is needed,"[7] but may take a very long time to develop as communication grows increasingly difficult, research is noncumulative, and identifications are increasingly attenuated.

- The processes of extraordinary or revolutionary science really begin only *after* an alternative paradigm is sufficiently developed to attract adherents.

- At some point, the processes of normal science can again begin, but only in the context of testing and refining the alternative paradigm or paradigms.

This view of scientific development provides not only significant interpretations of what is going on in public administration, but also prescriptions of what should be going on. There can be no doubt as to the significance of the position on paradigms, then.

Some implications of the usual paradigmatic concept are also very important. Consider only three examples. First, this use of paradigm implies that scientific progress is accompanied by—may even depend upon—major communication failures or gaps, as between generations of scholars. Second, the notion of revolutionary paradigms implies that scientific progress is discontinuous and noncumulative at times, and that normal scientific criteria and methods are of no clear relevance during such periods. Third, and paramountly, the definite premium is placed on the development of alternative paradigms, specifically, the most comprehensive paradigm possible and at the earliest possible time. As Ostrom notes: "If Kuhn's theory of scientific revolutions is correct, we can anticipate a resolution of the intellectual crisis in public administration only if an alternative paradigm is available."[8]

Paradigms as Evolutionary and Particularistic

As straightforward as it seems, however, Kuhn's view of scientific development is a questionable guide. And some exuberant extensions of his position pose even greater problems. That is, Kuhn's view appears in significant particulars to be an awkward description of how science does develop. Consequently, the search for paradigms as usually defined also seems at least a questionable prescriptive guide for the development of public administration, if it is not ironically an invitation to neglect the central issues and a temptation to expend energy in a self-defeating enterprise. This combination is both likely and awkward, as the following analysis seeks to establish.

Philosophers of Science Take a Second Look

After the early blush of enthusiasm about Kuhn's interpretation of paradigmatic advance in science as revolutionary and comprehensive, the opinion of specialists in such matters is that major qualifications in Kuhn's argument are necessary. So pervasive are these qualifications by philosophers of science, in fact, that they destroy the very quality of what in the 1960s was most attractive about Kuhn's distinction between normal and extraordinary science. Notably, Kuhn is among the prominent revisionists of interpretations of his own work.

A sufficient appreciation of the nature and extent of the revisionism can be presented economically, relying heavily on Toulmin's major critical synthesis.[9] Four emphases will do the job. Basically, these emphases argue that common paradigmatic views are more exuberant than descriptive of scientific progress. Perhaps the spirit of the times surrounding the development of these views was overpowering. But major conceptual retrenchment seems in order.

First, Toulmin stresses a major distinction in what he calls the "classical revolutionary view"—that normal science and extraordinary science stand in stark contrast. As he explains, the tasks of normal science "are essentially consolidatory, with all the scientists . . . operating according to a common framework of rational ground-rules. . . . fundamental concepts are shared, they will have a common vocabulary of debate and common procedures for resolving their differences."[10] Extraordinary science is something else again. Toulmin explains:

> . . . the displacement of one fundamental paradigm by another represents an absolute and complete change. Newthink then sweeps aside Oldthink entirely; so much so that . . . the reasons for replacing Oldthink by Newthink can be explained in the language of neither system. [The] commitment to incompatible 'paradigms' is then reflected in unavoidable incomprehension.[11]

Second, Toulmin sees elements of throwing out the baby with the bath water in common interpretations of scientific progress as revolutionary. Granted, he implies, there is no ultimately satisfying theory in any area of knowledge. Even the best product is subject to revision and refinement and—usually sooner rather than later—replacement by more comprehensive and often radically different formulations. But the usual interpretation of paradigmatic revolution goes far beyond challenging the *product* of scientific progress at any point in time. That interpretation also suspends the *processes* of science for some indeterminate period.

This suspension of the processes of science is meta-significant and became an integral part of many brave demands for "new science." To be fair, Kuhn's writings are difficult to interpret on the point. For example, early on, he equates paradigm and "dogma."[12] This identification at least suggests that paradigms are like religious dogmas around which loyalties develop, with any changes being tantamount to religious conversion with its attendant change in loyalty. But this usage is ambiguous. Does it apply only to the extant *products* of science, which evidence establishes are often held fervently and mistakenly? Or does the usage also apply to the *processes* of science, the long-tested agreements about how to establish whether mistakes have been made in connection with specific products of science? Kuhn's usage is unexceptional if it refers only to products, but his several treatments are not consistent or clear on the point.

No such questions apply to many of Kuhn's interpreters. They commonly see him as tarring both scientific products *and* processes with the same brush, defiantly. And therein lie some embarrassing and crucial problems with the approach to extraordinary science. As Toulmin puts the point, the notion of revolutionary paradigm precludes justification in rational terms or in the light of accepted processes of scientific exploration. That is, in the very definition of extraordinary science, "no common set of procedures for judging this rationality are acceptable, or even intelligible, to both sides in the dispute." The implication is both obvious and portentious:

> So the considerations operative within a revolutionary change must be interpreted as causes or motives, rather than as reasons or justifications. . . . At this fundamental level, conceptual changes can be discussed only in terms of unconscious thoughts, socio-economic influences, and other such causal processes. . . . Only after the victorious new paradigm is securely enthroned in acknowledged power can the rule of rationality be restored.[13]

In short, the basic choice process relevant to a revolutionary paradigm rests in people rather than in nature. At one level, this is both comforting and self-evident. Only people can accept paradigms or test them. At another level, however, the position implies sophisticated nonsense in relation to empirical theory. For example, the reality of what will happen to a free-falling body does not reside in persons but in nature, whose relationships are the ultimate arbiter, whatever paradigms people accept. The situation is more complicated in the case of values, or social theory. Men can build diverse castles to personal or social preferences. When values or social theory are to be acted upon, however, relationships in nature are again the ultimate arbiters of how, and perhaps whether, the preferred states can be achieved. Sometimes these relationships in physical nature are quite intractible; moreover, experience implies they are discovered by basic processes that are substantially invariable. In more or less direct contrast, the revolutionary paradigm assumed that only social reality was involved in scientific progress, whether as facilitator or roadblock.

This bias of the revolutionary paradigm toward people rather than nature often was expressed in extreme forms that transformed limited common sense into cosmic license. The reader is referred to Chapter 4 dealing with the new public administration, especially to the section entitled "If I Say It Is, It Is." Some interpretations of the revolutionary paradigm seemed to say that in order to change what exists, we need only to change the minds of people. There is much wisdom as well as major potential for tragedy in such a position. It all depends on where you draw the line. Many interpreters of the revolutionary paradigm were not very careful about drawing that line.

Third, Toulmin is leery about what this rejection of scientific *process* as well as *product* implies, but the acid test for him still remains. For the theory of paradigmatic revolution to apply, he notes, it will be necessary to show that some "theoretical change within a given scientific discipline has ever in fact produced so radical a discontinuity" as extraordinary science requires. A survey of the historical record, he notes, will determine whether such cases actually exist or "whether this fully-fledged definition does not exaggerate the depth of the conceptual changes actually occurring within the natural sciences."[14]

By a wide margin, Toulmin sees the historical record as lacking any such cases. Indeed, he puts Thomas S. Kuhn the historian to work in establishing the lack of support for Thomas S. Kuhn the philosopher of science. One focus is the "Copernican Revolution," which lasted a century and a half, by Kuhn's and Toulmin's mutual reckoning. Toulmin concludes: "The world-view that emerged at the end of this debate had—it is true—little in common with earlier pre-Copernican conceptions. Yet, however radical the resulting change in physical and astronomical *ideas and theories,* it was the outcome of a continuing rational discussion and it implied no comparable break in the *intellectual methods* of physics and astronomy."[15] All in all, Toulmin could make the theory of paradigmatic revolution fit the historical data only by severely qualifying the original interpretation. He concludes:

> ... paradigm-switches are never as complete as the fully-fledged definition implies; ... rival paradigms never really amount to entire alternative world-views; and that intellectual discontinuities on the theoretical level of science conceal underlying continuities at a deeper, methodological level.[16]

In this view, paradigm for Toulmin comes to mean much the same as "conceptual system," changes in which are clearly a part of normal science and imply no massive, discontinuous revolution.

Fourth, as Toulmin emphasizes, Kuhn himself has seen fit to modify the usual Kuhnian interpretations in significant ways. We can only sample this revisionism here, but even a glimpse is revealing. Consider Kuhn's treatment of "revolutionary" as applied to paradigms, which went through several major variations,[17] beginning with his original and sharp 1962 distinction between normal and extraordinary science. By 1965, Kuhn's meaning had shifted substantially to cases involving less drastic conceptual changes than the theoretic Armageddon central to his original formulation.[18] He freely concedes that his earlier distinction between normal and extraordinary science is sharper and more dramatic than historical experience warranted. Moreover, he also newly argues that scientific revolutions occur far more frequently than he had appreciated. Kuhn came to describe scientific progress as a continuous series of minirevolutions, rather than profound conceptual change every century of two. As Toulmin notes:

> This emendation at first looked innocent enough, yet its consequences went to the heart of Kuhn's theory. For it transformed the historical development of scientific theory into a 'revolution in perpetuity,' even in the cases hitherto labelled as 'normal'; and, in the process, it quietly abandoned the central distinction around which his whole theory had been built in the first place—viz., that between conceptual changes taking place within the limits of an overall paradigm, and those involving the replacement of an entire paradigm.[19]

Kuhn himself notes that many of his readers had interpreted him too broadly, asserting, for example, that he never intended that scientists in successive generations were to be understood as having any more than partial communication blockages.[20] Moreover, Kuhn comes to see extraordinary science as "revolutionary" in a very limited sense only.[21]

Toulmin comes down hard on Kuhn's revisionism and reinterpretations. He notes:

> ... this final account reduces the difference between 'normal' and 'revolutionary' changes to the distinction between *propositional* changes which involve no conceptual novelties, and so lend themselves to some kind of deductive or quasi-deductive justification, and *conceptual* changes which go beyond the scope of all merely formal or deductive procedures. So interpreted ... any scientific change whatever will normally have something 'normal,' and something 'revolutionary' about it.[22]

All of this is to say that the common understanding of revolutionary paradigms has had much of the support swept from beneath it, in no small measure by the scholar most closely associated with describing scientific progress as revolutionary change in comprehensive paradigms. Toulmin concludes that the later Kuhn had to be read quite differently than the earlier one. The later Kuhn, that is:

> ... recognized that a complete body of scientific theory ... is not a single, coherent logical system, which must be accepted or rejected

in its entirety, but rather something in which we can make radical changes piecemeal. So long as the switch between alternative paradigms was seen as a change between complete 'systematic structures' or concepts and propositions, the classical distinction between revolutionary phases is forced on us, with all its paradoxical consequences.[23]

Toward a "Viable Center" through "Active Peripheries"

The reevaluation of paradigms as revolutionary and comprehensive by specialists in the philosophy of science occupied some ten to fifteen years, and much thrashing around in public administration occurred under the heady influence of early versions long after major revisions had been made by philosophers of science.[24] That reflects an unfortunate lag in the transmission of knowledge.

Even if it is late, the point here is to translate the basic impact of the more recent ferment in the philosophy of science into a context and vocabulary familiar to public administrationists. This translation here will will feature two aspects. First, some problems with the classic revolutionary view that are unique to public administration will be detailed. Second, an argument will be made to reverse the usually accepted direction of how scientific progress will occur in public administration. The usual prescription has been to develop a "viable center" for the field with the presumption that an "active periphery" would result as a matter of course. The focus here is on active peripheries whose sum over time may support a vital center for public administration.

Practical Problems with Comprehensive Paradigms

In addition to the generic difficulties with comprehensive paradigms sketched earlier, the search for them in public administration implies some special problems. Consider only three concerns. First, most proponents of *a* public administration paradigm want things to happen quickly, almost instantaneously. In place of the gestation periods of a century or more that Kuhn originally estimated for major change in the physical sciences, the time frame is a matter of years.[25] Two consequences are most prominent. Full-fledged, alternative comprehensive paradigms are generated quickly, as illustrated in Chapter 2 by the Humanist/Systemic paradigm. Moreover, this time pressure was exacerbated by a large number of recently trained public administrationists who were trying to find a place and status in the field, as Chapter 2 sketches.

Second, a variety of features—reinforced by the time pressure—serve to raise the probability that self-limiting choices of paradigms will be made. Primarily, the natural sciences have longer histories than the social sciences, and hence are more protected against the ultimate consequences of the concept of extraordinary science. Specifically, the natural sciences have long track records that permit (in Toulmin's vocabulary) new *ideas and theories* to be tested in terms of relatively stable *intellectual methods and processes.* Even in natural science, it has often been touch and go. In public administration, where far less durable moorings of relatively tried and true intellectual methods exist, the choice between proposed paradigms is far more chancy and capricious.

Consider another perspective on why public administrationists are especially vulnerable to methodological humbug. The problems with ideas and theories in public administration are exquisitely more complicated than in the natural sciences. Briefly, public administration faces three related but distinct questions:

- What is the good state and how is it to be managed?

- What relationships in nature are relevant to management?

- How are the relationships in nature to be manipulated so as to achieve the vision of the good state that is well managed?

The first question is value-loaded; the second is empirical, whose exploration is by intellectual methods ideally influenced only in selected ways by the "values of science"; and the third is of the goal-based, empirical variety that seeks to prescribe how specific values can be achieved, based on a knowledge of empirical reality.

Such distinctions proved difficult to respect in the blush of public administration's romance with revolutionary paradigms, if they were not considered absolute evasions of essential responsibilities. As in the Humanist/Systemic Paradigm discussed in Chapter 2, for example, the distinctions are neglected, eroded, or even turned topsy-turvy. That is, to explain by contrast, the *use* of knowledge in the natural sciences proceeds in some form such as this: Given what we know about relationships in nature, this is how to go about achieving certain desired or valued states. In revolutionary public administration, the form sometimes became: Given our values, this is how relationships in nature will be, or at least should be. Given three facts of life—the complexity of phenomena in public administration, the very incomplete knowledge about them, and the uneven acceptance of common intellectual and analytical methods—exuberant public administrationists could more eaily be propelled into dead-end formulations than could scholars in the natural sciences. More critically still, the lack of agreement about criteria for choices between paradigms made it more unlikely that public administrationists would realize early that they had accepted a dead-end paradigm.

Of Center and Circumference

In terms probably more congenial to most public administrationists, the issue of scientific progress in public administration was expressed in such terms as a "viable center" and "active circumference." As Waldo notes, a healthy discipline can be visualized as having "a solid center as well as an active circumference,"[26] a view most congenial to those steeped in the tradition of Aristotle. Moreover, there was a clear certitude as to which is cart and which is horse. The viable center was the prerequisite; an active circumference would result. Taken together, both would signal a healthy discipline or field of inquiry.

The position here is that this basic view is awkward in multiple dimensions. The search for a viable center essentially seeks to start with the comprehensive definition of the field, as contrasted with starting with a process or a set of guidelines for working toward such an eventual center. The bias is understandable, and even would be preferable, were it practical. The view here is that it is not practical, based on ample evidence and experience, four aspects of which will be sketched.

First, and paramountly, the clamor for a comprehensive paradigm implies major dilemmas. Conceptually, for example, the fixation on *the* answer poses real cross-pressures. A narrow concept would be most defensible and easiest to formulate. But it might be stultifying. A very broad concept would be most satisfying, on the other hand, but it would be hard to lay credible claim that any Brobdingnagian definition was clearly within the real or foreseeable competencies of public administrationists. Mosher catches the delicious irony in these words:

> Public administration cannot debark any subcontinent as its exclusive province—unless it consists of such mundane matters as classifying budget expenditures, drawing organization charts, and mapping procedures. In fact, it would appear that any definition of this field would be either so encompassing as to call forth the wrath of ridicule of others, or so limiting as to stultify its own discipline.[27]

For Mosher, that is, to succeed in articulating a comprehensive paradigm is to inevitably fail in establishing a credible claim to the analytical territory thereby circumscribed. Failure is inevitable, in such a view.

Second, awkward consequences lay ready to ambush the many who believe it either limiting or ludicrous to lay prior claim to some paradigm for public administration, and who yet see the need to emphasize some viable center. No graceful escape seems possible from the inherent double bind. Thus Mosher concludes that "perhaps it is best that [the center] not be defined." Public administrationists, Mosher advises, should see their field as only "providing a way of looking at government."[28] Waldo is even more definitive:

"What I propose," he wrote, "is that we try to act as a profession without actually being one and perhaps even without the hope or intention of becoming one in any strict sense."[29]

Third, by implication, the fixation on a viable center is pitched at a highly general and abstract level, which at first blush seems beyond denial or even criticism bu which provides little or no direction for what should be done, by whom, or how. That is, the emphasis on a vital center is very far removed from the development of specific skills and technologies that might permit a credible claim by public administrationists—if not necessarily an exclusive claim—to some areas of proficient inquiry. To simplify, it is almost as if the need were framed in terms such as this: Give us an area within which we can do our thing, whatever that is. The neglected theme is: With these specific tools and technologies, we can help analytically to cope with these relatively specific areas.

Fourth, fixation on a viable center also makes public administration especially receptive to allures of paradigmatic revolution, yet relatively insensitive to the need for technologies and skills. More seriously, public administrationists generally lack the traditions of inquiry—the specific skills and technologies—that permit some reasonable test of proposed comprehensive formulations such as those idealized by the notion of revolutionary paradigmatic change. The very probable consequence is frustrated overexuberance rather than scientific progress.

Rationale for Miniparadigms

The emphasis here is not on a "center." On the contrary, the emphasis here is on one specific portion of the "active circumference" that Waldo sees as needed in today's public administration. Attention focuses on understanding the specific skills and technologies required in that portion of the disciplinary circumference, as well as on developing public administrationists who are competent in those skills and technologies. A viable center for public administration may eventuate from the success of public administrationists in dealing with several such portions of the circumference. Or results may generate some new or novel discipline or field. Only the future will tell.

Whatever the eventual outcome regarding a center, an emphasis on an active circumference has much to recommend it. Consider two attractions. Such an emphasis will discourage premature closure on a comprehensive paradigm, the search for which is likely to be futile even if it does not create more problems than it solves. More basically, the circumferential emphasis implies the need to develop skills and interests in appropriate technologies, as applied to public loci. Whatever else happens, that investment in technologies and skills will not be lost. Somewhat more specifically, the focus here on peripheries or miniparadigms rests on three sets of notions.

Why a Comprehensive Paradigm? Despite the alarm in much of the literature, it is not obvious that *a* comprehensive paradigm is either timely or necessary. Kuhn is definite as to timeliness in observing that: "It remains an open question what parts of social science have yet required such paradigms at all."[30] Realistically, public administration is less methodologically advanced than at least most of the social sciences. So this is not likely to be public administration's time.

Necessity is a far more complex issue, if only because a paradigm can serve various mixes of task and maintenance. It is at least probable on the historical record that paradigm pushers have got their priorities wrong way around. Their premise is that a prior paradigm is required to generate cumulative research; it should be the front load, as it were. An opposed premise has far more historical support, however.[31] Almost all paradigms worthy of the name have been the result of long periods of gestation and a plethora of relatively specific and often conflicting researches. A paradigm is the back load, in this view. Relatedly, because of a paradigm's dual impact on task and maintenance, pressures encouraging premature closure toward a paradigm coexist with conclusive historical evidence of the common danger of so doing. The Traditional Paradigm well served maintenance needs for nearly half a century, for example, but it made few contributions to the task of analyzing the phenomena of public management. That neglect of task needs basically explains why public administrationists are in their present predicament, as comfortable as it may have been to support a definition of the field that for so long met maintenance needs with respect to political science. At the very least, moreover, the several patent paradigmatic weaknesses sketched in previous chapters do not encourage a wholesale commitment to any of the paradigms, or to all of them.

Further, fixation on the absence or coming of a comprehensive paradigm also can inhibit the development of such a paradigm in a more insidious sense. The lack of a paradigm can serve as the excuse for the poor quality of the available literature. According to such a rationale, that poor quality is an understandable result of the lack of a comprehensive paradigm. Moreover, by implication, that quality of research and thought will improve dramatically once a "grand theory" somehow gets set in place. Even careful statements admit such an interpretation, as in the case with the following statement by Kronenberg: "The lack of clarity in the specifications of public administration as a field of empirical theoretical inquiry is part of a process of paradigmatic change of major intensity."[32] Less careful views might even rationalize a standstill status for the literature as we all await the coming of the new paradigm.

The view here is in sharpest opposition. The quality of the available literature will have to be sharply improved *before* any serious pretentions to even middle-level paradigms can be entertained. Public administration is where it is today in a task sense, basically, not because of the lack of a comprehensive paradigm. It is more correct to note that public administration got where it is because of the inadequacy of paradigms that many believed to be comprehensive. Little confidence is appropriate that today's forced choice of a paradigm would be any more fortunate. Rather, it is more appropriate to argue that the lack of sophistication about empirical research is such that it is unlikely that a wise choice can be made as to a guiding paradigm, considering only its task features. Of course, *any* accepted paradigm can serve in maintenance senses to define a field, to contribute to the self-esteem of professionals, to indicate who is "in" and who is "out," and so on.

Why Not Several Miniparadigms? The fixation on a comprehensive paradigm is understandable, of course. Some guides for both inquiry and identification are not only useful but necessary. The position here is that such guides can now better be provided by several miniparadigms that will help avoid the major scholarly warfare associated with the effort to choose *a* paradigm whose value at this time is very problematic. This is not only convenient, but it also seeks to recognize the field's diversity and early stage of development as well as to facilitate later movement toward a comprehensive paradigm. The position here is very much like that of Beardsley, who argued:

> Any attempt by political scientists to achieve a uniparadigmatic condition for their discipline would be morally indefensible and ultimately self-defeating. For such a uniformity of perspective could be achieved only by arbitrarily choosing one viewpoint and excluding all others. But the latter device, in turn, could be put into operation only by suppressing the analysis of the values and causal assumptions which inevitably comprise a significant part of any candidate for paradigm in political science, and therefore by depriving the would-be dominant paradigm of that high degree of explicitness which is characteristic of all genuine paradigms.[33]

There exist no definitive answers as to what structuring concepts are appropriate for providing balanced attention to the five phenomenal classes seen in Chapter 2 as central in public administration. The reader may recall that these classes included:

- Internal processes of any public administrative system
- Output measures
- Transactions with other systems
- Environmental or institutional envelope within which systems exist
- Value or normative criteria necessary to evaluate the above classes

The lack of comprehensive structuring concepts is seen as the gospel here; but that does not mean that no first approximations are available to help organize the field. Later sections of this chapter will specify substantial content for miniparadigms that can serve for a useful anchoring point for work in public administration. Immediate attention will be given to two classes of first approximations for embodying multiple miniparadigms into the mission and role of public administration viewed as both study and practice.

First, substantial and reasonable precedent exists for approaching public administration via several overlapping and competing paradigms. For example, Waldo at times reacts in such a way to the lack of a "new synthesis," following Simon's powerful 1948 challenge to the "principles" of public administration. Waldo notes that public administration is "anything but stagnant," that it has "grown by 'receiving' this bundle of data, that body of concepts, the other disciplinary perspective," and so on. But "no new synthesis." He adds that *"perhaps* none should be expected, would be undesirable if achieved." Basically, that is, many public administrationists have not treed their quarry because they were following the wrong track. The mistake may lie in seeking a grand theory, or a unified theory, as in some of the physical sciences. Waldo concludes: "The proper orienting analogy" for public administration may not be ". . . astronomy . . . but medicine, law and other professions. Schools of medicine, for example, use data and theory from dozens of fields, these data and theories change frequently and are never fully reconciled one to the other."[34]

Similarly, Heaphey has suggested that the principle of complementarity—drawn from the study of physics—can be a useful guiding metaphor for comparative administration. That is, Heaphey sees several "dominant visions" in the field:[35]

- "Academic analysis" following Riggs[36]
- A "quest for measurable data," which will permit the "creative juxtapositions" of theories with data[37]
- A comparison of selected values or institutional practices between two or more countries or cultures[38]
- An emphasis on administrative action whose "meaning is found in the world of action, not in the world of thought"[39]

Rather than taking these "visions" as evidence that *a* supratheory is needed, Heaphey notes the reaction of physicists who developed the law of complementarity, which stands as an alternative to *"a* precisely definable conceptual model." The physicist Niels Bohr explains that evidence "obtained under different experimental conditions cannot be comprehended within a single picture, but must be regarded as complementary. . . ." Hence comparisons are limited "to complementary pairs of inherently imprecisely defined concepts, such as position and momentum, wave and particle, etc." Concerning comparative administration, Heaphey concludes: "Applying this metaphor, . . . we could

say that complementary visions are involved. In terms of each vision, some kind
of evidence is gathered; what is evidence for one vision is not necessarily
evidence for another."[40]

Given such a view, *the* paradigm neither comes first nor is it the result of
some well-defined process. As Friedland notes, if such a paradigm should ever
develop, it "will not come into being because we need it to, nor because of our
unanimity in perceiving the problems to be solved or methods to be employed,
but rather, because our theoretical findings prove intellectually useful to one
another."[41]

Second, concerning teaching and curriculum rather than research, similar
first approximations are suggested by much of the preceeding analysis. At the
University of Georgia, for example, the working approach at both the doctoral
and master's level is to organize around three perspectives on the public
manager's job:

- *Public Management Core,* which can be fulfilled by such courses: a broad
  public administration survey course; public personnel; organization theory
  and behavior; and public budgeting and finance

- *Management Specialization,* which involves work in one of a wide range of
  functional activities: for example, data-processing finance, planning,
  personnel, and so on

- A *Policy Specialization,* which requires work in one of a wide range of
  substantive areas of greater or less specificity: the environment; neighborhood control; urban politics; housing and real estate; civil-military
  relations; intergovernmental relations; natural resources; social welfare;
  government regulation of business; international relations or politics;
  among many other potentials

This program is a crude amalgam of the latter two paradigms discussed in
Chapter 2. The framework attempts to meld the universal and scientific
emphasis in the Social-Psychological Paradigm with the programmatic and
"political" thrusts of the Humanist/Systemic Paradigm. The core is relatively
fixed; the two specializations can be highly variable. Practically, the range of
alternatives available is a function of the range of course and faculty resources
available, which means that the model above is suitable only for either a very
large school of public administration or public affairs or a large university with
a substantial public administration staff and fluid interdepartmental and inter-
school relationships.

Paradigms Imply Skills and Technologies. The public administration literature
tends to neglect the crucial point that a paradigm should be more than direc-
tional, more than an orientation to phenomena of concern. That is, the meaningful choice of a paradigm implies the growing specification and commitment to a

complex of skills and associated technologies, a commitment to learn such skills and to integrate them in practice as well as in principle. Thus, the Humanist/ Systemic Paradigm described in Chapter 2 implies the integration of a broad range of skills, including those of various branches of economics as well as the more or less full range of behavioral sciences.

Public administrationists, as has been variously demonstrated, are quite cavalier on this point. They are more likely to emphasize verbalisms than skills and technologies. This is meant in two senses. Public administrationists are likely to import broad concepts—like "confrontation" or "participation"—from other fields of research, while leaving behind the associated research technologies and the assumptions of fact and value often suffusing them. Relatedly, home-grown guiding concepts are likely to be stated in ways that do not encourage testing or even defy it. Much of Riggsian comparative administration has this quality, for example.

This is no casual matter. For a paradigm has to be more than a shopping list of items that are unavailable now, and may never be. The complex association between a paradigm and skills and technologies is here understood to motivate taking *the* pie—if that is what it turns out to be—one bite at a time. This will also permit the development in public administration of the specific skills and technologies appropriate to various specific miniparadigms, the testing of which may eventually lead to that "grand theory" so much desired. Friedland provides wise counsel on the point. While acknowledging the difficulties associated with its unavailability, he also cautions that "unified theory is not developed by exhortation," or "because we need it." Nor is its development likely to be a linear one "originating from a single well-defined notion of relevance and culminating ... in the unified theory...." Rather, theory will evolve by successes and misadventures alike, because of the accumulating usefulness of minitheories.[42] Demonstrating this usefulness, in turn, requires competence in appropriate technologies and skills both for research and application.

Guidelines for Miniparadigms

Because it purports to provide direction as well as criticism, this analysis will henceforth be preoccupied with specifically how to move toward a miniparadigm that may later contribute to a vital center for public administration. Directly, the analysis in the preceding pages does not generate a specific mission and role for public administration. But that conceptual history does imply a set of guidelines for orienting that development. These guidelines should apply whether public administration is organizationally tied to political science, whether it is an autonomous academic department or school, or whether it is an organizational component of some supradiscipline like "prescriptive policy sciences" or of some aggregate like a "public affairs" school.

Nine guidelines are offered here, criteria that can serve as standards against which to evaluate approaches for building content into public administration. The guidelines also permit a subtle but significant shift in approaching the field. That is, conceptual definitions of public administration typically stress classification, the separating or integrating of distinct realms of phenomena. Oppositely, the present approach is less concerned with isolating discrete realms than it is with indicating useful ways to approach broadly defined phenomenal mazes.

1. *Public administration should be defined in terms of the issues faced by public administrators, rather than in terms of attempted in/out classifications.* The total sense of it is a phenomenal area distinguished in complex ways from, for example, business administration more by degrees than by inclusion/exclusion. When the focus is on internal processes of administration, the degree of overlap is substantial. When public laws and institutions are focal, that overlap is much reduced.

Experience clearly suggests this point. For example, Simon realized the synthetic nature of his distinction that any decisions that implement "final goals" are "factual judgments"; and he sometimes was explicit in severely restricting the applicability of his distinction between fact and value. But this clarity is not of much practical help. As his critics often noted, there will always be meta-goals and meta-meta-goals, ad infinitum. Similarly, Simon himself took Goodnow to task because the latter's two central concepts were not precise enough to support inquiry. When Goodnow's *Politics and Administration* was written and read, a political decision still had to be distinguished from an administrative one. "Apparently it has been assumed that the distinction was self-evident, so self-evident as hardly to require discussion,"[43] was Simon's way of saying that Goodnow provided too little help in managing that challenge.

Most experience, unfortunately, reflects reliance on circumscribing public administration by inclusion/exclusion. Some have carelessly argued that if it is not "scientific," it is not public administration. This justifiably raises the hackles of those interested in values[44] and even demeans their efforts. More recently, some observers have argued that public administration should assume a "policy orientation" that is "macro-analytical," to distinguish it sharply from the "micro-analysis" of economics, psychology, and sociology.[45] Such a view is suspect, for at least two reasons. Rather than being concerned about what is "macro" and what is "micro," why not get on with the integration of levels of analysis that clearly will be necessary? It does not much matter which specialty brings off that integration. Moreover, I am anxious lest a kind of back-door, latter-day politics/administration dichotomy may be encouraged by a micro/macro distinction.

2. *A useful, working boundary definition of public administration must facilitate application as well as analysis; it must support "applied" as well as "pure" effort.* The point has caused much mischief. Moreso than many areas in

political science, that is, the *use* of the results of *research* is an issue close to the surface of the developmental history of public administration. The struggle essentially involves making reseach useful without converting researchers either into low-level gatherers of data or into working administrators. The needed work is perhaps most descriptively labeled "action research," with equal attention going to both its central aspects.

More or less universally, the literature of public administration fails to provide or even encourage action research. Little of it is rooted in empirical research; still less of that literature has a clearly developed sense of application or action as a central challenge; and the contemporary emphasis on methodologies like that underlying democratic administration (analyzed at length in Chapter 5) implies that much attention is being devoted to approaches that will not produce such empirical research, and may indeed hinder such research in profound ways. So the results of past effort are inadequate to provide action research; and some signs imply that future progress will have to run counter to such popular emphases in the literature as the work of Ostrom or the new public administration.

Despair is not yet appropriate, however. Indeed, action research has only recently gained wide acceptance via demonstrations of its great usefulness, as in medicine, weapons systems, and still more recently in the behavioral sciences.[46] Moreover, the conclusion in the paragraph above must be qualified, area by area, even in public administration. For example, various approaches to decision making do better than average on this score, with qualifications. Thus the usefulness of various statistical and mathematical tools in management is patent. And case studies, with their distinct decision-making orientation, also have a substantial usefulness in training managers or would-be managers.

3. *Any viable miniparadigm for public administration must be capable of being tied in to broad cultural values.* Public administration as both pure and applied is and should be culture-bound. The point has become manifest in recent work in comparative administration,[47] but it applies generally. To insist that public administration be determinedly value-free, in short, is to condemn it to lessened impact and even to irrelevance.

Having said this much, and so bluntly, care is necessary lest the present point be interpreted too broadly. There are delicious ironies in the insistence that public administration should not be value-free; and care is necessary lest the point be seen as a caricatured plea for a kind of "socialist reality." So let us be clear about what the present emphasis does not mean. The point here is not a pronouncement that what exists is normatively good; even less is it the enticing promise that what we prefer not only should exist, but will exist; and most certainly the argument here is not the classic one that, because it must deal with values, public administration therefore cannot be a science or scientific.

It will not be possible to briefly develop the more specific sense of what the present point does mean, but two broad emphases suffice to circumscribe in general terms what is meant by the pronouncement that public administration is and should be culture bound. The two emphases deal with:

- Public administration and science
- Public administration and its institutional context

Public Administration and Science

This first perspective on the specific ways in which public administration is and should be value-loaded is straightforward, although it does go against the grain of some historic thoughtways in the discipline. Those thoughtways generated much early debate and essentially conflicted over the issue of whether or not public administration is culture bound. If it were culture bound or value-loaded, went the terms of the debate, public administration would thereby be disqualified from becoming a science.[48]

This was a historic debate, but it was posed in awkward terms. For public administration is culture bound, and also *must be,* if it is to exploit its full scientific potential. Consider but three points. First, public administration *as pure research* is and always should be culture bound, even though in limited ways. For any empirical theory rests upon a set of "values of science" that guide the processes of gathering data and analyzing results. Hence, all empirical research is, or should be, guided by those values of science. At another level, the choice of subjects for study also will—and should, up to a substantial degree—reflect the needs of the host society or organization. Any other general bias legitimate thumb twiddling on a massive scale.

Second, any organizationally relevant science must be culture bound in another sense. *When man is the object of study,* his values, opinions, and feelings must be part of the target data for inquiry. Empirical regularities in one such normative/opinional "field" need not exist in all others any more than similarities need exist in the behavior of the same physical object in different gravitational fields.[49] To call someone an SOB in a trusting and friendly environment is one thing, for example. Quite different effects are probable when the environment is suspicious and defensive. In such cases, in essence, sets of values become critical intervening variables in predictive linkages.

Third, public administration *as applied* must rest on a statement of values or goals that are to be approached via knowledge of empirical regularities. The *use* of the results of any empirical inquiry, in short, must always be culture bound. More broadly, values should be integrated with empirical regularities in comprehensive theoretical networks for guiding action. Hence, I have elsewhere argued that the development of "goal-based, empirical theories" must be a major order of business in public administration.[50]

Unfortunately, the public administration literature more or less stumbles badly when it comes to providing a clear and explicit place for values in all three of these senses. For example, Ostrom's democratic administration reviewed in Chapter 5 clearly rests on an ideational structure that seeks to do the job of dealing with values by avoiding most of the issues associated with them, by fixating on only a very narrow range of values. Moreover, all three major paradigms in public administration reviewed in Chapter 2 have treated values inadequately. In the Social-Psychological Paradigm, as it were, the "science" tended to drive out or devalue the "value." The Humanist/Systemic Paradigm seeks to direct forceful attention to values, overall, but significant questions are still outstanding. Thus it remains to be seen whether "value" in the Humanist orientation will inhibit the development of "science."[51] And the Systemic orientation has tended to accent only a narrow range of values, much like those underlying the Traditional Paradigm. Hence, one of the essential counter-arguments arrayed against that once potent expression of the Systemic orientation in public administration, PPBS, is that it gained apparent specificity only at the expense of so narrowing its attention as to miss much of the value-related questioning that is at the heart of politics.

Public Administration and Its Institutional Context

This second perspective on how and why public administration is and should be value-loaded is more subtle, or perhaps the proper word is "ephemeral." Whether subtle or ephemeral, however, the issues of relevance here are at the dead center of our contemporary problems of governance and management. In introductory sum, the "North American" public administration of the past was tailored to an existing "institutional context"—complex manifestations of what objects or symbols were infused with specific value, which infusions were more or less definite and stable. Today, many of these ascriptions of value are matters of serious question, even if the old gods have not necessarily fallen and may possibly regain their hold on the collective consciousness. Consequently, new miniparadigms in public administration cannot simply rely on common under-standings of a supporting institutional context. Those paradigms may have to—in fact, probably will have to—contribute to the development of a modified institutional context, or even of a somehow new context. This task is of the highest order of difficulty and importance, raising as it does critical issues of who, and how, and when—a sense of everything having to be done at once because older understandings are not sufficient to help us over the rough spots, and also because developing understandings tend to come undone even under moderate stress and press. The appropriate posture for public administrationists is a difficult one: We have to be concerned about draining the swamp, that is to say, not only *while* we are up to our hips in alligators, but especially *because* we are up to our hips in alligators.

Three emphases provide perspective on this subtle and significant point. First, although observers differ on the timing of the disease, virtually all social commentators stress our loss of a sense of community[52] or the collapse of a "communal sense of order."[53] The beginning of the trend was clear, for example, to those early observers who saw industrialization and nationalism in the process of converting social life from an essentially gemeinschaft to more of a gesellschaft basis, from a value nexus based on long historical development and personal contact to a more sudden and mechanical restructuring of human relationships to better suit the twin demands of industrialization and nationalism.[54] The adjective appropriate to gemeinschaft and gesellschaft are, respectively, natural or organic as contrasted with artificial or artifactual.

As Barry D. Karl perceptively encapsulates the administratively relevant sweep of the last half-century or so in America, those early processes were at first resisted and later put out of mind by an act of will, but they have more recently become awesome and perhaps out of control. Briefly, he argues that our present institutional context for public administration was passed on to us by a generation that had a personal experience with an "old local-regional morality" and an associated "communal sense or order."[55] That sense of order was often more myth than reality, even then; and what was order for some might have been enslavement or a dismal quality of life for many others. But such fine points did not carry the day: That morality-with-order nonetheless became the wish foundation of an institutional context for public administration principles and practices that it supported and ineluctably shaped.

But events marched on, and an expanding gap came to develop between our inherited institutional context and evolving realities and preferences, even as they coexisted with a variously desperate longing for the "good old days" and for the sense of community so dearly missed.[56] Industrialization and nationalism continued to impact on these bedrock definitions of the desirable social life. Moreover, two major macro-forces have lately joined in that assault—professionalism and internationalism. For example, racial discrimination was one of the products of our "old local-regional morality,"[57] and that bastion was finally breached (although not yet defeated) by a combination of those four fearsome horsemen of today—industrialization, nationalism, professionalism, and internationalism. In public administration, for example, perhaps professionalism was the dominant motivator for reducing racism, professionalism being related to how a job is done rather than to the color of the skin of the person who does the job. No doubt, however, professionalism got powerful reinforcement from the other macro-forces, as from our growing internationalism and the patent fact that the international world is far more technicolor than it is white.

The issues are not yet decided, to be sure. It is possible that the last decade or two reflect more aberrations than they do central tendencies for the future. Hence, careful observers like Karl still withhold judgment, even as they are convinced that many contemporary versions of "doing your own thing" will not be sufficient for "the order necessary for the sustaining of community life," let alone for "efficient order."[58]

One point does seem clear, however. Developments in public administration can no longer merely rely on the traditional institutional context, with "developments" to be draped like conceptual tinsel on some hardy fir tree. Future developments in public administration must actively contribute to the evolution of a somehow redefined institutional context, as well as aid in the elaboration of the values that underlay that context. This is the essence of Karl's important conclusion: "It is perhaps the leading paradox of our age that all of the approaches to social system built up over the last century—whether one calls them social science, public administration, or industrial management—are in a state of crisis."[59] They all need to be reinfused with value, that is to say, having lost the support of a once-potent set of institutions and traditions.

It would be presumptuous here and now to argue that any miniparadigm has a lock on that challenge. What seems certain is that the approaches detailed earlier are not up to that task. More basically, in fact, they may be directly counterproductive to doing what must be done. For example, comparative public administration provides a model in this regard only by implying what should not be done. Recall that comparative administration sought to graft North American institutions on alien values and traditions. Similarly, Ostrom's democratic administration does not seem up to the task of providing the required set of bedrock values. Indeed, it seeks to finesse that significant issue, and perhaps thereby runs the risk of triggering that "rugged individualism" which can be a replacement for community but is never a basis for it.[60]

Second, although opinions clearly differ, the dominant intellectual view here is that it is advisable in the ongoing redefinition to preserve the value paradoxes built into the American form of government. Thus Caldwell concludes: "Examination of . . . American political ideals readily reveals their paradoxical character. As propositions underlying American constitutional theory, none are definitive, none absolute, and all are paralleled by contradictions in theory or in practice. Yet paradox from one viewpoint may be logic from another."[61]

Caldwell is almost certainly correct as to what exists. Usefully, Caldwell traces major paradoxical outcomes in governance to these ideological crosscurrents (among others) in the basic value preferences undergirding the dominant American approach to government:

1.   Sovereignty is vested exclusively in the entire people.

3.   Individuals possess "rights" which government ought to observe and protect. . . .

6.   The Legislative is the most democratic and representative branch of government, but is least able to fulfill its responsibilities.[62]

It requires no great insight to isolate tendencies at cross-purposes in these basic preferences. For example: Sovereignty resides in the people; but their representatives in the legislature have serious problems in meeting their responsibilities, major among which is to control government; and government requires critical oversight, and especially so given an aggressive interpretation of what is meant by "protection of rights."

Although Caldwell's description seems beyond serious challenge, much of the public administration literature in effect rejects his prescription about the virtue of preserving the essential paradoxes in our form of government. Overall, in fact, that literature is given to defining away the paradox. For example, the Traditional Paradigm in effect resolves those paradoxes by consistent allegiance to a monocratic hierarchy, which gives much the better of it to "administration" than to "politics." Similarly, while rightly taking the Traditional Paradigm to task for its fixation on hieratics, Ostrom's democratic administration also on balance seeks to resolve the paradox by an emphasis on methodological individualism.

The bias here will be to preserve the essential paradoxes in our form of government, following Caldwell. The miniparadigm of concern in the second volume of this set, then, will be determinedly centrist in this basic sense.

Third, one special paradox in the American system is the shifting blend of democratic/populist and elitist tendencies. It is easy to overreact to the point, given the social and political dynamite involved. But the track record seems clear enough. The two are a kind of yin and yang, each of which can help balance the excesses of the other. Caldwell illustrates the broader point in this telling specific: ". . . while professionalism is not a democratic process—indeed the hierarchies of knowledge and judgment it is intended to reflect are the essence of elitism—the development of modern democracy would be impossible without professionalism."[63]

Again, much of the public administration literature seems to reject a balance in this regard, and most of that literature prefers resolving the paradoxes by overemphasis on democratic/populist or elitist themes. The former theme is sounded bravely in today's common demands for "power to the people," for example; and the elitist bias of the Traditional Paradigm is patent, as it also is in many practices and policies in public management such as a career service or a professional meritocracy.

4. *Any useful miniparadigm in public administration must be capable of being tied-in to prevailing organizational needs in public agencies.* The point might be made in many ways, but the present focus is on change versus stability. Today's public administrators patently must give unprecedented attention to change—change in missions and roles or in organization structure, as well as change in the knowledge, in the skills, and (perhaps especially) in the attitudes of most personnel at all levels of organization.

Derivatively, any useful conceptual definition of public administration must also encompass the conflict certain to be associated with pervasive and persistent change in dynamic tension with the need for some stabilization. For example, different patterns of organizational growth imply the need for different kinds of organization structure.[64] Structural change, in turn, requires different behaviors and attitudes. All three kinds of change may occasion painful, bitter conflict. Any relevant approach to public administration consequently must relate to that real world of change grappled with by public administrators, including the need to stabilize after a change or to provide some sense of stability against the onslaughts of future shock.

Unfortunately, public administration has been timid about dealing with the problems of change. Sometimes, the neglect is a by-product of a specific developmental history. Thus the decision-making approach implies the possibility of a strong emphasis on change. But change got short shrift in Simon, and sometimes by conscious design. In at least the case of early work on Human Relations and of Scientific Management, more clearly, neglect of conflict and change was no accident. Their dominant underlying model was preoccupied with stability. Finding and keeping a "quasi-stationary equilibrium" was the usual goal for work in Human Relations, for example, with conflict being the antigoal. Similarly, Scientific Management sought a single best way and, once found, advised holding tightly to it. Conflict, in this context, only signaled that the "way" had neither been found nor respected. Much the same static or steady-state bias seems to pervade such popular approaches in public administration as that of Ostrom reviewed in Chapter 5.

The major exception to this generalization about the steady-state bias of the literature is the new public administration, which is analyzed in Chapter 4. As the discussion there indicates, however, the thrust for change was not clearly tied to the values to be approached thereby. And even less was the emphasis on change related to a technology for inducing it, or for facilitating restabilization after the required change had been accomplished.

5. *A viable concept for public administration must permit useful attention to a variety of organization and analytic levels.* Large number of observers of public management are not satisfied with a concept of the field encompassing the "lower" part of such hierarchical notions as politics/administration or value/fact. Observers long have complained that, as in Scientific Management or

in Simon's treatment of factual judgments in decision making, the scope of the field was restricted to low-level phenomena. For a variety of reasons, no field can reasonably be so restricted for long. Thus, if administration really is not separate from politics, any viable field must be conceptually licensed to explore interactions of interest.

On this point, the public-policy approach is variably acute. The emphasis on the content of policy and on "high-level" phenomena is most useful. Still, some interpretations threaten only to emphasize high-level policy, rather than to seek an integration with other levels of analysis. This is the potential mischief in limiting the attention of public administration or political science[65] to macro-phenomena, when the world of the public administrator comes in ineluctable shadings of macro- and micro-phenomena.[66] The failure to acknowledge this shading is common in many versions of "public policy," for example, which is especially significant because of the contemporary prominence of that broad vision of the mission and role of public administration.

Despite the short-run convenience of a restricted approach, the alternative to multilevel attention is not very attractive. Thus, students of a field can only resign themselves to having defined significant phenomena out of their reach, and, very likely, they can later take credit for having killed off their field. Or—if they are lucky—they can rest easier with the memory that they only malnourished their field for a while.

6. *Useful miniparadigms for public administration will include as major multiple foci the individual, his interpersonal relations, his small groupings, and large organizations as well. Consequently, any paradigms useful in the field must provide meaningful research and applied technologies for coping with these complex multiple foci.*

This compound guideline seems reasonable enough, and, if it is, the conceptual approaches to public administration reviewed earlier generally do not recognize the reasonable. For example, Simon's decision-making schema defines its science of administration in terms of the rational intellective processes of the individual decision maker. Similarly, though still differently, Scientific Management sought to eliminate man's multiple social and psychological anchorages, and, thereby, it sought to tie the individual employee to some "grand designer of work." Perhaps most dramatically, the ideation underlying democratic administration, as Chapter 5 shows, reflects either a unilevel emphasis on the methodological individual or assumes that individual and group levels of analysis are somehow identical. In addition, the methodology underlying his approach inspires significant doubts as to whether it can support what requires doing, either in descriptions of what is, or in prescriptions of how desired conditions can be achieved in practice. Ostrom's approach violates the sixth guideline both coming and going, as it were.

Even when a concept of public administration does encompass this sixth guideline, moreover, that recognition tends to be variously limited. For example, concerns were expressed in Chapter 2 that the Humanist/Systemic Paradigm cannot provide useful analytic guidance because of its several inherent contradictions or tendencies in opposition. In a more limited way, early work in Human Relations patently was concerned with a greater fullness of "organization man." Being without a substantial undergirding research literature or a technology for inducing desired conditions, however, early work in Human Relations was largely restricted to trumpeting a major but narrow truth—that we often can get things done only through people. Similarly, the public-policy approach, rightly interpreted, would include the multiple foci detailed above, but most interpretations are variously narrower than one proposed by Dye. He argues:

> If public policy is to be the dependent variable in our research, we must be prepared to search for policy determinants among economic, social, cultural, historical, technological factors, as well as political forces. If public policy is to be the independent variable, we must be prepared to search for policy consequences which are economic, social, cultural, historical and technological, as well as political.[67]

7. *Even as the development of multiple foci must remain the long-run goal, a "law of tactical convenience" should govern the priorities accorded to various lines of development work.* That is, all choices between research or applied priorities must somehow reconcile two emphases in dynamic tension— the findings, technologies, and skills that it would be desirable to have, and some realistic assessment of what issues constitute a manageable "next bite" at some specific point in the development of public administration.

Nature is not benign in this regard. Neglect of the long-run goal can result in a pleasant state of going nowhere. Alternatively, too much concern about what findings, technologies, and skills should ideally be in hand often means only that the manageable next steps required to move toward some global ideal will not be taken. In this sense, paradoxically, fixation on the ideal may only raise the probability that the ideal will not be approached. The dilemma is especially profound in political science and public administration, both of which must comprehend the nation-state, which it would be delightful to be able to do. At the same time, that global focus is an awkward one with which to begin to establish the research methods and traditions that are significant in increasing major aspects of such comprehension. At its worst, there can be so much attention to reach that grasp increases but slowly as a result. To simplify, it is as if physicists insisted on a general theory, while failing to undertake the many steps intervening between such mundanes as the Brownian movement and that general theory.

More or less, public administrationists have fixated on what it would be nice to have, and have neglected the development of methods and cumulative findings that are the necessary foundations for moving the public administration literature from where it is to where it would be so nice to be. This is an understandable thing, of course, but its effects are nonetheless real even if the mistake is so charmingly human.

Illustrations abound. Much of the new public administration, for example, sought such a great leap forward from an undeveloped and, speaking more plainly, an unspecified analytical base. Consider the emphasis on "revolutionary science" and the comprehensive paradigm that was thought to be its major product. Revealingly, also, it was widely believed that such a comprehensive paradigm would develop only if the processes of "normal science" were suspended while the required consensus developed. The position is intriguing, to say the least. The special curiosity of it is that the acknowledged failure of the earlier public administration paradigm—the "principles of public administration"—itself derived essentially from a failure to respect the traditions of normal science.[68] Ironically, also, the public administration literature would not have to labor hard to suspend normal science, for examples of its conscious application were and are quite unusual in the discipline.

Such examples motivate the emphasis here on the "law of tactical convenience," which urges tackling problems that are now manageable, so as to build knowledge of, and experience with, broad methodology and specific methods that will permit swallowing ever-larger bites of reality without getting analytical indigestion. The chapters of the companion volume will illustrate one such tactical convenience.

8. *As difficult as it is, the development of public administration must self-consciously concentrate on its task aspects versus maintenance aspects.* As the preceding chapters variously detail, maintenance considerations often seemed to determine the choice of a guiding concept for public administration. "Maintenance" in this case refers basically to the desire to preserve identifications and loyalties with political science in the choice of a working definition of the scope of public administration. "Task" features are those related to comprehending the phenomena to be studied.

Task and maintenance are not always easy to separate, but the distinction helps characterize much work in public administration. For example, maintenance considerations encouraged the long-lived acceptance of the two varieties of politics/administration, for example, as well as the popularity of the several varieties of public policy. Similarly, Ostrom's democratic administration impressed me with its maintenance features far more than with its contributions to task. Elsewhere, to illustrate, I note that Ostrom seems so intent on maintenance that he often weakens his own argument. Early political scientist Woodrow Wilson becomes the prime nemesis for Ostrom, whereas the sociologist Weber gets far less attention, despite the curious fact that Wilson argued for congressional supremacy, while Weber argued for the executive as the central authority. One of the reasons the emphasis is paradoxical is that Ostrom's analysis is clearly directed at overblown executive authority, whereas Wilson's emphasis on the legislature is in America practically and institutionally associated with the kind of fragmented authority that Ostrom prefers. I proposed a hypothesis for Ostrom's focus on Wilson, when it would have been simpler and more direct to argue that the principles of Weberian bureaucracy were innocent about even the more obvious issues in political philosophy. My hypothesis reads: "Specifically, Wilson's contributions to legitimating the maintenance thrust of [Ostrom's analysis] . . . was perceived by Ostrom as overbalancing the obvious technical problems of [emphasizing] Wilson's centrality."[69]

Note also that the short flirtation with the Phase III Science of Management is *the* exception to the present generalization. That variety of Phase III was all task, and maintenance be damned. Hence, its rapid demise, I suppose.

As the notion is used here, more specifically, three features of task are most central. A developing discipline must emphasize and balance the following:

- The processes of empirical science, because much of public administration requires a purposeful manipulation of the world of people and things, for which broad purposefulness it is necessary either to possess an increasingly precise map of the major relationships that exist in nature or else to learn to tolerate chronic failure in attempting to make what happen is desired

- The processes of the specification and clarification of normative choices, because much of public administration deals with issues of value, of the characteristics of good administrative conditions upon which progress toward the just state will depend in critical ways

- The processes of the increasingly conscious and successful use of empirical knowledge to move toward the values of the just state through administration that is increasingly capable of achieving what is desirable

Having said this much it is necessary to note that not just any analytical focus will suffice to permit useful attention to task in public administration. Useful foci, in fact, will be quite special and specific to the developmental stage of the discipline at any point in time. Moreover, it will be a long time before any very comprehensive approaches can be attempted with any great confidence. Given that it will often be necessary in practice to do the best possible under difficult or impossible conditions, what will be most useful now for the development of the study of public administration are some manageable foci that will permit successful experience with the three emphases and balancings just listed.

This argues against nothing now, and pie in the sky, by and by. Public administration must always do its best to help approach the values of the just state, on a day-to-day basis, no matter how inadequate our existing knowledge, no matter how fuzzy our goals, and no matter how pitiful are the available technologies for making happen what we value or prefer. Sometimes, these short-run pressures may be overwhelming, in fact.

Nonetheless, humble beginnings will be necessary to provide early momentum toward those pure and applied sciences of public management that will substantially meet the lofty aspirations implicit in the goal of movement toward the *just* state through *good* administration.

The chapters of the companion volume reflect one such humble beginning. They seek to detail one tactically convenient approach to dealing with empirical regularities, with values, as well as with applied technologies for moving toward those values via a knowledge of empirical relationships. This tactically convenient example is the "laboratory approach to organization development," or, more conveniently, OD. Hopefully, also, those chapters will stimulate others to similarly elaborate additional ways of dealing with the recently discussed three critical task emphases for balancing the development of public administration as a discipline.

The public administration literature contains much evidence that to be more ambitious than developing numerous miniparadigms of the kind illustrated in the chapters of the companion volume is to risk a nasty circularity: Ambitious expectations to do wondrous broad-gauged things develop from time to time, but these expectations quickly die because they are so far from having a firm footing in middle-range methods and findings. Such a circularity well enough encapsulates the history of the new public administration, as well as the last decade or so of attention to comparative administration.

9. *Overall, the development of public administration will depend on the exploitation of what may be called "open systems," by which is meant theoretical networks that are rooted in experience and that are testable; in consequence, they are at least potentially self-correcting.*

Much of the public administration literature stands in marked contrast with the ninth guideline. Much of that literature reflects a substantial, and probably growing, bias toward a "closed-system" approach, which is rooted in ideas that are logical derivatives from assumptions or postulates, and which are typically untested or even untestable even when they are explicitly recognized.[70] Work in the closed-system or "self-sealing" tradition is illustrated by this approach to ideation:

> The relation between the significance of a theory and the "realism"
> of its "assumptions" is almost the opposite of that [expected.]
> Truly important and significant hypotheses will be found to have
> "assumptions" that are wildly inaccurate descriptive representations
> of reality, and, in general, the more significant the theory, the more
> unrealistic the assumptions. . . .[71]

There is some truth in such words, of course, but they also contain some nasty traps for those who are not extremely careful. The traps are especially treacherous for those in disciplines like public administration that have neither firm traditions nor time-tested skills for empirically testing such assumptions and their derivatives.

Early and late, the public administration literature is far more dominated by work in the self-sealing tradition than by work that is potentially self-correcting. The "principles of public administration" reflect such an approach, for example, at an earlier time in public administration's development. Their basic methodology was self-sealing in definite ways. For example, the principles purported to prescribe the conditions for effective management, in two no-fail senses. When the conditions did not exist, the standard response was that they should. Where those conditions existed, and where "effective management" did not result, the common explanation was that the principles could not "really take effect anywhere until they were in place everywhere." This is a heads-I-win, tails-you-lose methodology. More recently, much new public administration can be similarly characterized as self-sealing, if in different ways than the "principles." Chapter 4 makes that point, recall. Similarly, Ostrom at once sees the principles as the major villain in the contemporary troubles in public administration, and yet at the same time, as Chapter 5 establishes, his democratic administration rests on a methodology like that underlying the "principles." Progress is difficult or impossible in such cases, because both feet are figuratively planted in the territory that is ostensibly to be left behind.

Some care is necessary here about the ninth guideline's advice that theoretical networks be rooted in experience. To illustrate, normative propositions in public administration are not themselves testable in the same sense as are empirical statements. But even they can be variously related to experience, as in such questions as:

- How can specific preferred end states be approached, given the specific empirical conditions and relationships that exist in nature?
- Do we know enough to be reasonably certain of getting from where we are to where we prefer to be, at least without inducing major unattractive consequences?

Note several related points, in conclusion. The intent of these guidelines is not that all relevant work in public administration must meet each of them. Rather, the field's development is seen as being enhanced by the cumulative impact of all efforts to help meet the guidelines. Moreover, more than one discrete approach can meet the guidelines. Thus claims have been made that "development administration" in essence can meet many of these guidelines,[72] and more power to such approaches. I hope this treatment motivates aficionados of that approach—as well as of numerous other approaches—to attempt the same kind of specific illustration and analysis of their approach as that provided in the second volume of this set: *Public Administration as a Developing Discipline: Organization Development as One of a Future Family of Miniparadigms.*

Notes and References

1. Thomas S. Kuhn, *The Structure of Scientific Revolutions* (Chicago: University of Chicago Press, 1962, 1970).

2. Herbert A. Simon, "The Proverbs of Administration," *Public Administration Review* 6 (Winter 1964): 53-67.

3. Dwight Waldo, "Scope of the Theory of Public Administration," in *Theory and Practice of Public Administration,* ed. James C. Charlesworth (Philadelphia: American Academy of Political and Social Science, 1968), p. 5.

4. Vincent Ostrom, *The Intellectual Crisis in American Public Administration* (University, Ala.: University of Alabama Press, 1973), p. 11.

5. Ibid., p. 13.

6. Ibid., p. 14.

7. Ibid., p. 15.

8. Ibid., p. 16.

9. Stephen E. Toulmin, *Human Understanding,* Vol. I, The Collective Use and Evaluation of Concepts (copyright © 1972 by Princeton University Press). See also Fred A. Kramer, "Policy Analysis as Ideology, *Public Administration Review* 35 (September 1975): 509-517.

10. Toulmin, *Human Understanding,* pp. 100, 101.

11. Ibid., p. 101.

12. Thomas S. Kuhn, "The Function of Dogma in Scientific Research," in *Scientific Change,* ed. A. C. Crombie (London: Heinemann, 1963), pp. 347ff.

13. Toulmin, *Human Understanding,* p. 103.

14. Ibid., pp. 100, 102.

15. Ibid., p. 105.

16. Ibid., pp. 105-106.

17. Conveniently, compare the Appendix of the 1970 second edition of Kuhn's *Structure of Scientific Revolutions* with the 1962 edition.

18. Toulmin, *Human Understanding,* pp. 113-114.

19. Ibid., p. 114.

20. See the Appendix of the second edition of Kuhn's *Structure of Scientific Revolutions.*

21. Toulmin, *Human Understanding,* pp. 112-113.

22. Ibid., p. 115.

23. Ibid., p. 127.

24. As Norton Long reminds Vincent Ostrom in a review of the latter's *Intellectual Crisis in American Public Administration,* which review appears in *The Journal of Politics* 36 (August 1974): 804.

25. See Ostrom, *The Intellectual Crisis in American Public Administration,* p. 5, for example.

26. Dwight Waldo, *Perspectives on Administration* (University, Ala.: University of Alabama Press, 1956).

27. Frederick C. Mosher, "Research in Public Administration," *Public Administration Review* 16 (Summer 1956): 177.

28. Ibid., p. 177.

29. Waldo, "Scope and Theory of Public Administration," in Charlesworth, *Theory and Practice of Public Administration,* p. 10.

30. Kuhn, *The Structure of Scientific Revolutions,* p. 15.

31. Lewis S. Feuer, *Einstein and the Generations of Science* (New York: Basic Books, 1972).

32. Philip Kronenberg, "The Scientific and Moral Authority of Empirical Theory of Public Administration," in *Toward a New Public Administration,* ed Frank Marini (Scranton, Pa.: Chandler, 1971), p. 195.

33. This excerpt from "Political Science: The Case of the Missing Paradigm," by Philip L. Beardsley is reprinted from *Political Theory,* Vol. 2, No. 1 (February 1964) p. 60, by permission of the Publisher, Sage Publications, Inc.

33. Philip L. Beardsley, "Political Science: The Case of the Missing Paradigm," *Political Theory* 2 (February 1974): 60.

34. Dwight Waldo, "The Administrative State Revisited," *Public Administration Review* 25 (March 1965): 16-17.

35. James Heaphey, "Comparative Public Administration: Comments on Current Characteristics," *Public Administration Review* 28 (May 1968): 242-245.

36. Fred W. Riggs, *Administration in Developing Countries* (Boston: Houghton Mifflin, 1964).

37. Heaphey, "Comparative Public Administration," p. 243.

38. Ibid., p. 244.

39. Consult Milton J. Esman, "The Ecological Style in Comparative Administration," *Public Administration Review* 27 (September 1967): especially 273-278.

40. Quoted in Heaphey, "Comparative Public Administration," p. 245.

41. Edward Friedland, "Comment: The Pursuit of Relevance," in Marini, *Toward a New Public Administration,* p. 54.

42. Ibid., p. 54.

43. Simon, *Administrative Behavior,* p. 54.

44. Without doubt, the most prominent display of academic hackles was in Herbert Storing, ed., *Essays on the Scientific Study of Politics* (New York: Holt, Rinehart & Winston, 1962), especially pp. 142-149.

45. Theodore J. Lowi, "What Political Scientists Don't Need to Ask About Policy Analysis," *Policy Studies Journal* 2 (Autumn 1973): especially 65-66.

46. For comprehensive perspective on action research, see Robert T. Golembiewski, *Renewing Organizations* (Itasca, Ill.: F. E. Peacock, 1972); and Edgar F. Huse, *Organization Development and Change* (St. Paul, Minn.: West, 1975), pp. 89-244.

47. A. Dunsire, *Administration: The Word and the Science* (New York: John Wiley & Sons, 1973), pp. 133-137.

48. Most prominently, see Robert A. Dahl, "The Science of Public Administration: Three Problems," *Public Administration Review* 7 (Winter 1974): 1-11.

49. See the literature on cohesiveness, for example, and its significant differential effects, given differences in norms. For example, see Robert T. Golembiewski, *The Small Group* (Chicago: University of Chicago Press, 1962), pp. 149-170.

50. Robert T. Golembiewski, *Behavior and Organization* (Chicago: Rand McNally, 1962), pp. 48-57.

51. The anti-intellectual or at least affective thrust of the "encounter movement," a variant of "third force" or humanist psychology, provides a case in point. For a pessimistic evaluation of that aspect of the movement, see especially Kurt W. Back's "Beyond Science," in *Beyond Words* (New York: Russell Sage Foundation, 1972), pp. 201-212.

52. Robert A. Nisbet, *The Quest for Community* (New York: Oxford University Press, 1953).

53. Barry Dean Karl, "Public Administration and American History: A Century of Professionalism," *Public Administration Review* 36 (September 1976): 503.

54. Golembiewski, *The Small Group,* especially pp. 12-18, provides overall perspective.

55. Karl, "Public Administration and American History," p. 502.

56. Perhaps the most characteristic expression of the need is reflected in the massive growth of opportunities for group experiences in caring and supportive environments. See Arthur Blumberg and Robert T. Golembiewski, *Learning and Change in Groups* (New York and London: Penguin, 1976), especially pp. 9-21.

57. As Karl incisively notes. "Public Administration and American History," p. 503.

58. Ibid., p. 503.

59. Ibid., p. 499.

60. Ibid., p. 503.

61. Lynton Keith Caldwell, "Novus Ordo Seclorum: The Heritage of American Public Administration," *Public Administration Review* 36 (September 1976): 455.

62. Ibid., p. 483.

63. Ibid., p. 489.

64. Alfred D. Chandler, Jr., *Strategy and Structure* (Cambridge, Mass.: The MIT Press, 1962).

65. For a collection of research that implies the validity of multilevel attention, see Heinz Eulau, *Micro-Macro Political Analysis: Accents on Inquiry* (Chicago: Aldine, 1969).

66. For dramatic examples of the blending of macro and micro at the highest organizational levels, see Irving Janis, *Victims of Groupthink* (Boston: Houghton Mifflin, 1972).

67. Thomas R. Dye, "Policy Analysis and the Urban Crisis," mimeographed, n.d.

68. Golembiewski, *Behavior and Organization,* pp. 47-86.

69. Robert T. Golembiewski, " 'Maintenance' and 'Task' as Central Challenges in Public Administration," *Public Administration Review* 34 (March 1974): 171.

70. Generally, see Robert T. Golembiewski, William Welsh, and William Crotty, *A Methodological Primer for Political Scientists* (Chicago: Rand McNally, 1969), pp. 11-39.

71. Milton J. Friedman, *Essays in Positive Economics* (Chicago: University of Chicago Press, 1953), p. 14.

72. George K. Najjar, "Development Administration and 'New Public Administration': A Convergence of Perspectives," *Public Administration Review* 34 (November 1974): 584-587.

Index